Olympic Women and the Media

Global Culture and Sport

Series Editors: **Stephen Wagg** and **David Andrews**

Titles include:

Roger Levermore and Aaron Beacom (*editors*)
SPORT AND INTERNATIONAL DEVELOPMENT

Pirkko Markula (*editor*)
OLYMPIC WOMEN AND THE MEDIA
International Perspectives

Global Culture and Sport
Series Standing Order ISBN 978–0–230–57818–0 hardback
               978–0–230–57819–7 paperback
               (*outside North America only*)

You can receive future titles in this series as they are published by placing a standing order. Please contact your bookseller or, in case of difficulty, write to us at the address below with your name and address, the title of the series and the ISBN quoted above.

Customer Services Department, Macmillan Distribution Ltd, Houndmills, Basingstoke, Hampshire RG21 6XS, England

Olympic Women and the Media

International Perspectives

Edited By

Pirkko Markula
University of Alberta, Canada

palgrave
macmillan

First published 2009 by
PALGRAVE MACMILLAN

Palgrave Macmillan in the UK is an imprint of Macmillan Publishers Limited,
registered in England, company number 785998, of Houndmills, Basingstoke,
Hampshire RG21 6XS.

Palgrave Macmillan in the US is a division of St Martin's Press LLC,
175 Fifth Avenue, New York, NY 10010.

Palgrave Macmillan is the global academic imprint of the above companies
and has companies and representatives throughout the world.

Palgrave® and Macmillan® are registered trademarks in the United States,
the United Kingdom, Europe and other countries

ISBN-13: 978–0–230–22284–7 hardback
ISBN-10: 0–230–22284–6 hardback

This book is printed on paper suitable for recycling and made from fully
managed and sustained forest sources. Logging, pulping and manufacturing
processes are expected to conform to the environmental regulations of the
country of origin.

A catalogue record for this book is available from the British Library.

A catalog record for this book is available from the Library of Congress.

10   9   8   7   6   5   4   3   2   1
18 17 16 15 14 13 12 11 10 09

Printed and bound in Great Britain by
CPI Antony Rowe, Chippenham and Eastbourne

Contents

Acknowledgements

I would like to warmly thank all the contributors whose work has made publishing this book possible. In addition, I would like to acknowledge the Department of Education at the University of Bath as well as the Faculty of Physical Education and Recreation at the University of Alberta, for providing the necessary academic support for me to edit this book. I would also like to thank Nancy Spencer for providing invaluable professional advice and support during the process of completing this book and Judy Liao for her substantial help in the final editing. Finally, I would like extend special thanks to Jim Denison without whose personal and intellectual support it would have been impossible to complete this book.

Notes on the Contributors

Natalie Barker-Ruchti is a researcher and lecturer at the Institute of Exercise and Health Sciences at the University of Basel, Switzerland. Her research interests include the coach-female athlete relationship, athlete experiences and identity, and women as sport coaches. She has used Michel Foucault's work along with feminist theories and concepts to investigate these themes. Natalie is currently working on two projects: one examines social integration and sport; the other explores the experiences of sports coaches in Switzerland.

Toni Bruce is a senior lecturer in Sport and Leisure Studies at the University of Waikato, New Zealand. Her research interests focus on gender, national identity, race and ethnicity, particularly as these are expressed in the sports media and thought about by sports journalists. A former news and sports reporter, her PhD research (1995, University of Illinois) investigated women sports writers' experiences reporting on male sport. She has co-edited the *Waikato Journal of Education* for six years and is on the editorial board for the *International Review for the Sociology of Sport*. She has published in a wide range of sport and communication journals and is co-editor of *Outstanding: Research about New Zealand Women in Sport* (2008), with Camilla Obel and Shona Thompson.

Agnes Elling is senior researcher at the W. J. H. Mulier Institute, centre for research on sports in society in the Netherlands. She conducted several studies into in/exclusionary mechanisms in (media) sports with respect to gender, ethnicity and sexuality. Her theoretical and methodological perspectives and approaches are rather eclectic, ranging from discourse analyses to large quantitative studies, though mainly with a social critical touch.

Laura Hills is a lecturer in youth sport/sociology of sport at Brunel University. She came to Brunel from University of Durham, where she was the course leader for their Sport, Health and Exercise degree. Her research and teaching centres on gender, physicality, community sport, sports culture and social identities. Her recent publications have focused on social and embodied aspects of girls' physical education experiences and gender, class, ethnicity and body in mediated sport. She co-authored *Sport, Media, and Society* (Berg) with Eileen Kennedy and, as a US citizen living in the UK, sustains an interest in cross-cultural comparisons of mediated sport. She is also working on a project investigating mixed gender sport with the Football Association.

Eileen Kennedy is Director of the Centre for Scientific and Cultural Research in Sport in the School of Human and Life Sciences at Roehampton University, London. She has a background in Philosophy (BA, University of Essex) and Women's Studies (MA, University of Kent) and gained her PhD in Sociology of Sport from De Montfort University for her thesis, 'Gender in Televised Sport'. Since then, her research and publications have focused on the intersections of nation, class and race in the discursive construction of masculinities and femininities in the sport and exercise media. Eileen is interested in the significance of the body and the senses in the consumption of media sport, and has begun to focus on the mediation of sport through sporting spaces and digital sportscapes. She is co-author, with Laura Hills, of *Sport, Media and Society* (published by Berg, in press).

Eunha Koh is a senior researcher at the Department of Policy Research and Development, Korea Institute of Sport Science, South Korea. Her research interests include nationalism and globalisation in sport, gender and sport, and national/international sport policies/politics. She is an Extended Board Member of the International Sociology of Sport Association and serving on government advisory boards in South Korea, including Gender Equality Board (Ministry of Culture, Sport and Tourism) and the Advisory Board for Human Rights in Sport (National Human Rights Commission).

Judy Liao is currently a PhD student in the sociocultural studies of sport and physical activity at the University of Alberta, Canada. Her research interests include poststructuralist analysis of women's sport, specifically women's basketball, cultural analysis of media and psychoanalytical theories.

Roelien Luijt is a sports researcher and a sports journalist. She worked as a researcher at the W. J. H. Mulier Institute – Institute for Social Scientific Research in Sports – before she started her own company, ZEAL Sport & Media. Her research interests include mediated sports, women's sports, elite sports and lifestyle sports. During the Olympic Games in Beijing (2008), she worked as a copy editor. She edited the Olympic news special of nu.nl, the largest news website in The Netherlands. Recently she established SHEsports.nl, a Dutch news website about, for and by sportswomen.

Margaret MacNeill is an Associate Professor in the Faculty of Physical Education and Health at the University of Toronto, is cross-appointed to the Faculty of Medicine and is a Fellow of the American Association of Kinesiology and PE. She is affiliated with the Canadian Centre for Sport Policy Studies, serves as a research advisor to the Ontario PE and Health Education Association, and is the former Director of the Centre for Girls' and Women's Health and Physical Activity Research. Key areas of research include sport media studies, Olympic ethnographies, youth and physical activity, gender and health mediacy, health risk communication, and communication for social change. Currently, she is funded by the Canadian Institutes of Health Research and the Social Sciences and Humanities Research Council of Canada. Her work has been published in the *Journal of International Communication, International Journal of Sport History, Olympika, Journal of Urban Health, International Review for the Sociology of Sport, Studies in Physical Culture and Tourism, Sociology of Sport Journal, Brazilian Journal of Sport Sciences,* and *Media and Culture Reviews.*

Pirkko Markula is Professor of Socio-cultural Studies of Sport and Physical Activity at the University of Alberta. Her research interests include poststructuralist feminist analysis of dance, exercise and sport, ethnography, autoethnography and performance ethnography. She is the co-author, with Richard Pringle, of *Foucault, Sport and Exercise: Power, Knowledge and Transforming the Self* (2006), editor of *Feminist Sport Studies: Sharing Joy, Sharing Pain* (2005), co-editor, with Sarah Riley, Maree Burns, Hannah Frith and Sally Wiggins, of *Critical Bodies: Representations, Identities and Practices of Weight and Body Management* (2007) and co-editor, with Jim Denison, of *Moving Writing: Crafting Movement in Sport Research* (2003).

Montserrat Martin is currently a lecturer of Sociology of Sport in Physical Activity and Sport Sciences degree at Vic University, Catalonia. Her main research interests include writing narratives and performance texts of women's experiences in team-contact sport, specifically rugby and basketball. She follows sexual difference feminism, which is grounded in poststructuralist feminist theories.

Nancy E. Spencer is an Associate Professor in the School of Human Movement, Sport and Leisure Studies at Bowling Green State University, Ohio. Her research interests include autoethnography, critical race theories, feminist and poststructuralist analyses in the making of celebrity in professional women's tennis. She has published research articles in the *Journal of Sport & Social Issues, Sociology of Sport Journal, Journal of Sport Management* and *Sport Marketing Quarterly.* She also published a chapter about Venus Williams in D. L. Andrews and S. J. Jackson *Sport Stars: The Cultural Politics of Sporting Celebrity* (2001). Spencer is Past-President of the North American Society for the Sociology of Sport (NASSS), and served on the editorial board for the *Sociology of Sport Journal.*

Ping Wu is a senior lecturer in sports journalism and media at the University of Bedfordshire. She was a professional sports journalist in China between 1997 and 2003 and covered many international sports events, including the 2000 Sydney Olympic Games, the 2002 Men's Soccer World Cup and the 2002 Pusan Asian Games. In July 2007, Ping was awarded a PhD for her research on the complex relationship between the news media and sports administrative organisations in contemporary China. Her research interest is sport and media, specifically the sociology of mediated sports production. She has published in a range of books and journals on the interdependence between sport and the media, media treatment of women's sport and female athletes, the media build-up to the Beijing Olympic Games and the Chinese elite sports system.

1
Introduction

Pirkko Markula

The Olympic Games are among the major sporting events in the contemporary world. Olympic broadcasts and news media, accordingly, are followed by large audiences, which place sport momentarily at the centre of world's attention (Puijk, 2000). To highlight the visibility of the Olympics, Segrave (2000) points out that the total broadcast audience, including global newspaper readership, for the 1996 Olympic Games in Atlanta 'has been estimated at close to two billion, almost half of the world's population' (p. 268). It is also evident that while the Olympics are a global event, they can be represented in multiple ways to multiple audiences around the world depending on the different cultural contexts (e.g. Puijk, 2000). With such an expansive scope, the Olympic Games have become a part of a large commercial media complex which offers a global platform to showcase the achievements of athletes. In addition, the media are now a significant part of the politics around the Games. The media industry can now participate in the exclusion and inclusion of different sports; the scheduling of Olympic events according to the market requirements of large television companies or providing an advertising platform for large multinational companies sponsoring the Games (e.g. Lenskyj, 2000; 2002; 2008; Maguire, Butler, Barnard and Golding, 2008; Slater, 1998; Tomlinson, 2005). Televising the Olympics, in particular, has directed large investments to the Olympic Games governing body through the sale of televising rights and advertising space/time (e.g. Bernstein, 2000; Billings, 2008). While broadcasting has arguably shaped the mode of Olympic representation, newspapers still act as an important site for the representation of the Games. While newspapers have less financial power than television, they still reach large audiences interested in the Olympics and can play a significant role in shaping public opinion of Olympic sports (Lenskyj, 2000; 2002). For example, in her critical analysis of the role of the newspaper media in the Sydney 2000 Olympics, Lenskyj (2002) demonstrates how reporting both 'boosts' and 'critiques' the event. Bernstein (2000) adds that newspaper coverage tends to provide a 'local' (or, as she defines it, 'national') reading of the athletes in a global event. The newspaper coverage, however, also reflects a 'shared professional culture' of reporting (p. 367). It is, therefore, pertinent to analyse how newspaper coverage depicts Olympic athletes in their local, national context, but also provide comparison points regarding the commonalities between the news media in different countries.[1] In this book, we focus specifically on how women athletes are represented 'locally' in newspapers in Europe, North America, Asia and New Zealand, but also how these local reports provide a 'global' reading of the differences and similarities between different nations, their coverage of the Olympics and their representation of women athletes.

Women's participation in the Olympic Games has steadily increased, partly as a result of national Olympic committees sending more women athletes to the Games, but also because of the increased number of sports open to women in the Olympic Games. To locate our project within the existing research regarding women athletes in the Olympic media, I first review previous findings from quantitative, content media analyses of women's sport to demonstrate the need for further feminist perspectives in media analyses of women Olympians. This chapter aims, thus, to give an overview of the different feminist approaches to researching sportswomen's representation in the media. In addition, I aim to highlight how this book complements or expands on these theoretical assumptions.

Liberal feminist readings: equal media coverage for women Olympians

There is a substantial literature detailing the amount of coverage women receive in the sport media. In general, the results demonstrate that women are greatly underrepresented (e.g. Alexander, 1994; Bernstein, 2002; Bruce, Hovden and Markula, in press; Capranica and Aversa, 2002; Capranica et al., 2005; Duncan and Messner, 1998; Kane and Greendorfer, 1994; King, 2007; Lee, 1992; Pedersen, 2002). While the results differ depending on the cultural context, women generally receive less than 10 per cent of sport coverage in both newspapers and TV. While the coverage for women's sport remains low in comparison to men, it does tend to increase during major international events like the Olympic Games (e.g. Bernstein, 2002; Billings and Eastman, 2002; Lee, 1992; Tuggle and Owen, 1999; Urquhart and Crossman, 1999). For example, while there are significant variations among different countries, women's representation in North American and European newspapers comprises well over 20 per cent of the Olympic coverage (Bruce et al., in press; Capranica et al., 2005; Kinnick, 1998; Shields et al., 2004; Vincent et al., 2002). A recent study of the Athens Olympic Games reported over 30 per cent coverage for women Olympians in China and Japan, and 16 per cent in South Korea (Bruce et al., in press). In addition, while women's overall coverage is lower than men's, women tend to be represented relative to their participation to the Games or national Olympic teams (Bruce et al., in press). Women's increased coverage appears to pave the way towards gender equality during newspaper reporting of the Games. This development, some researchers conclude, is the positive result of several factors.

Women's increased media visibility demonstrates that some of the gender equality policies initiated by the International Olympic Committee (IOC) have taken effect. For example, Capranica et al. (2005) argue that these initiatives have increased not only women's participation but also the number of women's events in the Games and thus have enabled growing acceptance of women's sport in general. In addition, the increased visibility of women's sport in the Olympic movement has created a better market for women's mediated sport. Some researchers point out that at international-level competitions other factors than gender might create media visibility. For example, several studies demonstrate that women who are expected to win medals receive more attention in the media and successful athletes, regardless of their gender, are the focus of media interest (Wensing and Bruce 2003). In this sense, national identity overrides the athlete's gender. Consequently, women's increased Olympic success in a variety of sporting events has resulted in greater media coverage. While these are positive developments, most researchers are only cautiously optimistic about gender equality in sport media representation and question whether mere increase in the amount of coverage results in better representation of women's sports.

Some researchers warn that focusing on 'raw' numbers might provide a too encouraging picture of the equality of women's Olympic media representation. For example, North American data (e.g. Lee, 1992; Shields et al., 2004; Vincent et al., 2002) demonstrate that newspapers tend to focus on sports that are traditionally stereotyped as 'feminine', such as gymnastics, diving, swimming and figure skating. Shields et al. (2004) conclude that '[f]or women and women's Olympic sports/events, unless a "gold medal" was at stake, the coverage of less "feminine" sports/events was at best thin' (p. 94). Consequently, such a media message promotes an acceptance of sportswomen, as long as they participate in appropriately feminine sports, that is those that do not require strength, power or contact. Moreover, several researchers are concerned about the quality of the Olympic coverage. For example, the descriptors of women athletes tend to focus on appearance rather than skill (e.g. Bernstein, 2002; Capranica and Aversa, 2002; Eastman and Billings, 1999). According to Bernstein (2002), such representation 'continues to send a message that sport is in essence a male activity, in which women play only a subordinate and/or sexualized role' (p. 426). She asks: 'If more media coverage means more sexualized images is more necessarily better? Or is more even worse?' (p. 426). Does reporting that trivialises and sexualises women athletes, these researchers ask, promote women's sport in a positive light? Other researchers have questioned whether research that focuses on promoting an equal amount of media coverage for women and men also plays a part in perpetuating poor quality in favour of quantity in women's sport coverage.

Quantitative content analyses of sportswomen's media representation are grounded in liberal feminist ideals of equal access and equal opportunity in sport (e.g. Hall, 1996; Hargreaves, 1994; Pirinen, 1997): an equal amount of media coverage will reflect general equality between men and women in sport.[2] Much of Olympic gender equality policies are based on a similar assumption that equality of representation will resolve any issues regarding gender discrimination. Creating equal access and equal opportunity to sport is also among the most tangible points of action for decisions-makers at the higher levels of international sporting organisations. However, feminist critics of liberal feminist research and policy-making argue that campaigning for equal opportunity alone does not end gender discrimination because they do not question the hegemonic values that structure competitive sport. According to these critics, all women entering sport will face marginalisation unless the underlying structure that favours male sport changes. For example, even if there is greater coverage of sportswomen, they are marginalised in other, more subtle ways in a male-dominated system. Bernstein's (2002) concern with the sexualisation of women's sports coverage is one example of such a subtle way of discrimination. In line with Bernstein, many of the contributors in this book participated in a large international content analysis which tracked women's Olympic coverage in newspapers during the Athens Olympic Games in 2004 (Bruce et al., in press). While we were able to detect increased coverage of women's sports during the Olympics and present it in an easy-to-read numerical form, this analysis did not tell us much about how women athletes were actually represented. We noted that much of the coverage tended to focus on a few 'star' athletes, but we were unable to trace how and why some of these athletes appeared in the coverage. Did the increased coverage reinforce women's discrimination in a male-dominated sport system? To bring about lasting change in the media representation of sportswomen, we needed different feminist tools from the ones that simply advocate more media coverage.

I now turn to feminist research concerned with how structural constraints continue to marginalise, trivialise and sexualise women's sport media representation despite the increased visibility of women in the Olympic media. For further discussion of liberal feminism in sport studies, see chapter 5.

Critical analysis: ideological construction of male hegemony in sport media

There has been a recent surge of qualitative, textual analyses of women's sport in sport studies. While these studies approach sport media from a variety of theoretical perspectives, much of this research detects how sport is ideologically constructed as a male hegemony and how women's media coverage is formed within this structure.

A significant proportion of feminist sport media research is inspired by a Gramscian notion of how systematic relations of dominance are maintained in society, not through force, but through mutual consent by dominant and marginalised groups. This type of dominance appeals to common sense and the natural order of things, and tends to be accepted also by the subordinate groups. The concept of hegemony refers to dominance through ideological control. Ideology refers to 'a set of ideas that serve the interests of dominant groups but come to be understood and taken up as the societal common sense about the way things naturally are and thus should remain' (Theberge and Birrell, 1994, p. 327). From this viewpoint, sport is considered as a male-dominated or patriarchal system where women's oppression is maintained through the ideology of masculinity which reinforces men's natural superiority over women: while women now have increased access to sport, the ideology of masculinity works in more subtle ways to exclude them. For example, sport preserves male dominance by marginalising, trivialising and sexualising women athletes by ideological means. Media representation plays an important role in constructing the ideological meanings of femininity in sport. Birrell and Theberge (1994) argue that sport media reinforces the image of women as physically inferior to men, and thus works ideologically to construct male hegemony. One way to identify women as the 'weaker sex' is to structure women's sport as a discrete category of men's sport (e.g. Kane, 1995). Birrell and Theberge (1994, p. 346) posit that

> the artificial separation of the sport world into two separate spheres delineated by sex clearly marks gender difference as significant and worth maintaining. Consequently, sex difference is constructed as a logical and necessary part of our cultural world.

In addition, women's sport is considered to be not only separate, but also inferior to men's sport (Lee, 1992; Pirinen, 1997).

In practice, this leads to the structural marginalisation of women's sport, something that is also evident in media representation. As demonstrated at the beginning of this chapter, women's sport is generally underrepresented in the media, and while women receive increased coverage during the major events like the Olympic Games, women's sport remains vastly underrepresented in general sport media coverage. Feminist sport scholars argue that women's sport is 'symbolically annihilated': the media give the impression that women's sport does not matter or does not even exist. For example, Duncan and Messner (1998) showed that televised sport in the US was systematically constructed to marginalise women's sport by providing significantly less coverage of women's sport and, when it was aired, its technical quality was much poorer than men's sport (see also Messner, Duncan and Cooky, 2003). Such marginalisation is an important indication of how the ideology of masculinity operates through sport media. Therefore, the structural, ideologically-based marginalisation cannot be 'fixed' by merely increasing women's sport participation. In addition to marginalisation, women's sport is ideologically controlled by trivialising women's performances.

Trivialisation refers to the belittling of women's sport achievements. Messner, Duncan and Cooky (2003) demonstrate a form of trivialisation of women's sport in the televised coverage in the US, where a considerable proportion of women's sport coverage is devoted to humorous feature stories of non-serious women's sport. In addition, women athletes can be 'infantilised' by referring to them by their first names (male athletes are typically referred by their surnames), by calling them 'girls', or by prefixing women's teams with the term 'Lady' and thus establishing men's teams as the 'false generic'. Sport media that focus on women's personal lives, appearance and attractiveness trivialise women's athletic prowess, their ability to compete, and their strength, speed and tactical ability as sportswomen (e.g. Birrell and Theberge, 1994; Duncan and Messner, 1998; Stone and Horne, 2008). Duncan and Messner (1998) identify how differences between the ways that men's and women's sports are reported on US television trivialise women's performances: whereas the commentators focused on male athletes' strengths, women's weaknesses, emotionality or failures were discussed. Similarly, sport media that, instead of sport, write about the athletes' traditional gender roles as daughters, girlfriends, wives or mothers emphasise the differences between men and women and belittle women's athletic skill. Dallario (1994) observed that even women who competed in Winter Olympic sports that defied stereotypical notions of femininity, such as the biathlon, luge and alpine skiing, were described in the media through condescending descriptors and compensatory rhetoric, as 'adolescents' driven by cooperation rather than competition. Such representation, Dallario concluded, 'reinforced a masculine sports hegemony through strategies of marginalization' (p. 275). Pirinen (1997) summarises that in the trivialisation/marginalisation discourse, gender relations are constructed as hierarchical power relations. This means that women in sports are often portrayed as 'less than' and 'other than' their male counterparts by giving women's sports scant coverage and by framing women's achievements as inferior to men's with sarcastic comments on successful performances and by sexually objectifying women athletes. In this book Wu (chapter 4) demonstrates how Chinese female athletes are belittled by the media which prefer to emphasise their personal relationships and appearance rather than their athletic skills. Such a portrayal further reproduces the masculine hegemony of sport (e.g. Pirinen, 1997). Pirinen draws attention to sportswomen's sexual objectification in the media. This trend has been further evidenced by several feminist researchers.

Birrell and Theberge (1994) point out that often women's physicality is portrayed differently from men's. Women athletes are often depicted in a sexualised manner that has nothing to do with their sport performance. Such portrayals emphasise how women athletes look, instead of what they do (Hall, 1996). This supports the ideology of masculinity and its definition of women as passive objects of the male gaze (to be looked at). One of the seminal feminist qualitative studies of women's sexualisation in the Olympic media is Duncan's

(1990) study of sport photographs from the 1988 summer and winter Olympic Games as well as the 1984 summer Olympic Games. After analysing pictures from the US magazines *Life, Sports Illustrated, Newsweek, Time, MS.* and *Macleans* during the Olympics, Duncan found that sport photographs tended to emphasise stereotypical sexual difference between female and male athletes by focusing on female athletes' physical appearance, by depicting sportswomen in poses that resembled soft-core pornography, by placing women in submissive poses and by displaying women as above all emotional. These differences sexualised the sportswomen and downplayed their abilities as athletes. According to Duncan, sport photography constructed an ideological terrain that legitimated patriarchal relations. She concluded: 'Focusing on female difference is a political strategy that places women in a position of weakness. Sport photographs that emphasize the otherness of women enable patriarchal ends' (p. 40). Elling and Luijt (chapter 7 below), who ground their methodology on Duncan's study, examine Dutch photographic coverage during the Athens Olympics to find similar sexualisation of the Dutch swimmer Inge de Bruijn. Following Duncan, they conclude that the sexualisation of female athletes contributes to women's oppression in western societies. Messner, Duncan and Cooky (2003) note an additional tendency to indulge in humorous sexual objectification of women athletes on US television (see also Duncan and Messner, 1998), a trend generally absent in men's sport reporting.

In addition to the sexualisation of athletes' sport performances, feminist researchers point to the tendency of the sport media to employ sexualised images of non-sporting women or sportswomen outside of sport contests (e.g. Duncan and Messner, 1998; Messner, Duncan and Cooky, 2003). Davis (1997), for example, draws attention to highly sexualised images of women in the *Sports Illustrated* 'Swimsuit' issue and Lenskyj (1998) analyses how one Australian sport magazine, *Inside Sport*, exploited women through sexualisation. The marketability of such images has also evolved into the phenomenon of so-called 'naked calendars', which are produced (often by sportswomen themselves) to raise funds for women's sport (see also Lenskyj, 2008). Thus, Mikosza and Phillips (1999) examined the second 'Golden Girls Calendar', launched by the Australian heptathlete Jane Flemming in 1996, and drew several parallels to the *Sports Illustrated* 'Swimsuit' issue. The calendar used 'the traditional form of the "girlie" calendar' in its portrayal of 13 Australian women from 11 Olympic sports. The focus is on large colour images of these athletes 'modeling in skimpy or transparent swimsuits, underwear and evening gowns' (p. 7). The researchers characterise these pictures as "'soft-porn", with codes such as long styled hair, cosmetics and poses connoting the sexualized female' (p. 8). This portrayal invites the viewer to see each athlete as a sexual object and thus produces a femininity 'which views women as sexually active and available' (p. 8). In addition, the women depicted in the calendar all display the characteristics of 'traditional femininity': white, lean, toned, with long hair and wearing make-up. The 'Golden Girls' portrayal, then, reproduces femininity as defined by the ideology of masculinity. The researchers acknowledge, however, that the proponents of the sexualised images of feminine athletes proclaim that this is a way to get publicity and raise the profiles of women athletes who otherwise have been unable to obtain funding or access to media outlets. The sexy, feminine image has also been advantageous to certain female athletes, such as the tennis player Anna Kournikova, who have attracted media attention and consequently lucrative sponsorship thanks to their looks rather than their performance (e.g. Bernstein, 2002; Harris and Clayton, 2002).

According to Bernstein (2002), the media attention, particularly photographic coverage, devoted to the blonde Kournikova clearly demonstrates how looks and image are ranked above athletic skill in women's sport. Harris and Clayton (2002) add that the hegemonic construction of femininity is the only way to explain the media attention devoted to a relatively unsuccessful tennis player like Kournikova, who epitomises the sexualisation of the female body through her participation in photo shoots entirely unconnected to tennis. The positive emphasis on Kournikova's sexuality, the authors argue, transmits sexualised, heterosexual femininity as the acceptable athletic identity of women.

Feminist sport research demonstrates that the media prefer to construct sportswomen as heterosexually attractive. As Creedon (1998) succinctly observes: 'homosexuality doesn't sell' (p. 96) in the sport media, which want to frame their coverage to a heterosexual male audience (Duncan and Messner, 1998). This audience is expected to prefer 'little girls and sweethearts' (such as tennis players or gymnasts), heroines that overcome pain or other setbacks to succeed, or scandalised athletes such as the figure skaters Tonya Harding and Nancy Kerrigan, whose rivalry was eagerly reported and analysed (see e.g. Baughman, 1995) or the sprinter Marion Jones whose involvement with drugs was reported globally (see also Creedon,

1998). In this media climate, a lesbian athlete is either invisible or seen as a 'problem'. Kane and Lenskyj (1998) argue that a 'lesbian presence in sport is threatening because it challenges male hegemony by upsetting existing power structures based on gender and sexuality' (p. 189). Sport media react to this threat by emphasising female athletes' heterosexual roles and 'conventional femininity', or not covering women in so-called 'male sports' because, it is commonly believed, women must be masculine to be able to perform well in these sports and thus lesbian. Kane and Lenskyj label this strategy the 'erasure' of women in ice-hockey, softball and rugby (see also Wright and Clarke, 1999). In addition, sport media 'neutralises lesbian existence by severely underrepresenting images and narratives that reflect women's physical and emotional bonds' (Kane and Lenskyj, 1998, pp. 193–4). These erasure tactics serve to maintain the images of female athletes as firmly heterosexual and 'create a female sport culture in which traditional notions of heterosexuality are rigidly enforced' (p. 200).

Wensing and Bruce (2003) provide an apt summary of the framing techniques used by the media to promote appropriate femininity. First, the media use gender marking, by identifying an event as a women's event, to *marginalise* women's sport. Second, women's sport is *trivialised* by infantilising women athletes (by using terms like 'girls') and emphasising non-sport-related aspects, such as appearance, family relationships and personal life, that detract attention from women's sport achievement. Third, sportswomen are framed by 'compulsory heterosexuality': they are portrayed as the mothers/wives/girlfriends of men to ensure that women's sport is not a serious threat to men's sport and thus is of lesser importance. Finally, sportswomen are *sexualised* by focusing on 'traditional feminine' physical and emotional characteristics, thus emphasising their 'appropriate femininity'. All these journalistic techniques work to reinforce male sport as 'the pinnacle of sporting value and achievement' and thus help to construct sport as a male domain (p. 387). Although these framing devices effectively support the ideology of masculinity, Wensing and Bruce also point to increasingly positive descriptions and images of women athletes that introduce more ambivalence to the sport media representation. For example, they argue, the media tend to 'accommodate' successful, nationally important sportswomen during major sport events. Other factors that, in addition to gender, intersect with the ideological construction of women athletes in the media have been considered by feminist sport researchers.

Reading the 'power lines': intersectionality and women's sport media representation

To emphasise further the complexity of cultural and social life (Theberge and Birrell, 1994), feminist sport researchers are increasingly conceiving gender relationally to other social forces. Birrell and McDonald (2000) argue that a singular focus on gender will produce incomplete or even dangerously simplistic analyses of complex power relations (see also McDonald and Birrell, 1999). They advocate that structures of dominance are expressed around 'the power lines of race, class, gender, and sexuality (and age, nationality, ability, religion, etc.)' (p. 4), which work simultaneously and have to be conceptualised as interrelated. It is necessary to 'read sport critically' to capture the 'complex interrelated and fluid character of power relations' (p. 4). In chapter 12 below Spencer, drawing on Birrell and McDonald, critically reads sportswomen's media representation in *USA Today*. This approach is theoretically grounded in critical cultural studies that build on the previous insights of feminist theory, critical race theories, Marxist theories and/or queer theory (for a discussion of feminist cultural studies, see also Bruce, chapter 8 below). Engagement with power is understood as a central focus for understanding social life, including the construction of media images. Consequently, sport media representation also has to be considered as formed in the intersection of relations of class, race, gender, sexuality and nation to understand fully how its current meanings have become dominant. Several feminist sport scholars have elaborated on the notion of intersectionality by examining interlocking systems of power, such as race, class, gender, simultaneously within the sport media representation of women's sport.[3] For example, Birrell and Cole (2000), Lock (2003) and McDonald (2008) undertake a critical reading of the intersections of gender and sexuality; and Duncan and Aycock (2005) interrogate the construction of disability and gender, class, race and sexuality in sport advertising and media (see also Schell and Rodriguez, 2001). In the US context, the intersection of race and gender in women's tennis, with its highly visible and celebrated global stars, has attracted the attention of several researchers (e.g. Douglas, 2005; Giardina, 2001; 2005; Schultz, 2005; Spencer, 2001; 2003; 2004). Hills and Kennedy (2006) derive from Collins's notion of intersectionality and Puwar's ideas inspired by Bourdieu about 'space invaders' – how individuals negotiate their way within mainstream organisations – an analysis of how gender and race intersected with nation and class in televised and newspaper representations of the Wimbledon tennis semi-finals and finals in 2005. Hills and Kennedy continue their discussion of intersectionality in this book (chapter 6 below) by focusing on how Kelly Holmes, the English double gold medal winner, was constructed in the British media during the Athens Olympic Games. In addition, in chapter 7, Elling and Luijt locate the Dutch media coverage within the intersections of gender, race and nationality and compare the representation of three Dutch athletes in Athens. The impact of nationalism on the representation of women Olympians has also drawn the attention of other feminist media scholars.

Several feminist researchers have articulated how the power lines of nationalism, gender, race and class cross in the mediated sport to produce relations of dominance and subordination (e.g. Borcila, 2000; Elder, Pratt and Ellis, 2006; Hogan, 2003; Jamieson, 2000; Stevenson, 2002). As an ideological construction, nationalism is based on an 'imaginary' national unity that is created through a powerful 'narrative of the nation' by excluding 'Others' (Elder, Pratt and Ellis, 2006; Hogan, 2003; Stevenson, 2002). For example, Hogan (2003) argues that capital interests, socially dominant groups and the state benefit from the Olympic opening ceremony by 'constructing widely palatable gendered and ethnicized discourses of national identity' (p. 118). These discourses create an impression of a nation as a unified, homogeneous place, either by excluding women and ethnic minorities or by representing them in a form that supports masculine hegemony. In this book, Koh (chapter 9) demonstrates how South Korean newspaper coverage uses women athletes to celebrate nationalism, but at the same marginalises and trivialises their performance by emphasising their emotionality over achievements. Lippe (2002), who examined the broadcasts of five nations from the European handball championships in 1998, discovered that the image of the female athlete as the national symbol aligns with hegemonic masculinity: the women handballers were 'feminised', sexualised, emotional athletes in a male world of leaders, coaches and journalists. Adding nationality to the mix, however, creates a certain ambivalence in the representation of the female athletes: successful females athletes were described 'in terms of active agents, of aggression and toughness' (p. 382) similar to 'the hegemonic masculine logic of continual success' (p. 388). To become national symbols female athletes cannot be entirely constructed as the 'Other' (of the male) and therefore need to embody some masculine features. As Lippe explains: '"We" must succeed in contrast to the "others", at the same time as "the other" features "us" in what we lack in comparison to other countries. In these contexts issues of gender might be understood as denied, a doxa, or ambivalent' (p. 388). Stevenson (2002) identifies similar contradictory themes in the media representation of the Australian Open in 1999 in Melbourne. Although tennis Grand Slam players do not represent nations, Australianness, hyperfemininity and power intersected in the media representation of women's tennis, but did not freeze the players as passive recipients of 'feminised' media narratives. In her reading of the golfer Nancy Lopez, Jamieson (2000) found parallel 'oppression and opportunity' embedded in the power crossings for a female athlete: 'The intersecting forms of domination in Lopez's experience offer her privilege as a professional athlete, a financially secure woman, and a heterosexual woman, but oppression as a person of Mexican heritage and working class heritage' (Jamieson, 2000, p. 150; see also Douglas and Jamieson, 2006). As the Olympic Games constitute a globally transmitted megaevent, the construction of women athletes as symbols of nationalism in this context has interested several researchers.

Borcila (2000) examined how gymnastics, an individual, acceptably feminine sport, was used to frame a narrative of US nationalism in NBC's 1996 Atlanta Olympic Games coverage. In general, the gymnasts were presented, not as sexy, but as 'vulnerable yet invincible "little girls"' (p. 210). Through sentimentalised stories of injuries overcome, strong will and perseverance became central tenets of American national identity. In addition, the coverage worked 'hard at separating and distinguishing "America" from other nations' (p. 120) when the gymnastics coverage presented American 'vulnerability' in the context of 'tough warriors' versus children from 'other' countries beset by 'tyrannical' regimes and poverty. Echoing previous studies of nationalism and femininity, the American gymnasts were represented ambivalently as little girl warriors. Wensing and Bruce (2003), who examined the representation of the Aboriginal athlete Cathy Freeman in the Australian press during the 2000 Olympic Games in Sydney, saw the impact of nationalism in a more positive light (see also Elder, Pratt, and Ellis, 2006: Gardiner, 2003). Freeman received huge visibility during these Games and the reporting of her success emphasised the ambivalence of gendered identity construction. As an Australian hope for national success, Freeman was represented as an emotionally strong athlete fully in control of her performance as someone who made decisions in consultation with, and not dependent on, male support and '[r]eferences to the stereotypical female and Aboriginal inability to cope with pressure was markedly absent' (p. 390). Therefore, Freeman's status as a 'national hope' positively disrupted the stereotypical gender marking of female athletes by adding ambivalence to identity construction. In chapter 8, Bruce continues this research by analysing how the articulation of gender with nationalism could potentially mobilise forces in professional sport to bring about change in representations of sporting women in the New Zealand media.

Feminist sport research indicates that when the female athlete's identity is constructed in an intersection of gender, race and nationality, the media coverage tends to endorse male hegemony. Women athletes continue to be constructed as different from and inferior to male athletes. For example, nationalism acts to reinforce sport as a masculine domain by reproducing women athletes as heterosexual, traditionally 'feminine', 'sexy' and emotionally charged women who do not threaten male dominance. However, while the narratives of race and nationality act to support the ideology of masculinity, they, like all ideologies, can also generate critique. For example, the increased ambivalence created by nationalism that cannot distance women too much from the successful, male national hero allows for a different type of representation of sporting femininity where female athletes assume some of the characteristics typically preserved for male athletes. This emerging diversity has inspired media readings that expand the analyses of ambivalence of women's sport media representation to interrogate further the interplay between the textual construction and larger social forces around women's sport.

The intertextual analyses focus on how the ideologically constructed media messages are shaped within the complex web of the media production. For example, in this book MacNeill (chapter 3) analyses the construction of the Canadian Perdita Felicien in the interacting meaning-making by journalists, television broadcasters and young audience members. The media–sport cultural complex (Rowe, 1999) is understood as more than mere interplay between dominant ideologies and resistance from marginalised groups to construct gender, class, racial and national identities. The media are seen as transmogrifiers of cultural meanings into hyperreal narratives of iconic and supra-normal celebrity image identities which become more real than 'real' life. In this virtual environment 'mass-produced images replace personal lived experience with events where free-floating signifiers ... come to represent and stand in for an unquestioned social reality' (Giardina, 2001, p. 215). Sport plays an important role in the construction of these identities because of its remarkable media presence and its tendency to celebrate superlative, individual performances (e.g. Jackson and Andrews, 2001; Darnell and Sparks, 2005). In this context, contemporary forces, like globalisation, add complexity to the ways sportswomen are represented in the media. For example, the new communication technologies have enabled the creation of a global space: a placeless 'reality' that meets us on the television screen everywhere in the world (Hills and Kennedy, 2006). Giardina's (2001) study of the construction of Martina Hingis's transnational celebrity status serves as a case in point.

Giardina's (2001) seeks to 'deconstruct Hingis within an interpretive space that frames her as a free-floating commodity-sign' (p. 205) to reveal her 'flexible citizenship' which has resulted from her transnational celebrity status. When the media-assisted process of globalisation breaks down the 'old structures and boundaries of nation-states and communities' (p. 205), a new type of citizenship – the flexible citizen – that is unbound to a nation emerges. For example, Hingis, who was born in the former Czechoslovakia, but now has Swiss citizenship, and also maintains a home base in Florida, has managed to negotiate her cosmopolitan citizenship to her advantage in the economic conditions of the consumer market in the women's tennis tour, which moves and is broadcasted globally. Each of her 'locales' reflects differently from her identity. For example, while the European media portrayed her as an intellectual player playing near-perfect technical tennis, outside of Europe Hingis has been associated with traditional American values of heteronormativity: femininity, grace and success. In this global context, then, Hingis's representation is either 'resistant' to the ideology of masculine or entirely oppressed by it.

Nike advertisements that target female athletes have drawn the attention of a number of feminist scholars who read these advertisements as constructing both 'dominant' and 'alternative' feminine identities within post-Fordist, post-feminist, neoliberal consumerism (Capon and Helstein, 2005; Cole and Hribar, 1995; Giardina and Metz, 2005; Lafrance, 1998; Lucas, 2000; McKay, 2005). In these advertisements, 'femininity' and masculinity are no longer diametrically opposed: 'the New Age female athlete à la Nike is both "girly-girl" and "athlete"' (Giardina and Metz, 2005, p. 75).

Through intersectionality and intertextuality, feminist sport researchers have further highlighted the contradictions and ambiguities of sportswomen's media representation in the current global sport–media complex. As a result, they have begun to challenge the process of 'modern' identity construction confined between the two poles of dominance and marginalisation: while sport media representations continue to align with hegemonic masculinity, there is an added concern regarding multiple meanings created through the contemporary image culture of floating signifiers. Consequently, feminist researchers now draw from a variety of theoretical perspectives to understand further the complexities of women's (mediated) sport in the contemporary world.

Poststructuralist readings of women's sport media representation

While poststructuralism is not a unified theoretical perspective, such theoretical perspectives as Lacanian psychoanalysis, Derridean deconstruction, the Foucauldian theory of discursivity and Deleuzian rhizomatics have been classified to comprise poststructuralism. While poststructuralist feminist sport media research is still relatively new, there are some examples of how Derridean (Cole, 1998), Deleuzean (Markula, 2005), Foucauldian (Markula, 2000; Markula and Pringle, 2006; Thorpe, 2008) and psychoanalytic (Helstein, 2003; 2005; 2007) theories can be used to read women's sport media representation. This book contributes to feminist poststructuralist analysis through psychoanalytic readings of women's Olympic representation by MacNeill (chapter 3) and Martin (chapter 10), Derridean deconstruction by Markula (chapter 5) and Foucauldian discourse analysis by Barker-Ruchti (chapter 11).

While these theories differ from each other, poststructualism can be generally characterised as challenging the modernist notion of one truth in favour of an examination of multiple realities. Consequently, poststructuralists assume that meanings are not fixed, but always changing, in flux, depending on the context. For example, the meaning of what constitutes an 'oppressive' media image is not decided before the analysis. As the poststructuralists would put it: certain signifiers are not firmly attached to predetermined oppressive or oppressed identities but the definition of 'feminine' identity is always considered as changing and context-specific.[4] This does not, however, denote a denial of power relations in the contemporary world. Foucault, for example, asserted that 'although governments, social institutions, laws and dominant groups are commonly assumed to hold power' they actually represent only its terminal forms (Markula and Pringle, 2006, p. 34). To understand the existing social inequalities, it is more important to understand how power is exercised through the formation of influential social phenomena. For example, women's mediated images are formed within certain relations of power between the numerous individuals involved in the media, sport and the international and national politics around sport. Consequently, unlike the hegemony theory perspective, power is not considered a possession of a specified group of people, but rather dominant individuals, groups, corporations or states 'become influential due to the contingent workings and, at times, tactical usages of "discourses"' (Markula and Pringle, 2006, p. 34). For example, in chapter 3 MacNeill examines how the Canadian Olympic athlete Perdita Felicien's image is negotiated as a combined 'effort' within the power relations of media production, the audience's (anticipated) gaze and the larger context of race relations in Canada. A poststructuralist perspective further challenges the necessity of such binary opposition as oppressive masculine and suppressed feminine identity as a basis for feminist politics (e.g. Hekman, 1990). In chapter 5, for example, Markula uses Derridean deconstruction to discuss the limitation of the binary logic of assigning certain sports as masculine and others as feminine. Martin (chapter 10) looks at the difficulty of fixing the meanings of sporting femininity through the psychoanalytic feminist lens of Luce Irigaray.

When power can no longer be conceptualised as a position for a clearly identifiable dominant group, it becomes more difficult to determine how to understand women's 'liberation' in or through sport. Following Foucault, a poststructuralist would assume that '[e]ach individual is ... caught in a network of historical power relations through which s/he constitutes her/himself as a subject acting on others: s/he is subjected to control but also has some freedom to use power to control others' (Markula and Pringle, 2006, p. 138). Instead of a 'true' feminine self to be liberated from the clouding of the dominant ideology of masculinity, a sportswoman's identity is already continually being produced, 'in flux', within the current power relations of sport of which each athlete is a part. A poststructuralist, therefore, might question the assumption that if the patriarchal sport system is finally abolished, then a 'new', 'better' and 'truer' femininity, currently locked under false representation created by the ideology of masculinity, will emerge.[5] Rather, the meaning of femininity is always constructed within various social contexts and within the pressure of constantly changing power relations. For example, Barker-Ruchti (chapter 11) offers a Foucauldian reading of the Swiss triathlete Karin Thürig which departs from a classification of her representation as either oppressive or liberating to look at how Thürig's athletic identity is constructed through the broader discursive context of a highly technologised, international elite sport. When identity construction is dependent on specific power relations, unified meanings for such terms as gender, 'nationalism', 'race' or ethnicity become more difficult to maintain. Poststructuralism, therefore, aims to further sensitise sport media researchers to cultural context of meaning-making. In this book, we examine further how cultural contexts create different conditions for meanings even in the increasingly globalised world. For example, Wu (chapter 4), writing on the Chinese media representation of women Olympians, points to the very different development of feminism in China from 'westernised' countries. Therefore, women's media representation should not be read through western theoretical constructs either.

While it is more difficult to determine how relations of dominance operate, poststructuralism remains deeply committed to a politics of change. The solutions to changing unjust conditions or discrimination are less simple within fluid, constantly changing cultural conditions. However, the relations of power are also deemed to be productive rather than exclusively prohibitive or repressive to women (e.g., Pringle and Markula, 2006). This means that sportswomen are also producers of their identities and can thus have a positive influence on how they are represented in the media. While the current discursive construction of sport and media acts to limit an individual, neither are these fields closed for social action by sport feminists, sport media researchers, feminist activists or individual sportswomen. A feminist poststructuralist researcher, for example, might ask the following questions: What representation would change the cultural and social conditions that create the discursive field of sport? How would changing the competitive ethics of sport and sporting women affect the media representations? Why should we change the discursive field of sport? How can we examine media representation in the globalised, discursive field of sport where multiple power relations continually mould the athletes' identities and where the athletes themselves are, by necessity, parts of these power relations? Although not fully answering these questions, the contributors to this book have opened a discussion about further engagement of feminist theory and the analysis of sport media representation.

Structure of the book

While one aim of this book is to introduce a variety of feminist perspectives into sport media analysis, it also intends to map the differences and similarities of athletes' representation in different countries. Consequently, the book is organised based on the country of which newspaper representation women athletes were analysed. In addition, a chapter that provides methodological guidance for qualitative, textual analysis of media has been included.

With significant literature mapping women's representation in sport media from diverse feminist perspectives, there is a dearth of methodological texts for feminist sport media analysis. Liao and Markula (chapter 2) aim to provide a guide for qualitative methods specifically for sport media researchers. They draw on Fairclough's critical discourse analysis (CDA) and Foucaudian discourse analysis to develop methods for feminist textual analyses of sport.

In chapter 3, MacNeill analyses the construction of the Canadian hurdler Perdita Felicien who fell in the final of the women's 100 metres hurdles and failed to complete the race. MacNeill provides an intertextual analysis to look at how a 'failed' female athlete was represented in Canadian newspapers and TV, but also elicits how girls understood the meaning of Felicien as a Canadian, female athlete. MacNeill adopts a psychoanalytic analysis of 'gaze', combined with postcolonial reading of Felicien as a black, Canadian, female athlete to analyse the meanings of femininity, nationality and race in Canadian context.

Ping Wu (chapter 4) provides an analysis of two Chinese newspapers, the *Titan Sports Weekly*, a market-oriented tabloid, and the *China Sports Daily*, a 'party organ' newspaper supported by the ruling Communist Party in China. To contextualise her analysis, Wu also discusses the development of feminism and the current climate for sport media in China. She focuses particularly on the representation of Chinese female divers, table tennis players and weightlifters, all of whom were expected to win medals for China in Athens, 2004.

Markula focuses in chapter 5 on the coverage of a Finnish newspaper, *Turun Sanomat*, of women Olympians. In addition to textual analysis, she traces, through Derridean deconstruction, the development of the concept 'feminine appropriate sports' in feminist sport studies.

In chapter 6, Hills and Kennedy look at the narrative construction of double gold medal winner, the middle-distance runner Kelly Holmes, in four British newspapers: *The Sunday Times*, the *Observer*, the *Sunday Mirror* and the *News of the World*. Holmes' surprise success at the Athens Olympic Games caught the British media off guard, and Hills and Kennedy, while drawing from multiple theorists, locate the newspaper narratives within the intersections of race, gender, class and sexuality in the Great Britain.

Echoing Hills and Kennedy, Elling and Luijt (chapter 7) locate Dutch female athletes' representation within the intersections of gender, race and nationality. They compare and contrast three Dutch medallists: the 'white', ethnically Dutch swimmer Inge de Bruijn, the 'black' Surinam-Dutch judoka Deborah Gravenstijn (bronze) and the 'black'

Indonesian-Dutch badminton player Mia Audina in two national newspapers (*Het Algemeen Dagblad* and *NRC Handelsblad*).

In chapter 8, Bruce employs feminist cultural studies to examine how nationalism and gender are articulated into an ambivalent representation of the New Zealand gold medalists, the cyclist Sarah Ulmer and the rowers Caroline and Georgina Evers-Swindell. Such ambivalence, she suggests, can open up spaces for political strategies to change the routine practices of sport journalists who tend to follow the dominant cultural assumptions about women's sports as less interesting or exciting than men's sport.

Eunha Koh (chapter 9) also examines how the media representation of women athletes has been constructed within the intersection of nationalism and gender in a major South Korean daily newspaper, *Donga Ilbo*. Unlike in the 'westernised' countries, the South Korean media do not sexualise Korean women athletes because they are seen as national heroines. While Korean women athletes continue to be trivialised and marginalised, only foreign female athletes are sexualised in this newspaper coverage.

In chapter 10, Martin introduces Lucy Irigaray's psychoanalytic feminism to sport media analysis. She uses narrative writing techniques to map how one Spanish newspaper, *El País*, represents the star player Amaya Valdemoro, captain of the women's basketball. Through the eyes of an undergraduate sport student who is struggling with a media analysis assignment, Martin shows the need to look beyond the 'female–male binary' to provide an understanding of sexual difference as the original and primary human difference. Martin's aim is to illustrate what Irigaray's call for a focus on the radical difference between the two sexes and a theory based on the uniqueness and irreducibility of femininity might mean for feminist sport media studies.

Similar to Martin, Barker-Ruchti draws from poststructuralist theorising in chapter 11 to examine the Swiss media representation of the cyclist Karin Thürig, whose successful Olympic performance, despite cycling being an unfamiliar sport in Switzerland, attracted significant media attention. Barker-Ruchti reads this coverage through a Foucauldian lens to examine how Thürig's performance was 'normalised' through referrals to invaluable assistance from sport science and technology.

In chapter 12, Spencer focuses on a series of 'Olympic portraits' shot by the *USA Today* photographer Robert Hanashiro. These portraits conjured up images of the ancient Olympic Games through wreaths of vegetation; flowing robes worn by the athletes; and photographs printed in sepia hues with ragged borders. Spencer critically reads seven portraits – of the swimmer Natalie Coughlin, the fencer Sada Jacobson, the triathlete Barb Lindquist, the freestyle wrestler Patricia Miranda, the softball pitcher Jennie Finch, the gymnast Carly Patterson and the beach volleyball players Kerri Walsh and Misty May – through the concept of critical nostalgia to interrogate the meaning of such representations in contemporary American culture.

Notes

1. For more detailed discussion of the 'global–local' debate in sport media studies, see Bernstein and Blain (2003); Hoberman (2004); Maguire (1999; 2006); Rowe, 2003; Silk, Andrews and Cole (2004); Wamsley, Barney and Marty (2002); and Wenner (1998). From a feminist perspective, the theories of globalisation have served as a backdrop to 'transnational' feminism. While not a unified concept, this type of feminism, through intersectional analysis of women's condition in the globalised world, aims for social change in women's lives, particularly in the developing world. Mendoza (2002) asserts that transnational feminism 'points simultaneously to the position feminists worldwide have taken against the processes of globalization of the economy, the demise of the nation state and the development of a global mass culture as well as pointing to the nascent global women's studies research into the ways in which globalization affects women around the globe' (p. 296). Transnational feminism thus draws on the discussions of globalisation, from Third and First World feminist theorisation on race, class and sexuality and feminist postcolonial studies 'to make us aware of the artificiality of the idea of nation and its patriarchal nature' (p. 296). Several chapters in this book examine the media construction of sporting women through intersectional analysis and/or postcolonial theory, but as the focus is on national context, the authors have not identified their feminist approach(es) within transnational feminism.

2. So-called post-feminism can be seen as a continuation of liberal feminist ideals in consumer capitalism. However, instead of calling for equal opportunities and access for women, post-feminism implies that feminist activism and feminist movement are no longer needed because today's women have already achieved the equality fought for by earlier feminist movements. Newly achieved women's freedom, autonomy and liberation are often combined with a 'consumer lifestyle' which allows women to make choices and also experience personal freedom through numerous leisure pursuits. Consequently, women's liberation is now associated with freedom to be both powerful and sexual: experience success in the workplace, but still be 'feminine'. McDonald (2005) summarises: 'Post-feminism is not synonymous with the absence of feminism, but rather refers to the growing number of women who now take for granted some of the goals and achievements of the 1970's feminist movement while shunning the label of feminist' (p. 27). Post-feminist ideals have occupied especially North American feminists, who have examined contemporary media representations of women's sport and exercise (e.g. Cole and Hribar, 1995; Heywood and Dworkin, 2003; Lafrance,

1998; McDonald, 2005). For example, McDonald demonstrates how *Women's Sport and Fitness* in the US employs 'post-feminist ideologies' to depoliticise feminist critiques of gender, class and race-based oppression to promote a 'liberated' woman who personifies the 'traditional' form of femininity with a new-found self-acceptance and a freedom to consume. This includes the freedom to appear 'sexy' and heterosexually attractive, even when appearing in a traditionally 'male' environment such as sport, as a celebrated choice of an individual woman. Lenskyj's (2008) reading of the 'naked calendars', an increasingly popular practice for sportswomen to raise funds for their training and competition, reveals post-feminist attitudes used to defend this form of fundraising in the popular media. For instance, the production of these calendars is justified based on such rationales as defending the images as artistic and tasteful representations of athletes who 'really' are feminine and sexy and who have the self-confidence to 'show off' their beautiful bodies. These women can still be taken seriously as athletes and so be successful in their 'work'. This type of 'empowerment' is embedded in the post-feminist logic of individual athletes' celebrated choice to have their bodies consumed in the marketplace of sport.

Critical readings of post-feminist rhetoric reveal how the political aims of feminism have been turned against feminism by hijacking such terms as 'liberation' to serve the 'cult of American individualism through which consumer capitalism thrives' (McDonald, 2005, p. 26). In this way, feminism is stripped of its critique of social, political and economic inequality to promote forces benefiting from these social conditions. For example, Lenskyj (2008) asserts that the post-feminist readings of the 'nude calendars' continue to reflect and reinforce sexual exploitation and homophobia not different from representations of 'soft porn'. She concludes that 'few, if any, of the nude images challenge that longstanding underlying myth that a woman's appearance, and not her achievement, athletic or otherwise, is the only indication of her worth and the key to her success and happiness' (p. 147).

3. The term 'intersectionality' can be attributed to Patricia Hill Collins' groundbreaking work deriving from black female intellectuals' creative use of their marginality or 'their outsider within' status (Collins, 1986, p. S14) in the US academia. Collins demonstrated how sociology can benefit from the key themes central to 'Black feminist thought' (p. S16). One of these themes is the 'interlocking nature of race, gender, and class oppression' (p. S19). Collins has since developed this theme, which is now better know as intersectionality (Anderson and Collins, 2004; Collins, 1990, 1994). Race, gender and class are seen as forming a 'matrix of domination' through simultaneous overlapping and intersecting (Andersen, 2005). Consequently, 'gender can never be studied in isolation from race and class' (Andersen, 2005, p. 444) and should be analysed in the context of such structural changes as globalisation, redistribution of capital and wealth and inequality. Andersen (2005), however, distinguishes an analysis of intersectionality of race, class and gender from an 'additive model' of thinking where such 'new' categories as sexuality, disability and age are subjected to the analysis. In this model, identities are understood solely as 'a plurality of views and experiences' detached from the systems of domination that permeate society (p. 445). Intersectionality is concerned with structural inequalities caused by race,

gender and class relations, not 'comparative or additional' thinking were identity categories are simply added and compared through different experiences of diverse groups of people. For example, Andersen cautions against the simple addition of such identity categories as sexuality to the mix without explicating 'a political economy of sexuality and its connections to the political economy of race, class, and gender' (p. 449) because 'the appropriation and exploitation of racial/ethnic and gender labor makes race, class, and gender fundamentally different in their operation than sexuality' (p. 450). Instead, she calls for feminist theory and politics framed with political economy that 'connects sexuality to race, class, and gender in more than the ideological realm' (p. 452).

4. For readers interested in further readings of feminist poststructuralism, see Buchanan and Clairebrook (2000); Butler (1993); Diamond and Quinby (1988); Grozs (1994); Hekman (1996); Holland (1997); Irigaray (1985); Markula and Pringle (2006); Weedon (1987).

5. This understanding of identity formation challenges the 'essentialism' of which some forms of feminism are accused. Essentialism refers to the notion that there is an essential 'female nature' that is more virtuous than the 'male nature'. Consequently, masculine domination should be replaced with feminine virtues. While such a presupposition is often connected to so-called 'radical feminism', other feminisms have also been accused of reifying, while more implicitly, the notion of an essential female nature. For example, the notion of male hegemony has been argued to imply an essentialist notion of a 'real' femininity that is waiting to be discovered once the ideological clouding is removed. This currently hidden femininity would then take over the power position from masculine hegemony. Poststructuralist thought challenges the essentialist conceptual binary of masculine hegemony and oppressed femininity waiting to replace it by arguing, not for a 'feminine epistemology' (specific women's ways of knowing) or 'feminine ontology' (specific women's truth) that would replace the currently unfair masculine domination, but for multiple truths (some of which are currently privileged) that 'have been formed through discursive processes by which human beings gain understanding of their common world' (Hekman, 1990, p. 9).

References

Alexander, S. (1994). Newspaper coverage of athletics as a function of gender. *Women's Studies International Forum*, 17, 655–62.

Andersen, M. L. (2005). Thinking about women: A quarter century's view. *Gender & Society*, 19, 437–55.

Andersen, M. L., and Collins, P. H. (2004). *Race, Class, and Gender: An Anthology*, 5th edition. Belmont, CA: Wadsworth.

Baughman, C. (1995). *Women on Ice: Feminist Essays on the Tonya Harding/Nancy Kerrigan Spectacle*. London and New York: Routledge.

Bernstein, A. (2000). 'Things you can see from there you can't see from here': Globalization, media and the Olympics. *Journal of Sport & Social Issues*, 24, 351–69.

Bernstein, A. (2002). Is it time for a victory lap? Changes in the media coverage of women in sport. *International Review for the Sociology of Sport*, 37, 415–28.

Bernstein, A., and Blain, N. (2003). *Sport, Media, Culture: Global and Local Dimensions.* London: Frank Cass.

Billings, A. C. (2008). *Olympic Media: Inside the Biggest Show on Television.* London: Routledge.

Billings, A. C., and Eastman, S. T. (2002). Selective representation of gender, ethnicity, and nationality in American television coverage of the 2000 summer Olympics. *International Review for the Sociology of Sport, 27*, 351–70.

Birrell, S., and Cole, C. L. (2000). Double fault: Renee Richards and the construction and naturalization of difference. In S. Birrell and M. G. McDonald (eds.). *Reading Sport: Critical Essays on Power and Representation* (pp. 279–310). Boston, MA: Northeastern University Press.

Birrell, S., and McDonald, M. G. (2000). Reading sport, articulating power lines: An introduction. In S. Birrell and M. G. McDonald (eds.). *Reading Sport: Critical Essays on Power and Representation* (pp. 3–13). Boston, MA: Northeastern University Press.

Birrell, S. and Theberge, N. (1994). Ideological control of women in sport. In D. M. Costa and S. R. Guthrie (eds), *Women and Sport: Interdisciplinary Perspectives* (pp. 341–59). Champaign, IL: Human Kinetics.

Borcila, A. (2000). Nationalizing the Olympics around and away from the 'vulnerable' bodies of women: The NBC coverage of the 1996 Olympics and some moments after. *Journal of Sport & Social Issues, 24*, 118–47.

Bruce, T., Hovden, J. and Markula, P. (in press). *Sportswomen at the Olympics: A Global Content Analysis of Newspaper Coverage.* Taipei, Taiwan: SENSE.

Buchanan, I. and Colebrook, C. (2000). *Deleuze and Feminist Theory.* Edinburgh: Edinburgh University Press.

Butler, J. (1993). *Bodies that Matter: On the Discursive Limits of 'Sex'.* New York: Routledge.

Capon, D. A. and Helstein, M. T. (2005). 'Knowing the hero: the female athlete and myth at work in Nike advertising. In S. J. Jackson and D. L. Andrews (eds.). *Sport, Culture and Advertising: Identities, Commodities and the Politics of Representation* (pp. 39–58). London: Routledge.

Capranica, L. and Aversa, F. (2002). Italian television sport coverage during the 2000 Sydney Olympic Games: A gender perspective. *International Review for the Sociology of Sport, 27*, 337–49.

Capranica, L., Minganti, C., Billat, V., Hanghoj, S., Piacentini, M. F., Cumps, E. and Meeusen, R. (2005). Newspaper coverage of women's sports during the 2000 Sydney Olympic Games: Belgium, Denmark, France, and Italy. *Research Quarterly for Exercise and Sport, 76*, 212–23.

Cole, C. L. (1998). Addiction, exercise, and cyborgs: Technologies of deviant bodies. In G. Rail (ed.), *Sport in Postmodern Times* (pp. 261–76). Albany, NY: State University of New York Press.

Cole, C. L. and Hribar, A. (1995). Celebrity feminism: Nike style: Post-Fordism, transcendence, and consumer power. *Sociology of Sport Journal, 12*, 327–69.

Creedon, P. L. (1998). Women, sport, and media institutions: Issues in sports journalism and marketing. In L. A. Wenner (ed.), *MediaSport* (pp. 88–99). London: Routledge.

Collins, P. H. (1986). Learning from the outsider within: The sociological significance of Black feminist thought. *Social Problems, 33*(6), S14–S32.

Collins, P. H. (1990). *Black Feminist Thought: Knowledge, Consciousness, and the Politics of Empowerment.* New York: Routledge.

Collins, P. H. (2004). *Black Sexual Politics: African American, Gender, and the New Racism.* New York: Routledge.

Dallario, G. (1994). Chilly scenes of the 1992 Winter Games: The mass media and the marginalization of female athletes. *Sociology of Sport Journal*, 11, 275–88.

Darnel, S. C. and Sparks, R. (2005). Inside the promotional vortex: Canadian media construction of Sydney triathlete Simon Whitfield. *International Review for the Sociology of Sport*, 30, 357–76.

Davis, L. (1997). *The Swimsuit Issue and Sport: Hegemonic Masculinity and Sports Illustrated.* Albany, NY: State University of New York Press.

Diamond, I. and Quinby, L. (1988). *Feminism & Foucault: Reflections on Resistance.* Boston, MA: Northeastern University Press.

Douglas, D. (2005). Venus, Serena and Women's Tennis Association: When and where 'race' enters. *Sociology of Sport Journal*, 22, 256–82.

Douglas, D. D. and Jamieson, K. M. (2006). A farewell to remember: Interrogating the Nancy Lopez farewell tour. *Sociology of Sport Journal*, 23, 117–41.

Duncan, M. C. (1990). Sports photographs and sexual difference: Images of men and women in the 1984 and 1988 Olympic Games. *Sociology of Sport Journal*, 7, 22–43.

Duncan, M. C. and Messner, M. (1998).The media image of sport and gender. In L. A. Wenner (ed.), *MediaSport* (pp. 170–85). London: Routledge.

Duncan, M. and Aycock, A. (2005). Fitting images: Advertising, sport and disability. In S. J. Jackson, and D.L. Andrews (eds.), *Sport, Culture and Advertising: Identities, Commodities and the Politics of Representation* (pp. 136–54). London: Routledge.

Eastman, S. T. and Billings, A. C. (2000). Sportscasting and sports reporting: The power of gender bias. *Journal of Sport & Social Issues*, 24, 192–212.

Eastman, S. T. and Billings, A. C. (1999). Gender parity in the Olympics: Hyping women athletes, favoring man athletes. *Journal of Sport & Social Issues*, 23, 140–70.

Elder, C., Pratt, A., and Ellis, C. (2006), Running race: Reconciliation, nationalism and the Sydney 2000 Olympic Games. *International Review for the Sociology of Sport*, 41, 181–200.

Gardiner, G. (2003). Running for country: Australian print media representation of indigenous athletes in the 27th Olympiad. *Journal of Sport & Social Issues*, 27, 233–60.

Giardina, M. (2001). Global Hingis: Flexible citizenship and the transnational celebrity. In D. L. Andrews and S. J. Jackson (eds.), *Sport Stars: The Cultural Politics of Sporting Celebrity* (pp. 201–17). London: Routledge.

Giardina, M. (2005). *Sporting Pedagogies: Performing Culture and Identity in the Global Arena.* New York: Peter Lang.

Giardina, M. and Metz, J. (2005). Women's sports in Nike's America: Body politics and the corporo-empowerment of 'everyday athletes'. In S. J. Jackson, and D. L. Andrews (eds.), *Sport, Culture and Advertising: Identities, Commodities and the Politics of Representation* (pp. 59–80). London: Routledge.

Grosz, E. (1994). *Volatile Bodies: Toward a Corporeal Feminism.* Bloomington, IN: Indiana University Press.

Hall, M. A. (1996). *Feminism and Sporting Bodies.* Champaign, IL: Human Kinetics.

Hargreaves, J. A. (1994). *Sporting Females: Critical Issues in the History and Sociology of Women's Sport.* London: Routledge.

Harris, J. and Clayton, B. (2002). Femininity, masculinity, physicality and the English tabloid press: The case of Anna Kournikova. *International Review for the Sociology of Sport*, 37, 397–413.

Hekman, S. J. (1990). *Gender and Knowledge: Elements of Postmodern Feminism.* Boston, MA: Northeastern University Press.

Hekman, S. J. (1996). *Feminist Interpretations of Michel Foucault.* University Park, PA: Pennsylvania State University Press.

Helstein, M. T. (2003). That's who I want to be: The politics and production of desire within Nike advertising to women. *Journal of Sport & Social Issues, 27,* 276–92.

Helstein, M. (2005). Rethinking community: Introducing the 'what ever' female athlete. *Sociology of Sport Journal, 22,* 1–18.

Helstein, M. (2007). Seeing your sporting body: Identity, subjectivity, and misrecognition. *Sociology of Sport Journal, 24,* 78–103.

Heywood, L. and Dworkin, S. L. (2003). *Built to Win: The Rise of the Female Athlete as Cultural Icon.* Minneapolis, MN: University of Minnesota Press.

Hills, L. and Kennedy, E. (2006). Space invaders at Wimbledon: Televised sport and deterritorialization. *Sociology of Sport Journal, 23,* 419–37.

Hoberman, J. (2004). Sportive nationalism in the age of globalization. In J. Bale and M. K. Christiansen (eds.), *Post Olympism: Questioning Sport in the Twenty-first Century* (pp. 177–188). Oxford: Berg.

Hogan, J. (2003). Staging the nation: Gendered and ethnicized discourses of national identity in Olympic opening ceremonies. *Journal of Sport & Social Issues, 27,* 100–23.

Holland, N. J. (1997). *Feminist Interpretations of Jacques Derrida.* University Park, PA: Pennsylvania State University Press.

Irigaray, L. (1985). *This Sex Which Is Not One.* Ithaca, NY: Cornell University Press.

Jackson, S. J. and Andrews, D. L. *Sport, Culture and Advertising: Identities, Commodities and the Politics of Representation* (pp. 59–80). London: Routledge.

Jamieson, K. M. (2000). Reading Nancy Lopez: Decoding representations of race, class, and sexuality. In S. Birrell and M. G. McDonald (eds.), *Reading Sport: Critical Essays on Power and Representation* (pp. 144–65). Boston, MA: Northeastern University Press.

Kane, M. J. (1995). Resistance/transformation of the oppositional binary: Exposing sport as a continuum. *Journal of Sport & Social Issues, 19,* 191–218.

Kane, M. J. and Greendorfer, S. L. (1994). The media's role in accommodating the resisting stereotyped images of women in sport. In P. J. Creedon (ed.), *Women, Media and Sport: Challenging Gender Values.* Thousands Oaks, CA: Sage.

Kane, M. J. and Lenskyj, H. J. (1998). Media treatment of female athletes: Issues of gender and sexualities. In L. A. Wenner (ed.), *MediaSport* (pp. 186–201). London: Routledge.

King, C. (2007). Media portrayals of male and female athletes: A text and picture analysis of British national newspaper coverage of the Olympic Games since 1948. *International Review for the Sociology of Sport, 42,* 187–99.

Kinnick, K. N. (1998). Gender bias in newspaper profiles of 1996 Olympic athletes: A content analysis of five major dailies. *Women's Studies in Communication, 21*(2), 212–37.

Lafrance, M. (1998). Colonizing the feminine: Nike's intersections of postfeminism and hyperconsumption. In G. Rail (ed.), *Sport and Postmodern Times* (pp. 117–39). Albany, NY: State University of New York Press.

Lee, J. (1992). Media portrayals of male and female Olympic athletes: Analysis of newspaper accounts of the 1984 and 1988 Summer Games. *International Review for the Sociology of Sport, 27,* 197–219.

Lenskyj, H. J. (1998). 'Inside Sport' or 'on the margins'? Australian women and the sport media. *International Review for the Sociology of Sport*, 33, 19–23.

Lenskyj, H. J. (2000). *Inside the Olympic Industry*. Albany, NY: State University of New York Press.

Lenskyj, H. J. (2002). *The Best Olympics Ever? Social Impacts of Sydney 2000*. Albany, NY: SUNY Press.

Lenskyj, H. J. (2008). *Olympic Industry Resistance: Challenging the Olympic Power and Propaganda*. Albany, NY: SUNY Press.

Lippe, G. van der (2002). Media image: Sport, gender, and national identities in five European countries. *International Review for the Sociology of Sport*, 27, 371–95.

Lock, R. A. (2003). The doping ban: Compulsory heterosexuality and lesbophobia. *International Review for the Sociology of Sport*, 38, 397–411.

Lucas, S. (2000). Nike's commercial solution: Girls, sneakers, and salvation. *International Review for the Sociology of Sport*, 35, 149–64.

Maguire, J. (1999). *Global Sport: Identities, Societies, Civilizations*. Cambridge: Polity Press.

Maguire, J. A. (2006). Sport and globalization. In A Raney and J. Bryant (eds.), *Handbook of Sports and Media* (pp. 435–46). Mahwah, NJ: Erlbaum Associates.

Maguire, J. A., Butler, K., Barnward, S. and Golding, P. (2008). Olympism and consumption: An analysis of advertising in the British media coverage of the 2004 Athens Olympic Games. *Sociology of Sport Journal*, 25, 167–86.

Markula, P. (2000). 'I gotta do the Marathon:' Women's running as a truth-game. *Aethlon*, XVIII(1) (Fall), 89–106.

Markula, P. (2005). 'Cute with vague feminist gender shift': Posh and Becks united. In D. L. Andrews (ed.), *Manchester United: A Thematic Study* (pp. 160–72). London: Routledge.

Markula, P. and Pringle, R. (2006). *Foucault, Sport and Exercise: Power, Knowledge and Transforming the Self*. London: Routledge.

McDonald, M. G. (2005). Model behavior? Sporting feminism and consumer culture. In S. J. Jackson, and D. L. Andrews (eds.), *Sport, Culture and Advertising: Identities, Commodities and the Politics of Representation* (pp. 24–38). London: Routledge.

McDonald, M. G. (2008). Rethinking resistance: The queer play of the Women's National Basketball Association, visibility politics and late capitalism. *Leisure Studies*, 27(1), 77–93.

McDonald, M. G. and Birrell, S. (1999). Reading sport critically: A methodology for interrogating power. *Sociology of Sport Journal*, 16, 283–300.

McKay, J. (2005). Enlightened racism and celebrity feminism in contemporary sports advertising discourse. In S. J. Jackson, and D. L. Andrews (eds.), *Sport, Culture and Advertising: Identities, Commodities and the Politics of Representation* (pp. 81–99). London: Routledge.

Mendoza, B. (2002). Transnational feminisms in question. *Feminist Theory*, 3, 295–314.

Messner, M. A., Duncan, M. C., and Cooky, C. (2003). Silence, sports bras, and wrestling porn: Women in televised sports news and highlights shows. *Journal of Sport & Social Issues*, 27, 38–51.

Mikosza, J. M. and Phillips, M. G. (1999). Gender, sport and the body politics. *International Review for the Sociology of Sport*, 34, 5–16.

Pedersen, P. M. (2002). Examining equity in newspaper photographs. *International Review for the Sociology of Sport*, 37, 303–18.

Pirinen, R. (1997). The construction of women's positions in sport: A textual analysis of articles on the female athletes in Finnish women's magazines. *Sociology of Sport Journal*, 14, 290–301.

Puijk, R. (2000). A global media event? Coverage of the 1994 Lillehammer Olympic Games. *International Review for the Sociology of Sport*, 35, 309–30.

Rowe, D. (1999). *Sport, Culture and the Media: The Unruly Trinity*. London: Oxford University Press.

Rowe, D. (2003). Sport and the repudiation of the global. *International Review for the Sociology of Sport*, 38, 281–94.

Schell, B. L. A. and Rodriguez, S. (2001). Subverting bodies/ambivalent representations: Media analysis of a Paraolympian. *Sociology of Sport Journal*, 18, 127–35.

Schultz, J. (2005). Reading the catsuit: Serena Williams and the production of Blackness at the 2002 U.S. Open. *Journal of Sport & Social Issues*, 29, 338–57.

Segrave, J. (2000). The (neo)modern Olympic Games: the revolutions in Europe and the resurgence of universalism, *International Review for the Sociology of Sport*, 25, 268–81.

Shields, S., Gilbert, L., Shen, X. and Said, H. (2004). A look at print media coverage across four Olympiads. *Women in Sport & Physical Activity Journal*, **13**, 87–99.

Silk, M., Andrews, D. L. and Cole, C. L. (2005). *Sport and Corporate Nationalisms*. New York: Berg.

Slater, J. (1998). Changing partners: The relationship between the mass media and the Olympic Games. In R. K. Barney, K. B. Wamsley, S. G. Martin and G. H. MacDonald (eds.), *Fourth International Symposium for Olympic Research* (pp. 49–69). London, ON: University of Western Ontario.

Spencer, N. E. (2001). From 'child's play' to 'party crasher': Venus Williams, racism and professional tennis. In D. L. Andrews and S. J. Jackson (eds.), *Sport Stars: The Cultural Politics of Sporting Celebrity* (pp. 87–101). London: Routledge.

Spencer, N. E., (2003). America's sweet heart and 'Czech-mate': A discursive analysis of the Evert–Navratilova rivalry. *Journal of Sport & Social Issues*, 26, 115–35.

Spencer, N. E. (2004). Sister act IV: Venus and Serena Williams at Indian Wells: 'Sincere fictions' and white racism. *Journal of Sport & Social Issues*, 28, 115–35.

Stevenson, D. (2002). Women, sport, and globalization: Competing discourses of sexuality and nation. *Journal of Sport & Social Issues*, 26, 209–25.

Stone, J. and Horne, J. (2008). The print media coverage of skiing and snowboarding in Britain. *Journal of Sport & Social Issues*, 32, 94–112.

Theberge, N. and Birrell, S. (1994). The sociological study of women and sport. In D. M. Costa and S. R. Guthrie (eds.), *Women and Sport: Interdisciplinary Perspectives* (pp. 323–9). Champaign, IL: Human Kinetics.

Thorpe, H. (2008). Foucault, technologies of self and the media: Discourses of femininity in snowboarding culture. *Journal of Sport & Social Issues*, 32, 199–229.

Tomlinson, A. (2005). The commercialization of the Olympics: Cities, corporations and the Olympic commodity. In K. Young and K. B. Wamsley (eds.), *Global Olympics: Historical and Sociological Studies of the Modern Games* (pp. 179–200). London: Elsevier.

Tuggle, C. A. and Owen, A. (1999). A descriptive analysis of NBC's coverage of the centennial Olympics. *Journal of Sport & Social Issues*, 23, 171–83.

Urquhart, J. and Crossman, J. (1999). The *Globe* and *Mail* coverage of the Winter Olympic Games: A cold place for women athletes. *Journal of Sport & Social Issues*, 23, 193–202.

Vincent, J., Imwold, C., Masemann, V. and Johnson, J. T. (2002). A comparison of selected 'serious' and 'popular' British, Canadian, and United States newspaper coverage of female and male athletes competing in the Centennial Olympic Games. *International Review for the Sociology of Sport*, 37, 319–35.

Wamsley, K. B., Barney, R. K. and Marty, S. G. (2002). *The Global Nexus Engaged. Sixth International Symposium for Olympic Research.* London, ON: University of Western Ontario.

Weedon, C. (1987). *Feminist Practice & Poststructuralist Theory.* Oxford: Basil Blackwell.

Wenner L. A. (1998). *MediaSport.* London: Routledge.

Wensing, E. and Bruce, T. (2003). Bending the rules: Media representations of gender during the international sporting event. *International Review for the Sociology of Sport*, 38, 387–96.

Wright, J. and Clarke, G. (1999). Sport, media and the construction of compulsory heterosexuality. *International Review for the Sociology of Sport*, 34(3), 227–43.

2
Reading Media Texts in Women's Sport: Critical Discourse Analysis and Foucauldian Discourse Analysis

Judy Liao and Pirkko Markula

This chapter provides a methodological guide for researchers interested in conducting qualitative media analysis in sport studies. Instead of asking each contributor to include a method section in their chapters we have chosen to devote a whole chapter to the methodological aspects of feminist sport media analysis. While there are several qualitative methods that are designed for analysis of language, we have chosen to focus on critical discourse analysis (CDA) developed by Norman Fairclough and a modified form of Foucauldian discourse analysis. Several of the contributors analyse media content through a critical feminist lens and it is, therefore, pertinent to introduce CDA in this chapter. In addition, Barker-Ruchti (chapter 11) uses Foucauldian analysis in her examination of Swiss media coverage of the triathlete Karin Thürig so that the readers can witness a further example of this type of media analysis. Where the contributors use other analytical methods, they introduce their theoretical perspectives in more detail in their chapters. These include Derridean deconstruction (see Markula, chapter 5), psychoanalysis (see MacNeill, chapter 3) and narrative writing (see Martin, chapter 10). As this book intends to celebrate theoretical variety, we do not argue for the 'best way' to analyse media, but wish to draw attention to the interconnectedness between theoretical premise and method in feminist sport media analysis.

Neither Fairclough nor Foucault is considered a feminist and their works do not consider gender issues directly. In this sense, the focus on these methods might appear out of place in a book about feminist interpretations of female athletes at the Olympic Games. Both Foucault's approach and Fairclough's critical model, however, have been appropriated for feminist use (e.g. Chouliaraki and Fairclough,

1999; Hekman, 1996; Weedon, 1997) and thus are also appropriate for feminist analysis of the sport media. We first introduce Fairclough's CDA, which is one of the few established methods developed specifically for analysis of texts. We then discuss a modified Foucauldian archaeology and genealogy for the purpose of analysing media. To compare and contrast these two methods, we provide a clear example of an analysis of a TV commercial featuring Women's National Basketball Association (WNBA) players. We conclude by evaluating appropriate ways of using each method.

Fairclough's critical discourse analysis

Critical discourse analysis (CDA) is a general term which encompasses a variety of methods for social critique (Blommaert, 2005). Among various scholars working with CDA, Fairclough has systematically developed 'a set of philosophical premises, theoretical methods, methodological guidelines and specific techniques' to analyse texts (Jørgensen and Phillips, 2002, p. 60). Fairclough (2006) characterises his theoretical approach as a 'transdisciplinary' one (p. 12) which distinguishes between discursive (society and culture) and non-discursive material (e.g. economic and governmental systems) worlds. The relationship between the discursive and non-discursive worlds is dialectical: while they constitute two discrete terrains, they interact in various ways. For example, if women's sport in understood as less important than men's in the cultural, popular media discourse, the organisational and commercial practices are also likely to treat women's sport as secondary. Similarly, scant attention in the media or in the commercial marketplace (e.g. endorsements, sponsorships) creates an understanding of women's sport as unimportant and unpopular. Such perceptions, Fairclough argues, are ideologically constructed.

Ideological working of discourse

The central focus of CDA is to critically investigate and address social problems by examining the *ideological workings* of discourse. For Fairclough (2006), discourse is a 'particular way of conceptualizing … language' (p. 9). Language here exceeds written texts, or spoken words, and includes visual images, body language and various semiotic forms. Fairclough's method is designed to disclose the ideologies and thus make explicit how dominance works through texts and language.[1] With its focus on the ideological construction of textual content, CDA appears to lend itself well to feminist examinations of how sport media representations carry the ideologically constructed meanings of femininity, such as marginalisation, trivialialisation and sexualisation, which work to subordinate women and preserve male dominance in sport (see also chapter 1). Fairclough (1995; 2002) further considers that ideology is located in both semiosis (the structural meaning-making system) and communication events (the forms and contents of texts as used in a certain situation). Therefore, it is important to analyse both how ideology constrains discursive practices and how discursive practices of communication events transform meanings. Based on these principles, Fairclough has developed a specific CDA method to analyse the ideological content of a media event.

Fairclough's three-dimensional model for CDA

Fairclough's CDA comprises three steps designed to analyse how ideology(ies) operate through a communication event. (A communication event is an event where language is used. For example, a newspaper article, a commercial, a television programme or an interview can be considered as communication events (Blommaert, 2005; Jørgensen and Phillips, 2002).) Fairclough defines the three analytical steps as a description of the content of the communications event, intertextual analysis and connection to ideological dominance. We now introduce each step separately and demonstrate how to use CDA through a concrete analysis of a TV commercial of the Women's National Basketball Association (WNBA), 'This is Who I am 2003'.[2]

The first step is to analyse the *contents of the communication event*. The prime method used in this phase of the CDA is 'description'. Fairclough proposes that we describe linguistic characters of the text, such as vocabulary (e.g. wording and metaphor) and grammar (e.g. transitivity and modality),[3] and its textual organisations beyond sentences, for instance, cohesion (e.g., conjunction and schemata) and structure[4] (e.g. turn-taking) (Blommaert, 2005; Fairclough, 1995; Jørgensen and Phillips, 2002). Although Fairclough often focuses on linguistic aspects of texts, this step concerns more than a description of merely written or spoken words. For example, photographs, which are often analysed by researchers in sport studies, can be described in similar detail to language in CDA. For example, Duncan's (1990) article introduced in chapter 1 is concerned with the pictorial content of Olympic Games[5] photographs. Her descriptors include physical appearances, poses and body positions, facial expressions, emotional displays and camera angles. The analysis of the textual organisation includes visual groupings (how multiple photos are grouped together), captions, surrounding texts and titles. In this book, Elling and Luijt use Duncan's descriptors as a basis for their analysis of photographs in the Dutch newspaper coverage of the Olympic Games (chapter 7). A TV commercial can also be understood as a communication event which is comprised of spoken and written language as well as visual content. We now attempt a description of a commercial where we have to consider both of these aspects of communication.

The WNBA TV commercial 'This is Who I Am 2003' depicts seven WNBA basketball players (in alphabetical order – Jennifer Azzi, Sue Bird, Swin Cash, Lisa Leslie, Tichia Penicheiro, Sheryl Swoopes and Tamika Williams) and is composed of individual montages of the players. Among the seven, Penicheiro is the only non-American player;[6] Cash, Leslie, Swoopes and Williams are African Americans; and Azzi and Bird are Caucasians.

To ensure we have provided a detailed enough description for the further analysis we have listed our descriptors in Table 2.1. The table allows for an easy check of the original descriptions at the later stages of the CDA. We have further divided the descriptions into audio texts, visual texts (which include physical appearances of the athletes), body language, written texts and camera angles in this 1-minute 2-second TV commercial. We have presented as much detail as possible about the appearance of the athletes (e.g. facial expression), their clothing (e.g. colour and style) and their surroundings (e.g., objects, background, other individuals).

Fairclough (2005) describes the second step of CDA as an analysis of the *processes of production, circulation and consumption of discourses or intertextuality*. This can be an analysis of the actual physical processes of publishing or consuming texts (e.g. who watches TV or reads newspapers), but can also refer to an examination of how the discourses in the communication event relate to prior ones. At this stage, the researcher has first to connect the descriptions of the communication event from the first stage of the CDA to a discourse and then to look for links to other discourses used to shape the particular discourse under analysis. Therefore, the purpose of the second stage is to interpret the possible meanings embedded in the event. Fairclough refers to the discursive connections as the intertextuality of the text and further distinguishes between two forms of intertextuality. A manifest intertextuality refers to how a text is 'overtly drawing upon other texts' (Blommaert, 2005, p. 29) by, for example, directly quoting from other texts or discourses. A newspaper article of women's sport might overtly quote from legislation of Title IX or refer to nutrition texts to promote sport as a 'healthy' activity for women.

Table 2.1   The content of 'This is Who I Am', 2003

Visual	Audio (Dialogue)	Camera Angles
P is driving a sports car in a black, skin-tight leather outfit.		Neutral Above eye-level
L is on a catwalk by a swimming pool wearing a stylish dress.		
A is standing in a desert wearing a leather vest.		Neutral
B is leaning against a wall in a stylish evening dress with an icy expression.		Neutral
S is dancing on a cliff in a red gauzy dress.		Slightly below eye-level
C puts on a pair of blue carpenter jeans:	I'm part of the new revolution.	Neutral
C is posing against a white backdrop in a red dress.		Above
L is posing with a basketball in a tight blue outfit.		Above
By the pool, L shrugs her shoulders:	I'm glamorous, so what?	Neutral (Close-up)
B is in a pink sport bra and looking up.		Below
P stands by the sports car:	I'm always looking ahead, never behind.	Neutral
A is wearing a red sport bra and lifting weights with a voiceover:	I'm not afraid to lose, but I don't like it.	Above
Then A looks into the camera C's game highlights. (Clenches her fist to celebrate).		Neutral
C wearing a red dress:	I'm not a diva	Neutral
P stands by the car:	I'm a diva	Neutral
P's game highlights. (Cheering up the team).		
B is leaning against the wall, and smiling.		Slightly above
S stands by a cliff wearing a red sport bra:	I'm responsible, 'cause I know my son is watching	Neutral
S's game highlight. (Driving in for a lay-up).		
S in a red dress is posing with a basketball:	I'm in the spotlight, but I still have my secrets.	Below
A video clip of L slamming the ball through the net – or 'dunking'.		Neutral

Table 2.1 (Continued)

Visual	Audio (Dialogue)	Camera Angles
By the swimming pool, L is wearing a long, low-cut evening dress.		Neutral
W is smiling and throwing a basketball up, she is wearing a blue denim jacket:	I'm a shining star.	Neutral
L is posing with a basketball in a tight blue outfit with a voiceover:	I'm your sister.	Neutral
S stands by the cliff:	I'm your daughter.	Neutral
P stands by the car:	I'm the girl next door.	Neutral
C is posing in front of a gate of a factory look-alike.		Above
B is stretching in a pink sport bra and tights.		Below, then neutral
B's game highlights. (Driving in for a lay-up).		
A stands in the desert wearing a leather vest:	I'm a believer in myself	Neutral
A is running in the desert wearing a red sport bra and tights.		Neutral
B is in a silver dress:	I'm not as sweet as you think I am	Neutral
L is striking a pose by the pool in a dress:		Slightly below
L is posing with a basketball in a tight blue outfit:	I'm on a journey,	Neutral
(on the screen): FEARLESS **I AM POWER** WARRIOR **DAUGHTER** PRIDE **THIS IS WHO I AM** JOURNEY **GLAMOROUS** I AM CONFIDNET STRENGTH SHINING STAR REVOLUTION (All other texts fade away) THIS IS WHO I AM	but I am not alone (voiceover)	

Interdiscursivity, or constitutive intertextuality, is a more subtle form of intertextuality which focuses on how different genres, discourses and styles are employed in a communication event to articulate with specific characteristics. For example, a segment of sport news might contain an interview that includes discussions of an athlete's performance, her current sponsorship contract and details of her family life. These discourses or topics then articulate her with certain characteristics (e.g. high performance, successful funding, motherhood). Each segment might use a different narrative style (such as a one-to-one interview, narration of facts, slow motion). This interdiscursivity constructs the athlete drawing from her private and public life as a female, an athlete and a business-woman to provide an authentic understanding of what it means to be a woman in competitive sport. In photographs constitutive intertextuality can be analysed through different camera angles from which the objects are pictured. For example, a shot taken at a below eye-level angle implies the photographed individual has an inferior status to the viewer, whereas an above eye-level angle suggests a superior status. In addition, different facial expressions, poses, positions of body and physical appearance convey different meanings. We now continue our CDA of the WNBA commercial to demonstrate how to analyse intertextuality. We first examine what discourse(s) can be detected in the descriptions from our first analytical step and then analyse its manifest intertextuality (i.e. how these discourses might draw on other discourses). We then focus on the constitutive intertextuality by detailing the different genres and styles of the commercial by focusing specifically on the camera angles, the body positions and the physical appearance of the players.

Based on our description, the WNBA commercial does not explicitly quote from any other discourse. However, the audio-dialogue contains references to a 'new revolution'. This reference has been often quoted by women's sport in general and especially the WNBA. The league has frequently linked itself to the groundbreaking legislation, Title IX, and to successful women in various fields in the US. In this sense the term 'new revolution' in this commercial connects to the idea that the WNBA is a successor of feminist 'revolutions'. Secondly, there are sev-eral statements that refer to glamour or diva-like behaviours that can be connected to the looks of the players. Thirdly, we can detect statements that refer to sport performance ('I'm not afraid to lose; I'm a shining star') or the mental toughness required in sport ('I'm always looking ahead; I'm a believer in myself'). Moreover, statements like 'I'm your daughter', 'sister', 'the girl next door' and 'mother' link the players to their family and community. In sum, the discourse in the commercial connects with other discourses that define women's elite sport and fem-inist movements (e.g. Title XI), but also locate the athletes within the narratives of feminine beauty and family roles.

To examine constitutive intertextuality, we first focus on the visuals of the commercial. Most are 'beauty shots' in which the athletes pose in non-sport outfits. Most of these outfits are tight and many denote a 'traditionally' feminine style. Even when the players are pictured doing physical activity, they wear tight, scant clothing or a feminine, evening dress. In addition, the players pose with basketballs (a frequently used portrayal of a basketball player), but none appears in her jersey or any sport outfit. These images present them as, first and foremost, pretty women, but not necessarily as athletes. In one scene, however, Azzi lifts weights in a sport bra and asserts her determination and desire to win. When Cash puts on the carpenter jeans, her image can be connected to tough, traditional men's work. The camera angles in the commercial are mostly neutral. It is possible that this pictorial technique have been chosen to depict the players as strong and powerful athletes and not sexual objects. There are, however, few sport scenes (e.g. various highlights of the players actually playing basketball) compared to the NBA's commercials, where nearly all of the content is composed of highlights from the basketball games. Overall, the commercial depicts the WNBA players as strong and empowered, yet glamorous, 'ordinary' women.

After detecting what themes emerge from the text and how they link with other discourses around women's sport, the third step of CDA demonstrates *how the communication event connects to hegemonic ideology.* The starting point is that hegemony works through integrating subordinate classes into the social order by articulating meanings that appear as common sense. Therefore, to reveal how hegemony works through a communication event, it is necessary to re/articulate its ideological structure. The ultimate aim is to disclose ideological operations of hegemony in the discourse to change the ways we use language. These changes would lead to further changes in the practices of the material world and thus contribute to 'social emancipation' (Fairclough, 2002, p. 127).

As the third step for our analysis of the WNBA commercial, we align intertextuality with the ideological construction of gender in sport. While we acknowledge that a female athlete's identity is constructed in the intersections of several ideological forces, we focus on the ideology of masculinity for the sake of brevity in our example (for examples of analysis of intersectionality, see Hills and Kennedy, chapter 6; Elling and Luijt, chapter 7; Bruce, chapter 8; Koh, chapter 9). As discussed in chapter 1, ideology of masculinity works, subtly, to keep women subordinate to men. For example, sportswomen's performances are rendered inferior to men's by marginalising, trivialising and sexualising women athletes in the media. We now analyse whether the WNBA commercial works along these lines.

The WNBA commercial contains a high proportion of sexualised images which focus on depicting the players as 'pretty' women rather than serious basketball players. Their role off the court as daughters, sisters, mothers, divas or girls next door are emphasised, which further articulates the players with 'acceptable', traditional femininity as defined by the hegemonic ideology of masculinity. Their athleticism is trivialised by the lack of sport-related images which appear odd in a promotional video for a sport league. In addition, wearing stylish dresses even when posing with basketballs, a symbol of their athletic identity, detracts from the players' athleticism and muscularity. The female athletes in the commercial perform 'female apologetic': they have to be pretty to be strong athletes. Such representation preserves the hegemonic ideology of masculinity, although superficially celebrating the emergence of successful female basketball players. In the end, these players are *female* athletes, who might be good players, but are definitely pretty and feminine. Our CDA has revealed a form of gender discrimination in the WNBA commercial which now, as a result, should be corrected.

Summary

Following Jørgensen and Phillips (2002), the main tenets of CDA system include:

1. CDA critically uncovers social problems. Our analysis demonstrates that the WNBA commercial promotes gender difference in a subtle manner. We acknowledge that CDA could have potentially helped us further critique issues around race, sexuality or nationalism which we left unanalysed due to shortage of space.
2. Discourse works ideologically. The discursive aspect of society helps maintain material dominance by conveying hegemonic ideologies which are produced in the interests of dominant classes. Hence, a goal of CDA analyses is to reveal underlying ideologies through an examination of certain discourses. Our analysis demonstrates that although the discourse in the WNBA commercial appears empowering to women, it is actually a strategic production of ideology of masculinity to cope with the emergence of strong women.
3. An analysis of discourse should be conducted within its historical context through an investigation of manifest intertextuality of the discourse. We examine how various historical events around women's sport in the US (e.g. Title XI), and their discursive practice, shaped the discourse of the commercial.
4. The relationship of social and cultural structures and material world is dialectical. Through examination of intertextuality, we can understand how the communications event is given meanings in relation to the material world. For example, the connection of Title IX in the WNBA commercial can be linked to a material change in social gender relations.

The goal of CDA is to disclose ideologies that serve the interest of dominant groups through certain discursive practices. In the following section, we turn to Foucauldian discourse analysis to detail how this methodological approach might serve researchers interested in sportswomen's representation in the media.

Foucauldian discourse analysis

At the beginning of this chapter, we noted that both Fairclough and Foucault ground their methods on the concept 'discourse'. We now begin our discussion of Foucault's discourse analysis by comparing his notion of discourse with Fairclough's use of the same term to illustrate the theoretical premise of each method. Fairclough actually borrows the term 'discourse' from Foucault and in many ways his CDA and Foucault's method appear very similar. However, there is a profound difference in how they understand the impact of power and the role of language as part of the power relations. If Fairclough's CDA is helpful for feminist researchers who aim to uncover how hegemonic ideologies work through language, Foucault's method is suitable for poststructuralist examinations of how language structures reality (see also Barker-Ruchti, chapter 11). Before embarking on actual methodological differences, however, it is important to highlight the concept of power in each scholar's theoretical schema.

Power relations and discourse

Fairclough draws from the Gramscian theory of hegemony where ideologies are understood as systems of beliefs that the powerful use to maintain their dominance over the subordinate groups. Ideologies are transmitted through language, which gives meanings to individual experiences. CDA reveals these meanings and thus exposes the ideologies that permeate language and maintain the hegemony of a certain group and oppress others. Foucault understands power quite differently: instead of a possession of a certain group, he sees power as relational.

Foucault advocates that power 'exists only as exercised' within relationships with people (Foucault, 2000, p. 340). Power, therefore, is everywhere and anyone who is not physically confined is able to exercise it in relations to others. This also means that from Foucault's point of view we cannot simply divide individuals into those who 'possess' power (and thus oppress others) and those who are without power and thus are innocent victims of the powerful. Neither is anyone outside of power relations or 'free' from power, but are always necessarily involved in the use of power due to one's relationship with other people. In Foucault's (2000) own words, he rejects the idea of 'false consciousness' and, at the same time, the utopian idea of power as 'the renunciation of freedom' (p. 340). Consequently, while Fairclough's position assumes that the dominant classes actively *create* particular types of language to convey hegemonic ideology, Foucault asserts that certain groups become powerful and influential by *tactically using* discourses. Foucault asks 'how' power is exercised instead of 'who' has power and 'what' power is (Cole, Giardina and Andrews, 2004). It is crucial to note, however, that Foucault does not assume that all individuals and groups are 'equal'. On the contrary, he asserts very strongly that imbalances in power relations exist and devotes much of his research to examining how individuals are disciplined through discursive formations in society. For Foucault, discourses in conjunction with relations of power influence people's experiences and social practices. Discourses, however, comprise more than ideologies disguised by a particular use of language.

In essence, discourses are ways of knowing and everyone using language participates in the circulation and creation of these knowledges. For example, what we currently know as 'sport' is considered professional, often international, competition where successful participation requires serious training and time commitment. From a Foucauldian perspective, sport comprises a field where practices are defined through discourses. The best athletes, for instance, are professionals who need to train effectively in order to be successful. Training as a practice requires knowledge from several experts such as sport scientists, coaches, trainers, managers and businessmen. However, a certain type of sport science knowledge, for example, dominates the field of sport because we tend to define 'effective training' in a particular way. Sport media reporting can also be considered as a practice that is defined through discourses or ways of knowing what is worth reporting in a newspaper or in a television newscast. Everyone who talks or writes about sport participates in circulating this knowledge. For example, sport fans often debate the effectiveness of certain training techniques or lament the fate of an athlete who sustained an injury due to over-training. Newspaper articles regularly reveal training details from an athlete's programme. Foucauldian discourse analysis aims to detect what knowledges dominate particular fields, where they come from and how they have become dominant. In other words, a Foucauldian would ask: why do we consider certain ways of knowing about sport as important?

Where ideologies are defined as tools for oppression, no discourse is good or bad in itself. What matters is how a discourse is used within power relations. For example, training knowledge based on sport sciences is not bad *per se* – on the contrary, it certainly has improved results in many sports – but if it becomes the 'only true way of knowing' about athletes' preparation for competitions, it suppresses other knowledges in the field. Similarly, an athlete's identity is formed within the nexus of power relations and discourse(s) that structure sport as a field. The media play a part in this construction by representing athletes in certain ways. Again, for a Foucauldian, no representation is good or bad *per se* but its impact on the discursive field depends on how it is used. For example, if newspaper stories focus only on slender, blonde, 'sexy' women athletes when the best competitors appear very different from this representation, a Foucauldian discourse analysis would aim to uncover why such an understanding of women athletes dominates the media when success in the field of sport is defined by a winning performance, not through appearance. In other words, a Foucauldian would be interested in what discourses define a female athlete's identity in media and how these discourses have become dominant within current power relations that structure elite sport. The next question is: How do we detect the discourses that define sport women's media representation?

Foucauldian discourse analysis as method for sport media analysis

Foucault's methods to analyse language were not developed as clearly as Fairclough's. However, he details two approaches as methodological bases for his work. Foucault's earlier work was based on what he called the 'archaeology' through which he examined how discursive formations accumulated meanings within a specific cultural and historical context. At this point Foucault focused on written statements in the scientific works to specify further that discourses in these texts could consist of either general domain of statements, individualisable groups of statements or groupings of specific 'rules' all of which defined a practice. To examine what statements link with each other into discourses an archaeologist should identify the objects, enunciations, concepts and theories that inform a particular discursive practice such as sport media reporting. At this point, Foucault did not clearly connect the formation of discourses with relations of power, but later developed his 'genealogical' method to specify this nexus.

Both of Foucault's methods require an examination of the historical development of discourse(s) into technologies for exercising power. Therefore, an analysis faithful to Foucault would require an historical examination of a large sample of data. For example, to understand how the practices of the WNBA have been formed within the discourse/power nexus of professional (women's) sport in the US, we would need to collect texts broadly around the organisation since its formation. It would be hardly sufficient to focus on one communication event like a commercial to fully comprehend the discursive construction of women's basketball within its social context in the US. Foucauldian discourse analysis can nevertheless benefit sport media analyses which are less ambitious in scope. In this chapter we present a modified version of Foucauldian discourse analysis to illustrate how a researcher can adopt Foucauldian theoretical principles for media analysis.

In our textual analysis we combine the archaeological (what discourses define the WNBA commercial 'This is Who I Am') and genealogical (how discourses link with the power relations that currently define women's professional sport) methods. Foucault begins his archaeology by identifying *objects* for his analysis. Objects are the specific topics to which the texts refer; in our case, these would be specific issues regarding women's professional sport. Next, we need to look for sources, or *enunciations*, where these issues are talked about. In a sense, we have already taken these steps as we have identified that women have few professional sporting opportunities in the US and thus, if we want to understand issues around professionalism, the WNBA is one of the options. Notably, basketball is a team sport and we could have opted for an individual professional sport like tennis or golf that receives significant media attention. Our decision to analyse women's team sport will, nevertheless, reveal details regarding discourses structuring specific understandings of women in a profession requiring working as a part of a team in a social context like the US where individualism is very highly valued. We chose this TV advertisement as the source of analysis instead of an internet site, a series of newspaper articles or the TV broadcast of a basketball match because this particular advertisement was aired frequently during broadcasting of NBA games on major TV channels, such as ABC and ESPN, months before the WNBA 2003 season officially started. In this sense, the visibility of the commercial might be higher than other related media sources. Therefore, it might have more influence on how people understand the WNBA and its athletes.

Next we need to examine what *concepts* are developed during the commercial and how these are organised. This step will help us identify how concepts form *individualisable groups of statements* by defining the rules for their coexistence. At this level, various statements might refer to the same object, but these statements do not need to be unified. We identify such concepts as 'revolution' and 'journey' in the commercial. In addition, various poses performed by the athletes, the assertion of being a diva, a term often used to describe women in the entertainment business, and an open declaration by Leslie on a catwalk allude to the phenomenon of 'modelling'. At the same time, the players are referred to as girls, sisters, mothers or daughters, which might hint at the concept 'family'. Various statements such as 'do not like to lose', 'always looking ahead never behind' and 'a believer in myself' refer to the players' mental state. Finally, while not very visible in the commercial, the players' sport performances are represented through selected highlights of the athletes' performance and the presence of a basketball in other contexts during the advertisement. This stage of the analysis appears very similar to our previous CDA. However, we need to expand on this stage of analysis by looking at how these concepts form meaningful theoretical formations.

Our next focus is the *theoretical formations* that are structured based on the concepts. In the WNBA commercial, the concepts connect to themes that allow us to link the individual statements (e.g. 'I am glamorous') to the *general domain of statements* and further to discourses that structure women's professional sport. This level of analysis is 'concerned with statements that coalesce within specific social contexts' (Markula and Pringle, 2006, p. 29). For example, the commercial tells us something about the discursive formation of women's professional sport in the US. It appears that the main concepts refer to women's involvement in a revolution through engagement in various 'professions'. This narrative of revolutionary journey is composed of concepts of mental toughness, sport performance and modelling. This narrative depicts the women as glamorous, but not as sweet, competitive and tough professional basketball players who can also succeed in other professions such as modelling. This success is a result of 'knowing what one wants', whether one is a glamorous diva, caring mother or driver of a sports car. This is a self-confident, determined and successful professional who believes in herself. Winning matters. That is why the players work out, play ball and 'dunk'. The idea that one can achieve whatever one wants through determination and hard work is commonly celebrated in American society: the American dream of success through individual perseverance. In the commercial, the players' professional success is not divorced from their families. When enjoying their successful professional lives (having glamorous clothing, being a diva, driving a sports car and playing professional sport) the players are still daughters, sisters and mothers. While the concept of family could be interpreted as a construction of 'new women' who have to take care of business and the household at the same time, we argue that 'family' might be also read as an alternative form, 'sisterhoods', a kind of female bonding. This idea of 'sisterhood' is prevalent in American popular media about professional women, such as in the popular TV series 'Sex and the City'. In this sense, people who are on this revolutionary journey are not simply WNBA athletes, but every (professional) woman in the US.

To further locate the representation of the basketball players within its context, we now connect the 'discourses' of professional women's sport to the power relations that define professional sports in the US. The exploration of *operations of power* from transmissions and transformations of discourse constitutes the genealogical phase of the analysis. It is important to note again that in Foucault's view, power is relational and therefore is exercised to create certain practices. Consequently, our objective is to understand what effect or practice is produced through the discourses instead of disclosing who is in the possession of power to create discourses (Kendall and Wickham, 1999). To link the discourses of women's professionalism to larger power relations defining sport, we first situate the WNBA in its social and historical context. The WNBA was created, partly, due to the success of the American women's basketball team in the 1996 Olympics in Atlanta.[7] This team won a gold medal and was also successful in terms of broadcast ratings. We could argue that athletic and strong female athletes, such as basketball players, gained more visibility and thus were deemed more acceptable to American society which has traditionally favoured individual, 'aesthetic' women's sports. This set up the condition for the possibility of a 'female professional basketball athlete'. The professionalisation of women's basketball makes it necessary for the league to sell its product. In order to be more profitable, the league, in its commercial, strategically allies itself to the discourses of a successful business ethos: determination, professionalism and individualism even as a part of a team sport.

While female professional basketball players are presented as business professionals, they are also defined as glamorous divas, girls next door or dutiful mothers. These images connote the traditional options for women that obviously still have a strong presence in the lives of contemporary working women in America. Deriving from the 'dual' identity of women and packaging it with the American understanding of 'success', the league is able to mould a commercial product that has developed into the most successful women professional sport league in North America. Nevertheless, this discursive context reinforces certain type of professionalism – one that considers sport and modelling as the primary forms of professionalism – for women. Both of these professions, at least in this popular consciousness, are 'body'-related professions. There is no allusion that professions that might require more 'intellectual' capacity or rigorous education instead of the visibility of the body can be desirable options for women. In this sense, the formation of other identities is not possible in this power/discourse nexus.

This WNBA commercial can be further understood against so-called 'post-feminism', a term coined by some feminist researchers to denote an understanding that (liberal) feminism has already reached its goal of equal opportunities for women. Lafrance (1998) defines post-feminism more formally as a belief that 'everyone who deserves to be equal is indeed equal' (p. 120) (for a further discussion of post-feminism, see chapter 1). Therefore, women's oppression, as described by previous feminist movements, no longer exists in today's society. In popular consciousness, this translates into young women's claim that they are free to choose their options in life as long as they as they know what they want. In this discourse, the successes and failures are personal responsibilities, but women's successes are still defined through 'traditional' definitions of beauty and motherhood combined with the self-confidence of business ethics. This strand of 'feminism' overlaps in many ways with neoliberalism, which promotes and celebrates personal achievements, and demands limited governmental interventions but greater personal responsibility. This neoliberal attitude of personal responsibility also reflects on apathy of 'welfare mothers' and their often troubling children in the US. Needless to say, feminist research continues to demonstrate that 'post-feminism' is hardly possible within the current power relations of the neoliberal ethics where there is only an illusion of individual choice. This Foucauldian analysis clearly illustrates how the young women's choices are limited by the discursive construction of 'feminism' as professionalism that actually allows for very few options. Contemporary femininity is then created by the discourses within the power relations of current American society as the 'post-feminist' superwoman who is able to act as a determined 'body' professional, look good and be a good mother all at the same time.

In summary, the main tenets of our adapted version of Foucauldian discourse analysis include:

1. A Foucauldian discourse analysis attempts to highlight how identities are structured with a particular power/discourse(s) nexus. Because power is understood as relational, the analysis focuses on how power is used through discourses instead of who 'possess' power to oppress others. In this sense, the aim of a Foucauldian discourse

analysis of the WNBA commercial is to understand what discourses might act as technologies of dominance that discipline athletes into a limited identity.

2. Discourses can be identified by analysing language and text through the two-tiered analysis of archaeology and genealogy. Although discourse encompasses several levels of daily practices, in this analysis of media we are limited to language and text.

3. The archaeological phase focuses on how discourses are formed by identifying the object, enunciations, concepts and theories that then constitute discourse(s).

4. The genealogical analysis links the discourse(s) to the power relations determining their specific cultural and historical context. If an archaeological analysis identifies discourses, a genealogical analysis connects the discourses to the operation of power at its cultural and historical context. In this analysis, we situated the discourses of the WNBA commercial into the post-feminism and neoliberalism of the contemporary United States. With the strategic alliance of certain popular discourses in the society, the WNBA has become one of the most successful women's professional sports in the US. However, these discourses legitimate only certain images of women professional athletes.

Conclusion

In this chapter, we have introduced CDA and Foucauldian discourse analysis as tools to analyse sport media content. Because these two methods assume a different theoretical understanding of power, they result in different foci for a media researcher. CDA aims to disclose how ideology works through language. Consequently, the ultimate goal is to reveal how the hegemonic groups ensure their power positions through communication events ultimately to work towards social justice. For example, the starting point of our example of CDA was to reveal how the ideology of masculinity operated in the WNBA commercial to oppress women athletes through sexualisation, trivialisation and marginalisation of women's sport. While our CDA revealed some contradictions in the media representation, the Foucauldian discourse analysis provided a more complex mapping of how women's basketball is constructed in the contemporary US.

Although Foucauldian discourse analysis focuses on examining the complex interplay of how power relations operate through discourses, the goal is not to challenge the 'hegemony' of a certain group *per se* but to map how power is used through discourses that define practices in certain fields like sport or news reporting. Therefore, a Foucauldian analysis does not begin with a preconceived assumption of oppressive and oppressed groups, but attempts to understand the effects, both productive and repressive, of discourse and through them, the use of power. In this sense, a Foucauldian takes a political stand through an analysis of the multiple possibilities for discursive operation. It also assumes that all the groups involved in this production participate in the formation of discourses to some extent. For example, the players participate in the construction of the WNBA commercial, and although we were unable to analyse their impact in the discursive construction of women's basketball in this chapter, a Foucauldian would not assume them as innocent victims who are tricked into taking part in their own oppression. The Foucauldian discourse analysis resulted in a more complex picture of the current condition of women's basketball in the intersections of neoliberal ethics of professional sport and 'post-feminist revolution' for women in contemporary America.

In conclusion, it is important to engage in a detailed process of analysis to provide as complete a picture of women's sport media representation as possible. In addition, it is crucial to understand the theoretical logic behind one's chosen method of analysis. While we focus on CDA and Foucauldian discourse analysis in this chapter, we do not want to advocate either method as superior to the other. We do wish to point out, however, that feminist media researchers should choose carefully a method of analysis to match their intended goal and, at the same time, recognise the limitations and possibilities of the theoretical premise underlining the particular method. Based on this chapter, it is clearly impossible to 'mix and match' concepts from different methodologies and produce a coherent and constructive analysis. A carefully conducted analysis that derives from a clearly defined theoretical premise can, however, provide further insights into the politics of women's sport media representation.

Notes

1. Discourse operates at different levels. First, discourse can be defined as an abstract noun, which refers to the so-called semiosis, the structure of meaning-making systems. Secondly, it can be understood as a concrete noun 'in the sense of particular ways of representing aspects of the world' (Fairclough, 2006, p. 11): 'the kind of language used within a specific field ... [or] a way of speaking which gives meaning to experiences from particular perspectives' (Jørgensen and Phillips, 2002, pp. 66–7). The ways women's sport and

women athletes are presented in the media can be understood as a concrete noun. For example, a 'glamour shot' of a female athlete could be understood to demonstrate how sport media, from its perspective, gives meaning to women athletes.

2. The WNBA produces a campaign with a main theme every year. For example, there have been campaigns around such themes as 'We Got Next', 'Have You Seen Her' and 'Expect Great'. 'This is Who I Am' is the theme in both 2003 and 2004. The commercial we analyse in this chapter was the main feature of the campaign in 2003. The campaign also included various segments of individual players talking about their personal interests and their personal lives with the central idea to reveal the off-court personalities of the athletes.

3. An analysis of transivity focuses on how events are dis/connected from/to subjects and objects. For example, in the sentence 'the coach was fired after the rumour about an inappropriate relationship with one of her athletes', the agent who took the actions (the person who fired the coach) is omitted. The event, therefore, is presented simply as 'natural phenomenon – something that just happened without a responsible agent' (Phillips and Jørgensen, 2002, p. 83). On the other hand, an analysis of modality focuses on the degree to which the speakers affiliate to their statements. For example, saying 'it is disgusting', 'I think it is disgusting' and 'some might find this disgusting' express different degrees of commitment the speakers make to the statements.

4. A 'structure analysis' can also refer to a way to analyse narratives (Smith and Sparkes, 2005).

5. Although Duncan did not refer to CDA, we have chosen her work to demonstrate CDA for several reasons. First, her understanding of power, hegemony and ideology appears to be close to Fairclough's position. Secondly, she analyses photographs as discursive, but also recognises their non-discursive social relations, such as the differences between men and women. Thirdly, her project obviously carries political aims to emancipate women athletes who are often sexualised and trivialised in the sport media. Lastly, her work is one of the seminal analyses of sport photographs within feminist sport studies.

6. Although Portuguese by nationality, she has played in the US since attending Old Dominion University, Virginia.

7. After the 1996 Olympic there were two professional women basketball leagues launched in the US, the WNBA and the ABL. The latter folded in 1998.

References

Blommaert, J. (2005). *Discourse: A Critical Introduction*. Cambridge: Cambridge University Press.

Chouliaraki, L. and Fairclough, N. (1999). *Discourse in Late Modernity: Rethinking Critical Discourse Analysis*. Edinburgh: Edinburgh University Press.

Cole, C. L., Giardina, M. D. and Andrews, D. L. (2004). Michel Foucault: Studies of power and sport. In R. Giulianotti (ed.), *Sport and Modern Social Theorists* (pp. 207–23). London: Palgrave Macmillan.

Duncan, M. (1990). Sports photographs and sexual difference: Images of women and men in the 1984 and 1988 Olympic Games. *Sociology of Sport Journal*, 7(1), 22–43.

Fairclough, N. (1995). *Critical Discourse Analysis: A Critical Study of Language.* London: Longman.

Fairclough, N. (2002). *Methods of Critical Discourse Analysis.* London: Sage.

Fairclough, N. (2006). *Language and Globalization.* London: Routledge.

Foucault, M. (2000). The subject and power. In J. D. Faubion (ed.), *Essential Works of Michel Foucault, Vol. 3: Power* (pp. 326–48). New York: New Press.

Hekman, S. J. (1996). *Feminist Interpretations of Michel Foucault.* University Park, PA: Pennsylvania State University Press.

Jørgensen, M. and Phillips, L. (2002). *Discourse Analysis as Theory and Method.* London: Sage.

Kendall, G., and Wickham, G. (1999). *Using Foucault's Methods.* London: Sage.

Lafrance, M. R. (1998). Colonizing the feminine: Nike's intersections of postfeminism and hyperconsumption. In G. Rail (ed.), *Sport and Postmodern Times* (pp. 117–39). Albany, NY: SUNY Press.

Markula, P. and Pringle, R. (2006). *Foucault, Sport and Exercise: Power, Knowledge and Transforming the Self.* New York: Routledge.

Smith, B. and Sparkes, A. C. (2005). Analyzing talk in qualitative inquiry: Exploring possibilities, problems, and tensions. *Quest, 57,* 213–42.

Weedon, C. (1997). *Feminist Practice & Poststructuralist Theories,* 2nd edition. Oxford: Blackwell.

3
Opening up the Gendered Gaze: Sport Media Representations of Women, National Identity and the Racialised Gaze in Canada

Margaret MacNeill

Sport media professionals and scholars need to open up the concept of gaze in order to understand media representations of women, race and national identity. Racialised minority groups have historically been depicted as a threat to the status quo by Canadian media (Fleras and Kunz, 2001) except in coverage of male athletic champions. Female athletes of colour are often considered an historic double threat to the hegemonic masculine order of the sport media, who rarely cover women's sport outside of Olympiads. The racialised figures of female athletes of colour are often portrayed outside of hegemonic notions of womanhood (Douglas, 2002). While past Canadian sport media studies have offered particular understandings of gendered codes and/or racialised codes (e.g. Abdel-Shehid, 2005; Crossman, Douglas, 2002; Lee, 1992; MacNeill, 1988; Sparks, 1992; Theberge and Cronk, 1991) the constitutive power of particular gaze is often ignored. Stuart Hall's examination of the representation of difference in the sporting 'spectacle of the Other' is one of the few exceptions to deploy a critical theory of gaze informed by cultural studies and postcolonial theory (1997; also see L. Davis's work on the ideal and colonising subject position constructed in *Sport Illustrated*, 1997).

Perdita Felicien – a Team Canada hurdler and the focus of this case study – ran and fell in the 2004 Summer Olympic championships. A half-page photograph of the fallen hurdler was printed above the fold on the front page of the *Toronto Star* the following day. Beneath the photograph columnist Rosie Demanno declared:

Perdita: *She who is lost.*
That's what her name means in Latin. And that's what Perdita Felicien was last night, a lost girl, wandering this way and that on the track, incredulity writ large on her stricken face, hands first on her head, then on her hips, then back on her head. Mouthing the words: Omigod, Omigod.

The race of her life, the race all Canada had been anticipating, had just ended in a disastrous clattering crash, barely seconds out of the block, this fine young woman's grand Olympic dreams repulsed by the very first obstacle in her path. The hurdle that she's never missed before.

Unbelievably, inconceivably her foot met it flush on, and suddenly Felicien was falling ... falling ... arms flailing, fingers grasping at air, a tangled heap of limbs and metal, her body twisting and contorting, stumbling on an awkwardly unbalanced leg, tumbling into the next lane, upending the hurdle and wiping out the poor Russian woman running alongside. Such a chaotic mess.
(DiManno, 2004, 25 August, p. A1, *Toronto Star*)

Felicien is clearly female, black, alone and out of the race. In Canadian mainstream media narratives, champion athletes tend to win for the nation but fail by themselves. As the reigning world champion in both indoor and outdoor 100-metre hurdles going into the 2004 Olympic Games, the *Toronto Star* explicitly chose her to occupy a marquee position during the Olympiad to 'tell an epic story of a Canadian athlete from a new immigrant family on the road to Olympic glory' (*Journalist*, 2007, 23 May). For the Olympic sports journalist Randy Starkman, she radiates Olympic success: 'The vibe she gives off is powerful: it is imprinted in her body language' (2004b, 12 August, p. J4). Felicien admits she is ecstatic to play the lead citizen role in the Olympic opera:

I've been to the Olympics before. I know the magic. I know the energy that you get from an entire nation. We're all looking for that gold to make our country proud. I love my role in life
(Felicien, cited in Starkman, 2004b, 12 August, p. J4).

The pre-Olympic anticipated glory storyline changes abruptly at the first hurdle of the Olympic 100-metre final when Felicien unexpectedly crashed. A headlining apology is boldly printed above the image linked to the story DiManno tells, 'Perdita: I'm Sorry' (*Toronto Star*, 25 August, cover headline). Is she sorry she fell? Sorry she let down her Mom, family and friends? Sorry she let down her team or coach? Sorry she knocked down the Russian? Or sorry she let down the nation? Like the voyeuristic driver who slows to look at an accident on the highway, the viewer of the image can gawk at the sporting wreckage: Felicien, with eyes closed, holding her head and belly with her hands, reclined backwards into a hurdle. This tragic and static representation of her lying on the track is placed by the editor in the coveted 'above the fold' half-page. Below the fold, Dimanno's textual accounting anchors the visual disaster. News hierarchies are also revealed in the photo's place-ment as success stories of Lori-Ann Muenzer (a gold medallist in a cycling event the same day) and of two women nominated to the Supreme Court of Canada are fully contained below the fold. Clearly, tragedy trumps women's success in Canadian media codes of newsworthiness. Perdita Felicien, the quintessential multicultural citizen, becomes the 'Other'.

The purpose of this chapter is twofold: first, to present a qualitative case study of the *Toronto Star*'s coverage of the female hurdler Perdita Felicien to demonstrate the production, dissemination and audience reactions to visual images that produce particular gendered, nation-alised and racialised gaze; and second, to overview postcolonial cultural studies and feminist psychoanalytic platforms that lead us to particular questions about Olympic media texts and methodological approaches to help answer them.

Visual methods and the circuit of culture

> The relationship between what we see and what we know is never settled.
>
> (Berger, 1972, p. 7)

To pursue this case study of visual depictions of Perdita Felicien and the text that anchors the images during the 2004 Olympic period, I deploy a feminist cultural studies approach that appropriates key notions of 'Othering' from postcolonial studies, gaze from psychoanalysis and intertextuality from literary and discourse analysis. Cultural studies is concerned with the 'circuit of culture', which, according to du Gay (1997), involves moments of production, representation, consumption, regulation and identity. Cultural studies are necessarily a part of an interdisciplinary network to get at the complexity of the circuit. Textual analyses of media often involve analysis of other moments in the circuit and/or the circulation of the representations within the wider political economy of media institutions. Societies, nations, communities or locales are not considered to be merely the 'context' for viewing Olympic media texts. The production and consumption of texts are, instead, considered to be moments that play constitutive roles in cultural re/production of contexts, identities and power relations.

A strict methodological protocol does not exist in cultural studies of media. Rather this loose umbrella of disciplines appropriates a wide variety of methods, such as ethnographic, semiological, psychoanalytic, sociological and critical textual methods (Van Leeuwen and Jewitt, 2001). In this study, framing, narrative and discourse analysis are deployed to get at some select elements of the circuit of culture that *Toronto Star* newspaper texts are implicated in. I borrow from the work of du Gay (1997), van Leeuwen and Jewitt (2001) and Rose (2001) to read Felicien's story from a cultural studies perspective.[1]

For this case study, daily editions of the *Toronto Star* were collected between 7 August and 5 September 2004, the period spanning the week prior to the Athens summer Olympic Games, the Olympic period itself and the week after the Games. The most widely covered athlete of any sport or gender in this collection is Perdita Felicien (Wensing and MacNeill, 2009). She received coverage in 20 articles and 28 photographs and thus has been chosen as the focus of our attention. Textual analyses are often limited to the moment of representation in the circuit of culture. However, this case study includes some insights from producers and audiences of the Athens Olympics to get at the multiple moments in the cultural production of Olympic media. The following analysis examines how images of Felicien can be understood and the implication in relationships of power affecting the representation of gender, race and nation through applying the notions of gaze, the 'Other' and intertextuality.

Reading Felicien through gaze

Outside the field of sport studies there has been heated debate about the concept of gaze in art history, radical film studies, feminist media studies and Foucauldian scholarship (e.g. Carter, 2006; Loshitsky, 2003; Mulvey, 1988; Penley, 1988). Since the 1970s, the concept of gaze has been developed to analyse visual culture and how audiences relate to and/or are positioned by the person or people represented in the image.[2] Much of this analysis derives from Laura Mulvey's (1975) groundbreaking essay 'Visual Pleasure and Narrative Cinema' in *Screen*. It has since been canonised as a founding essay in feminist film and visual studies (Loshitzky, 2003). Drawing heavily on psychoanalysis, particularly Sigmund Freud's understandings of sexuality, scopophilia (taking people as desired objects in the image and subjecting them to a controlling gaze) and unconscious, and second on Lacan's mirror-phase, Mulvey seeks to question how women are positioned in a phallo-centric order and how narrative cinema structures a patriarchal gaze. Women on screen, Mulvey argues, are positioned as the objects of voyeuristic and fetishistic desire through the 'male gaze'. In mainstream (western) cinema gaze constitutes 'Woman as image, man as bearer of the look' (Mulvey, 1975/2001, p. 397). The world, she claims is

> ordered by sexual imbalance, pleasure in looking has been split between active/male and passive/female. The determining male gaze projects its phantasy on to the female figure which is styled accord-ingly ... to connote to-be-looked-at-ness.
>
> (Mulvey, 1975/2001, p. 397)

Mulvey's purpose is to call for the 'destruction of pleasure' in narrative conventions that reinforce patriarchy (1975/2001, p. 394). For Mulvey the 'male gaze' can be direct (the woman on screen performs directly for the assumed male in the audience) or indirect (the audience members identify with the gaze of the man on the screen towards the woman on the screen). Male gaze is ahistorically assumed to be related to a drive for mastery of the woman. The mutual constitution of both the text and the spectator is of importance to Mulvey and is explored by attention to how both representations of men and women and the gendering of viewers are affected by visual, spatial and temporal constructions of the text (Rose, 2001). Mulvey's contributions include opening up feminist cultural politics (Loshitzky, 2003), foregrounding how mainstream media conventions limit the on-screen power of female characters and seek to uncover how these conventions interpellate or hail the viewer to a gendered subject position.

Drawing from the notion of gaze can offer sport media case studies possibilities for seeing women in a variety of gendered positions in dif-ferent roles in the wider political economy of sport. Consider, for exam-ple, the *Toronto Star*'s television guide magazine. Leading up to the 2004 Summer Olympics, the cover displays Felicien hurdling directly towards the viewer to remind us that the Games are fast approaching: 'Going for Gold: Perdita Buoys Canada's Hope' (*Toronto Star, Star Week*, 2004, 7–13

August). This cover is devoid of male protagonists and voyeurs, as well as female competitors within the frame. In fact, only two out of 28 photos over almost a month of daily newspaper attention show her with others on the hurdling track. There are no coaches, officials, competitors or media personnel. She presents steely competitive individualism rather than traditional codes of fragile and docile femininity; she is offered as a significant figure on the national and international scene supporting herself. Perdita's foot is directed at us at the front of the cover; it keeps us off the race track in the position of the photographer or timekeeper, both of whom record and adjudicate her worth in our gaze, yet contain her successes to the track lane. The use of her first name 'Perdita' in the headline is not so much infantilising (as traditional media studies of gender would code a first name) as it is familiarising. Familiarity with the two-time world champion is expected in the reading of the cover. Her piercing gaze aligns with the next hurdle, not our eyes; yet we are free to visually surf the text of her body, to evaluate her technique, determination, gender, race or other possibilities of identification.

Felicien's powerful presence and determined gaze are harnessed by the media to declare her the great national hope for athletic glory on the international stage. However, to 'buoy' national hopes is also to buoy local media profits:

> You might wonder why we have a tv guide in the *Star* when it promotes our competitors television shows and sportsnews, but many who watch televised sport come back to the paper to check scores of games and events they've gambled on, and to see how Canada did at the Olympics in a different timezone.
>
> (*Journalist*, 2004, 27 May)

To account for the larger social order, a useful dialogue between psychoanalytic and cultural studies approaches has led to theoretical and methodological shifts in gaze and visual studies (Loshitzky, 2003). The flirtation of film and psychoanalysis is considered problematic for feminist approaches because gaze is theorised from the standpoint of male power and constructions of masculinity (Gledhill, 1992). Women can only be seen as castrated and see themselves as castrated within this Freudian-inspired psychoanalytic approach (Rose, 2001). Thus, theoretically, Mulvey's approach cannot raise such questions as: Can women be represented differently? Can women see actively? Can men only act as fetishising voyeurs when they look at women? Are other ways of seeing possible? Can men look at men, and women look at women pleasurably? (Rose, 2001, p. 115). Moreover, Mulvey's approach ignores historical specificity, denies female spectators agency, fails to consider how mainstream media viewers can be hailed to other subject positions based on ability, sexuality, age, class and race, and ignores the possibility of resistant and transgressive readings. Methodologically, Mulvey's own feminist psychoanalytic approach to gaze has been limited to examining the points of view of western, white, heterosexual male character towards female characters and the audience; the structure of space between characters; and how the camera moves and frames focus in response to male protagonists.

Considerations of how gaze is implicated in subjectification, identity and regulation using a wider cultural studies approach may help to overcome the essentialist assumptions of the earlier psychoanalytic approach. To rework Loshitzky's argument about a film's meaning, I suggest a sport photograph's meaning (or any media text's meaning) 'is produced in a context, and every photograph is historical in the way it situates the spectator in relation to the context of its production and reception' (2003, p. 255). Notwithstanding the serious limitations of essentialism in the psychoanalytic approach noted above, gaze continues to have relevance, particularly for the study of Olympic sport media who target and position different audiences during the Olympics. For example, Canadian media have long assumed the sport audience to be male (MacNeill, 1996); but in recent years, the *Toronto Star* has explicitly broadened its readership to different ethnic communities with a mandate to debate multiculturalism across all sections of the paper; to develop new lifestyle magazines like *Desi* to appeal to South Asian consumers; and to expand the sports audience to women before and during the Olympic period: 'Our look and mode of address is shifting' (*Journalist*, 2007, 23 May).

In addition to broader social relations, considerations of intertextuality may be one way to open up the gaze. This entails going beyond a visual text to dialogically study meanings, memories and potentially resistant meanings produced by both producers and audiences as they work to represent meanings within a system of discourse that regulate them. I shall continue reading Felicien's representation through intertextuality.

Intertextual liaisons: Felicien's gender, race and nation

Intertextuality is a term borrowed from literary studies. Mikhail Bakhtin's contentions that language is dialogic and that the history of particular bodies of literature (or genres of media) is a 'history of appropriation, re-working and imitation' (Bakhtin, 1981, p. 69) enticed Julia Kristeva to propose the notion of intertextuality. Kristeva (1967) suggests all media texts contain a 'mosaic' of elements and understandings from previous works. Rather than considering an individual text (such as the sports page) to be a discrete, distinct and unique composition, intertextuality directs our attention to how both the production and interpretation of texts are informed by other texts and systems of knowledge.[3] For example, prior to the opening ceremonies in Athens, the *Toronto Star*'s headline was atypically staggered vertically down the page with photos between the phrases (2004b, 12 August, p. A1):

READY
OR NOT

To understand this atypical headline, the reader needs knowledge of prior athletic successes of Felicien as world champion, a history of Olympic facilities construction delays, as well as Eurocentric memories of the refrain from a childhood game of 'Homefree tag': 'Ready or not, here I come'. After 'READY' is an image of reigning world champion hurdler Perdita Felicien standing between golden arches, her upper body centred in classical western architecture. This framing emphasises the competitive individualism of an athlete that is signified by the deep degree of muscular striation in her shoulders. Patriotism is symbolically represented through the red tank top and literal stamp of the nation-state, 'Canada', in white on her chest. With her relaxed gaze averted sideways into a golden glow of Olympic surroundings, the audience is expected to reflect on her past laurels and anticipate a gold medal success for the nation. Understanding the role of the arches in connoting anticipated Olympic glory requires a previous understanding of Athenian architecture and mythologised ancient Olympic images, and experience with previous visual media that use the upward tilt to signify dominance. In this case the tilt enables Felicien's short stature to appear to fill the arches that are much further behind her. To intertextually understand the lower part of the headline, 'OR NOT', *Toronto Star* readers are assumed to be well aware of slow Olympic bureaucracies. Below 'OR NOT' is an image of male construction workers scrambling to complete a $40 million IOC-approved Olympic Spirit building in Toronto. This harkens memories of many years of Canadian media criticisms of Athens Olympic building delays.

In the same daily edition of this broadsheet paper, the cover of the special 'Olympic Preview Section' widens the photographic frame to capture Felicien's whole body on the ancient site. The severe upward tilt exaggerates the muscularity of her legs, introduces a pierced and taunt mid-section not seen on the front cover, and elongates her overall stature to appear even taller and more imposing than the front page: Felicien and her hurdle among the columns of an ancient site signify her 'right' to a place in Olympic history (*Toronto Star*, 2004b, 12 August, p. J1). But the race has not yet been run. Her facial expression is less serene and contemplative than on the front cover (where she glimpses skyward within the frame). In this preview section, which offers stories about medal hopefuls, her furrowed brow and competitive 'game face' gaze away from the audience to a finish line elsewhere. In small font by her feet the words 'Perdita Felicien's Olympic plan: Go get the gold' is printed. In addition to the broader context of the Olympic Games, Felicien is firmly located within Canadian nationalism.

Sports readers, lookers and Olympic consumers are encouraged to bring their understandings of nationalistic codes into the *Toronto Star*'s telling of an Olympic journey to glory that promised to unfold from a trajectory of two world championships in the past to imminent Olympic glory. In a two-page centre-fold to this Olympic Preview Section, Felicien is named as one of the top ten medal hopefuls for Canada. Randy Starkman observes,

> It's hard to believe Canadians didn't even know who Felicien was just one year ago. The 23-year-old from Pickering flashed onto the scene at the world championships in Paris with a stunning victory in the women's 100-metre hurdles and followed it up at the world indoor championships in Budapest
>
> (2004a, 12 August, p. J7)

As the storyline approaches the opening of the Olympics, posed photographs of Felicien in her red Team Canada uniform from past championships and in current photo shoots anchor an official Canadian identity with a multinational corporate swoosh. The Nike white swoosh and red uniform achieve a level of symbolic equivalence by utilising the official colours of the Canadian flag. She is presented as the quintessential Canadian succeeding on the world stage. But comparisons to her main speed rivals on the track, such as Gail Devers of the United States, Felicien's childhood role model for sporting participation and competitiveness, slide into gendered comparisons of fingernails. As the semi-finals approach, Devers from the

United States is positioned as an arch-rival of Felicien. Devers's hands are depicted as inhuman claws in a close-up photograph (2004, 21 August). When Devers falls and is injured in the semifinals, the newspaper's front page trumpets a headline: 'Gold and Glory within Felicien's Grasp'. The headline is positioned over a photograph of Felicien, who displays her hands with the Canadian flag painted on each fingernail (2004c, 24 August, p. A1). She gazes at her hands, while we are brought in to inspect the gendered tools for the nation.

Overall, the newspaper's framing of photos attempts to reduce Felicien to an individual devoid of competitors on the track at her level of speed. While she is positioned as the poster athlete for Canadian sporting success, wider stories circulate around the Canadian media about her identification with an American track role model, her history of training at an American university for most of her high performance sport career, and her stories of family connections to St Lucia. These connections suggest a transnational identity rather than a narrower identification as Canadian. However, the tight framing by the *Toronto Star* attempts to close off multiple subject positions for the newspaper audience without fully succeeding.

When the print media use Felicien to prepare for the unfolding of a Canadian success story (rather than other possibilities such as a Caribbean-Canadian success story, diasporic or transnational success story), race enters the story. Racialised minority groups have historically been depicted as a threat to the status quo by the Canadian media (Fleras and Kunz, 2001) except in coverage of male athletic champions. Female athletes of colour are often considered an historic double threat to the hegemonic masculine order of the sport media, who rarely cover women's sport outside of Olympiads. The racialised figures of female athletes of colour are often portrayed outside of hegemonic notions of womanhood (Douglas, 2002). Several past Canadian sport media studies have offered particular understandings of gendered codes and/or racialised codes (e.g. Abdel-Shehid, 2005; Crossman, Hyslop and Gutherie, 1994; Douglas, 2002; Lee, 1992; MacNeill, 1988; Sparks, 1992; Theberge, 1991). In our case study, however, other media genres use representations of Felicien to problematise the image of women athletes of colour as strong. For example, a televised parody of pre-Olympic 'medal hoping' requires intertextual or interdiscursive[3] familiarity with traditional sexist, homophobic and racialised stereotypes twisted around Felicien's name in *The Canadian Air Farce*. Perdita Felicien's status as a strong and fast athlete on the track team bears the brunt of oppressive humour playing with many stereotypes:

Male Anchor: Canadian medal hopefuls are the Men's and Lesbians' Track Team.

Female Anchor: You can't say that!

Male Anchor: Canadian medal hopefuls are the Men's Track Team.

Female Anchor: Also hopeful is Perdito Felicien ... Perdildo Felice ... Felice Navida ... It doesn't really matter if Canadians medal.

Male Anchor: What really matters is they pass the urine test.

(Canadian Air Farce, 2008, 4 April)

This short clip moves from homophobic references to a denial of female athleticism, to racialised transgressions of Felicien's name, while mingling references to her name to a masturbatory device and a Hispanic Christmas carol. The comedy narrative colludes with cultural stereotypes to represent her as the 'Other' in contradiction to the *Toronto Star*'s coverage leading up to the 100-metre hurdling finals There are also other 'internal' voices that provide critique of the dominant media narratives.

In addition to the dialogic notions of language and the intertextuality of narratives in a culture, there is also a practical level of intertextuality between media. The sports media in Canada, including broadcast, online and print formats, are one of the few news beats that regularly report on and critique their media competitors (MacNeill, 1996). For example, the *Toronto Star* has a regular media 'armchair' critic in the sports section. On the same day the *Toronto Star* headlined with a half-page photo of a fallen Felicien, the media critic Chris Zelovich criticised television images that 'crossed the line between news and invasion of privacy' (2004, 25 August, p. D2). The CBC's 'shot of the day', Zelovich claimed, was 'a sobbing Felicien crying on the shoulder of former Olympian Charmaine Crooks with Olympic champion Donovan Bailey offering words of comfort'. For Zelovich, the problem came with the second longer replay of the post-race drama on the track sidelines when the longer replay also depicted 'a visibly distraught Felicien, shaking with emotion and apparently screaming in anger, no doubt at herself'. Not only does Zelovich reinforce traditional sport media narratives that stress athletes winning for the nation and failing as individuals, he also hails the reader to sexist assumptions that she is shaking with emotion and screaming at herself (rather than, for example, yelling in pain due to an injured ankle suffered in the fall). The armchair media critic, like the armchair sport media scholar, has much to speculate on if producers, key actors and audiences are not given voice in media studies.

Furthermore, media competitiveness may account for the armchair critic's claims of unethical intrusion into a bad news story moment. Print photos in the *Toronto Star* could neither capture 'shaking' nor the sound of 'screaming' that competitors in the broadcast media could convey live and replayed. His argument of invasion of privacy is at odds with dominant codes that privilege the 'thrill of victory and agony of defeat' moments in the public setting of the Olympic Stadium. Thus, it appears that sport media personnel report on each other's coverage to compete over professional status, practices and ratings.

Media representations, as demonstrated in my reading of Felicien, are steeped in struggles over the meaning of gender, race and nation. According to Bannerji, such visual images 'are congealed social relations, formalizing in themselves either relations of domination or those of resistance. The politics of images is the same as any politics' (1993, p. 20). To further interrogate the politics of media I locate the representation of Felicien within a theoretical framework of postcolonialism.

Postcolonial reading: Felicien as 'Other'

Postcolonialism offers one framework to further understand the representations of the 'Other' in sport (media) cultures that deploy stereotypes to exploit certain groups. Postcolonialism recognises difference, questions hierarchy and helps to move towards anti-essentialist conceptions of identity. In this sense, it also provides tools to widen my earlier discussion of 'gaze'. Using a postcolonial cultural studies framework, Hall (1997) demonstrates how a sporting spectacle of racialised athletes deploys tropes of representation, that is, binary significations of us/them, good/bad, normal/exotic, attractive/ugly. Drawing on colonialising imagery and narratives, athletes of colour are often depicted by sports media using 'classic stereotypes in reference to the primal physicality of black athletes and their pathological indolent, aggressive, naturalistic, exuberant and deviant character' (St. Louis, 2005, p. 122).

Hall's (1997) examination of the representation of difference in the sporting 'spectacle of the Other' is one of the few exceptions to deploy a critical theory of gaze informed by cultural studies and postcolonial theory (see also Abdel-Shehid, 2005; Davis, 1997; Douglas, 2002; Jiwani, 2008). For example, Hall analyses the cover of a *Sunday Times* magazine depicting the sprinter Ben Johnson winning the 100-metre sprint at the 1988 Summer Olympic Games. Johnson was soon disqualified for taking a banned substance. Hall describes the colour image as depicting this black Canadian runner beating four other 'superb athletes in action, at the peak of their physical prowess. All of them men and ... for the first time – all of them black!' (Hall, 1997, p. 226). The cover image is anchored by the headline 'Heroes and Villains'. Hall points out that the difference between heroes and villains is ambivalent; it can be both negative and positive. Johnson is valorised as a civilised multicultural Canadian success story when he wins, but stereotyped as a Jamaican immigrant when he fails (Jiwani, 2008).

As pointed out earlier, minorities, and minority women in particular, are typically represented as the 'Other' in Canadian media (Fleras and Kunz, 2001). In addition to Felicien, the only other front-page images of women of colour during the Olympic study period framed women as the victimised 'Other': one cover depicted a young black woman being held hostage at gunpoint by a black male in downtown Toronto (2004, 26 August), the other image framed two Sudanese women squatting in a refugee camp in Chad (2004, 9 August). The opportunity to gaze on a media representation of successful women of colour is rarely offered in the mainstream media.

Felicien as a successful athlete, therefore, does not fall easily into traditional, binary representations of gender and race typically produced in western media and exemplified by stereotypes of white cognitive abilities versus black physicality (Coakley, 1998). The sport media tend to draw on binary codes to celebrate male athleticism as stoic, aggressive and strong, whereas female athleticism is often depicted as graceful and visually attractive. Except for her long lacquered nails – a form of heteronormative gender marking based on Eurocentric ideals of beauty – appearance is not foregrounded in the framing of Felicien photos. Rather, the visual and written texts focus primarily on her technique, drive and attitude as a hardworking athlete. Here postcolonial approaches to cultural studies of sport can help move beyond simplistic readings of gender and race and instead foreground contradictory, ambiguous and binary representations of the colonial subject. For example, Felicien, the daughter of an immigrant from St Lucia, is imagined as an exotic and noble athlete in news coverage and images leading up to the 2004 Olympics. She is the ambassador for Canadian multiculturalism instead of a victimised 'Other'. The visual and textual newspaper coverage foregrounding her as a 'Canadian success story' never explicitly addresses sexuality or womanhood, nor hints of any type of steroid abuse, unlike the televised comedy clip. Instead, she is heralded as a clean technician of her sport and a fiercely competitive subject who, according to the *Toronto Star*, runs for Canada, Nike and her family. She is, however, concurrently demeaned as 'Other' in television humour.

Such an ambiguous representation provides multiple readings of Felicien's body. These multiple narratives can serve as resources for navigating relationships and understandings between audience members. For example, a previous study about youth constructions of health and fitness where girls between 13 and 15 years of age, without prompting, frequently deployed Olympic media memories can be of interest to my postcolonial reading of Felicien:[4]

> *MM*: What kinds of activities do your parents think are healthy for youth of your age?
>
> *Simone*: My Mom wants me to try everything I saw in the Olympics to see what I like the best. Right now I, ummm, play soccer for a rec team and sometimes swim. Kara Lang is from my neighbourhood and on the Olympic team so I kinda like to hope.
>
> *Carla*: Sometimes I think that all my family wants me to do is nothing. I want to play soccer like Simone but my Dad says that, ummm, back home football – you know, soccer here – is just for men. He says I'll get big legs like the women on the Olympic track team.
>
> *MM*: Does he think playing soccer or having big legs is unhealthy?
>
> *Carla*: I dunno. Soccer in gym class makes me breathe really hard so I think it's healthy for girls. It's just that it seems unnatural for him but he's, ummm, my Dad is old school Portuguese.
>
> *Pearla*: That's crazy. Is he really just lipping girls who are athletes and lezzies? Soccer and running in track should be okay for girls if boys can do it. If 'Dita – remember that black hurdler who fell? – has big muscles it's cause she works hard to get healthy and strong. That's, you know, not unnatural. That's work. Lots of hard work.
>
> *Carla*: But you can't change my Dad's mind. Sports are still a boy thing to him.
>
> (FG #3: 2005, 17 November 2005)

In this focus group discussion, media texts consumed by youth exist in their memories and have been reconstituted and materialised in their understandings of health. These polysemic representations are also grounded in their debates about homophobic and gendered stereotypes that affect power relations in their families and communities, and in the opportunities (or lack in Carla's case) to be active in response to media role models and narratives of success. It is obvious that representations of women Olympians in visual and written texts do not exist as stand-alone artefacts of sporting culture. All texts draw on cultural codes, discourses and often metaphors and stereotypes to dialogically communicate at the production and consumption moments.

Conclusion

Visual images offer a field where gaze and looks are exchanged and power relations are exercised (Sturken and Cartwright, 2001, p. 106). Complex images of gender, nation and race are social constructions that are regulated by broader cultural politics, media institutions and local negotiations. Media images of female athletes in Canada, and specifically of Perdita Felicien in this case study, can be deployed to invoke cultural identities around race, gender, nation and transnationality (as well as other identities), but their meanings are never fixed. The theories of gaze help us analyse how the textual representations of female Olympians by the media may construct particular and preferred subject positions for audiences. However, there is no guarantee they will be taken up. As Hall (1999) argues, cultural identity 'is a matter of "becoming as well as being". It is not something which already exists, transcending place, time, history, and culture. Cultural identities come from somewhere, have histories. But, like everything that is historical, they undergo constant transformation' (p. 225). Visual analyses of women in the sports media, therefore, require ongoing attention to historicising the circuit of culture, paying attention to intersecting relations of power and how gaze may implicated in positioning spectators. Questioning the making of meaning and cultural identities in an intertextual manner can increase our attentiveness to how we, as researchers, practise our own looking and to avoid conducting research with what Linda Tuhiwai Smith (1999) calls 'imperial eyes'. Furthermore, by integrating postcolonial and feminist approaches, sport media researchers can examine how the media represent some female athletes as racialised 'Other', how cultural hierarchies are reproduced or resisted, and begin to develop decolonising pedagogies for sport media literacy and media interventions.

Appendix: Visual analysis protocol

du Gay (1997), van Leeuwen and Jewitt (2001) and Rose (2001) offer a series of concerns that can be addressed in visual analysis from a cultural studies perspective, including the:

- history and circulation of the image in culture;
- cycle of production, distribution and consumption through which visual representations are encoded with meaning, decoded and transformed;
- specific material properties of the image;
- medium through which the image is produced and circulated;
- form of visuality required to look at the image;
- codes and conventions to make meaning in the visual representation;
- sensuous aspects of looking and emotional responses;
- consideration of how looking at media representations are embodied acts.

More specifically, Rose offers a useful set of technical, compositional and social questions that address the three key sites where the meanings of images are struggled over and produced: production site, image site, audience site. Not all of these concerns have been addressed in this chapter, however this short list of key questions from Rose are a good starting point for establishing a research protocol (see Rose 2001, pp. 188–90 for the full list):

Production of the image:

- When and where was it made?
- Who made it?
- What technologies produced it?
- What were the social identities and relations between the maker, the owner and the subject of the gaze?
- Does the form of the image reconstitute those identities and relations?

The image:

- What is being shown?
- What are the components of the image and what do they mean?
- How are they arranged?
- Where is the viewer's eye drawn to in the image and why?
- What is the vantage point of the image?
- What use is made of colour?

- What knowledges are excluded from this representation?
- Does this image dis/empower its subject?
- Are the relations between the components of the image un/stable?

Audiencing:

- Who were the original audiences for this image?
- Where and how would it have been displayed originally?
- How is it circulated?
- Where is the spectator positioned in relation to the components of the image?
- What relation does this produce between the image and its viewers?
- Is the image one of a series, and how do the preceding and subsequent images affect its meanings?
- Would the image have had a written text to guide its interpretation?
- Is more that one interpretation of the image possible?
- How actively does a particular audience engage with the image?
- How do different audiences interpret this image?
- How are these audiences different from each other, in terms of class, gender, race, sexuality, and so on?
- How do these axes of social identity structure different interpretations? (adapted from Rose, 2001, pp. 188–90).

Notes

1. See appendix.
2. Theories of the gaze and power arose simultaneously in French intellectual thought in the 1970s in the work of Michel Foucault and Jacques Lacan. In *The Birth of the Clinic* (1973) Foucault examines the emergence of the clinic as a site for new medical practices involving a medical gaze for diagnosis and teaching that ultimately fortifies a dominant medical discourse of seeing and categorising illness. *Discipline and Punish* (1977) examines the panoptic surveillance of prisons allowing wardens to view prisoners without being observed. The power of the warden's potential gaze ensures prisoners discipline themselves to abide by prison rules whether or not a warden is actually present in the observation tower. Gaze is thus implicated by Foucault in relations of power and the regulation of subject. Elsewhere, Jacques Lacan's (1979) psychoanalytic discussions of the mirror stage in the development of a baby's psyche, when identity is recognised and reflected back, conceptualises gaze on a different level. This is considered an important stage of human development because the gaze of recognition in the mirror allows us to theorise how humans enter the symbolic order of social life.
3. For Fairclough (2003), analysis of a text's interdiscursivity is 'analysis of the particular mix of genres of discourses, and of styles upon which it draws, and

of how different genres, discourses or styles are articulated (or "worked") together in the text. This level of analysis mediates between linguistic analysis of a text and various forms of social analysis of social events and practices' (p. 218; see also Fairclough, 1992). Some poststructuralist forms of discourse analysis use this term interchangeably with 'intertextual'.

4. This focus groups excerpt (17 November 2006) conducted in the Greater Toronto area of Canada is derived from a SSHRC-funded study, *Youth Constructions of Health and Fitness Project*, for which I wish to acknowledge the girls in this focus group and principal investigator Genevieve Rail and co-investigator Natalie Beausoleil.

References

Abdel-Shehid, G. (2005). *Who da Man? Black Masculinities and Sport Sporting Cultures*. Toronto: Canadian Scholars Press.

Bakhtin, M. M. (1981). *The Dialogic Imagination*. Austin, TX: University of Texas Press.

Bannerji, H. (1993). *The Gaze: Essays on Racism, Feminism and Politics*. Toronto: Sister Vision Press.

Berger, J. (1972). *Ways of Seeing*. Harmondsworth: Penguin.

Canadian Air Farce (nd). Olympic countdown, *Canadian Air Farce*. Rerun broadcast 1 April 2008, on the Comedy Network (Canadian cable channel).

Carter, C. (2006). The transformative power of cultural criticism: bell hooks's radical media analysis. In D. Berry and J. Theobald (eds.), *Radical Mass Media Criticism: A Cultural genealogy* (pp. 212–33). Montreal: Black Rose Books.

Coakley, J. J. (1998). *Sport in Society: Issues and Controversies*, 6th edition. Boston, MA: McGraw-Hill.

Crossman, J., Hyslop, P. and Gutherie, B. (1994). A content analysis o the sports section of Canada's national newspaper with respect to gender and professional/amateur status. *International Review for the Sociology of Sport*, 29(2), 123–31.

Davis, L. (1997). *The Swimsuit Issue and Sport: Hegemonic Masculinity in Sports Illustrated*. New York: SUNY Press.

DiManno, R. (2004). An Olympic dream dies at the first hurdle. *Toronto Star*, 25 August, A1, A16.

Douglas, D. D. (2002). To be young, gifted, black and female: A mediation on the cultural politics at play in representations of Venus and Serena Williams. *Sociology of Sport Online*, 5(2). http://physed.otago.ac.nz/sosol/v5i2/v5i2_3.html. Retrieved 11 December 2007.

du Gay, P. (1997). *The Production of Culture/Cultures of Production*. London: Sage and Oxford University Press.

Fairclough, N. (1992). *Discourse and Social Change*. Cambridge: Polity Press.

Fairclough, N. (2003). *Analysing Discourse: Textual Analysis for Social Research*. London: Routledge.

Fleras, A. and Kunz, J. L. (2001). *Media and Minorities: Representing Diversity in a Multicultural Canada*. Toronto: Thompson Educational Publishing.

Foucault, M. (1973). *The Birth of the Clinic: An Archaeology of Medical Perception*. New York: Pantheon.

Foucault, M. (1977). *Discipline and Punish: The Birth of the Prison*. London: Allen Lane.

Gledhill, C. (1992). Pleasurable negotiations. In F. Bonner et al. (eds.), *Imagining Women: Cultural Representations and Women* (pp. 193–209). Cambridge: Polity,

Hall, S. (1990). Cultural identity and diaspora. In J. Rutherford (ed.), *Identity, Community, Culture, Difference* (pp. 222–37). London: Lawrence & Wishart.

Hall, S. (1997). *Representation: Cultural Representations and Signifying Practices.* London: Sage.

Kristeva, J. (1967). Word, dialogue and novel. In T. Moi (ed.), *The Kristeva Reader* (pp. 52–77). Oxford: Basil Blackwell.

Jiwani, Y. (2008). Sports as a civilizing mission: Zinedine Zidane and the infamous head-butt. *Topia*, 19, pp. 11–33.

Journalist (2007, May 23). Personal communication with *Toronto Star* reporter.

Lacan, J. (1979). *The Four Fundamentals of Psycho-analysis.* New York: W.W. Norton.

Lee, J. (1992). Media portrayals of male and female Olympic athletes: Analyses of newspaper accounts of the 1984 and 1988 Summer Games. *International Review for the Sociology of Sport,* 27(3), 197–219.

Loshitzky, Y. (2003). Afterthoughts on Mulvey's 'Visual Pleasure' in the age of cultural studies. In E. Katz, J. D. Peters, T. Liebes and A. Orloff (eds.), *Canonic Texts in Media Research* (pp. 248–59). Oxford: Polity Press.

MacNeill, M. (1988). Active women, media representations and ideology. In J. Harvey and H. Cantelon (eds.), *Not Just a Game: Essays in Canadian Sport Sociology* (pp. 195–211). Ottawa: University of Ottawa Press.

MacNeill, M. (1996). Networks: An ethnography of CTV's production of the 1988 Winter Olympic ice hockey tournament, *Sociology of Sport Journal*, 13, 103–24.

Mulvey, L. (1975/2001). Visual pleasure and narrative cinema, *Screen*, 16(3), 6–18. Reprinted in M. G. Durham and D. M. Kellner (eds.), *Media Studies and Cultural Studies: Keywords* (pp. 393–404). Oxford: Blackwell.

Mulvey, L. (1988). Afterthoughts on 'Visual pleasure and narrative cinema' inspired by *Dual in the Sun*. In C. Penley (ed.), *Feminism and Film Theory* (pp. 69–79). New York: Routledge.

Penley, C. (1988). *Feminism and Film Theory.* London: Routledge.

Smith, L.T. (1999). *Decolonizing Methodologies: Research and Indigenous Peoples.* New York: Zed Books.

Sparks, R. (1992) Delivering the male: Sports, Canadian television, and the making of TSN. *Canadian Journal of Communication*, 17, 319–42.

St. Louis, B. (2005). Brilliant bodies, fragile minds: Race, sport and the mind/body split. In C. Alexander and C. Knowles (eds.), *Making Race Matter: Bodies, Space and Identity* (pp. 113–31). New York: Palgrave Macmillan.

Rose, G. (2001). *Visual Methodologies: An Introduction to the Interpretation of Visual Materials.* London: Sage.

Starkman, R. (2004a). 10 medal hopefuls, *Toronto Star*, 12 August, J6–J7.

Starkman, R. (2004b). A lesson in sporting life, *Toronto Star*, 12 August, J4.

Sturken, M. and Cartwright, L. (2001). *Practices of Looking: An Introduction to Visual Culture.* New York: Oxford University Press.

Toronto Star (2004a). Going for gold: Perdita buoys Canada's hope, *Star Week*, front cover. *Toronto Star*, 7–13 August.

Toronto Star (2004b). Ready or Not, *Toronto Star*, 12 August, A1, J1.

Toronto Star (2004c). Gold and glory within Felicien's grasp. *Toronto Star,* 24 August, A1.

Theberge, N. and Cronk, A. (1986). Work routines in newspaper sports departments and the coverage of women's sports. *Sociology of Sports Journal,* 5, 195–203.

Wensing, E. and MacNeill, M. (2009, in press). Canada: Gender differences in Canadian English-language newspaper coverage of the 2004 Olympic Games. In T. Bruce, J. Hovden and P. Markula (eds.), *Women in the Olympic Media: A Global Analysis of Media Coverage.* Taipei City, Taiwan: Sense Publishers.

van Leeuwen, T., and Jewitt, C. (2001). *Handbook of Visual Analysis.* London: Sage.

Zelkovich, C. (2004). CBC steps over line with replay. *Toronto Star,* 25 August, D2.

4
From 'Iron Girl' to 'Sexy Goddess': An Analysis of the Chinese Media

Ping Wu

This chapter focuses on media discourse of female athletes in contemporary China. First, the historical developments of Chinese women's liberation and feminist critique will be discussed to reveal the broad social background for my discussion. Next, academic literature on media treatment of women's sport and female athletes in China will be reviewed. Finally, a textual analysis will examine how the Chinese media portrayed Chinese female athletes in their reports of the Athens Olympic Games.

Women's liberation and feminist critique in China

The process of women's liberation and the evolution of feminist critique in China differ greatly from their counterparts in the West. At the beginning of the twentieth century, China was experiencing a huge national crisis. Chinese intellectuals who were bent on realising nation salvation and modernisation started to criticise Confucianism, the dominant and state-supported ideology in feudalist China for over 2000 years. According to Confucianism, men represent *Yang*, being bright, strong, positive and symbolised by the sun and the heaven. Women, by contrast, represent *Yin*, being dark, weak, negative and symbolised by the moon and the earth. Croll (1995) explains: 'Originally conceived as complementary, such oppositions were early arranged in a series of hierarchical relationships juxtaposing superiority with secondariness, authority with obeisance and activity with passivity' (p. 12). Although Confucianism also emphasises that the world is formed by the combination of *Yin* and *Yang*, the prerequisite of harmonious coexistence of the two sexes is women's absolute obedience to men. Therefore, women should have no place in social affairs and their activities and roles should be kept within the family. Confucianism defines an ideal woman as a 'virtuous wife and good mother [*xian qi liang mu*]'. In feudalist China, women had no sense of subjectivity, no self-worth and no self-identity, and the overwhelming majority of them were illiterate. The liberal intellectuals, most of whom ironically were men, regarded Confucian rhetoric of women as the shackles of inequality by which Chinese women had been bound for centuries and argued that 'women are also human beings' and therefore they, like men, should have human rights and be involved in social life (Wang, 1997). During the May Fourth Movement which started in 1919, Western feminism was introduced into China for the first time (Wang, 1997). However, Chinese feminist activists did not set up their own political agenda before 1949. Instead, women's liberation was thought of as part of the nationalistic movement for nation's liberation and independence (see Bao, 1995; Yang, 2004). In republican China (1911–49), although more and more Chinese women left their 'small family' for large society and became financially independent modern females with a clear consciousness of their subjectivity, these so-called 'new women' [*xin nüxing*] were still a small minority of the total female population in China.

It was in the People's Republic of China (PRC), which was established in October 1949, that Chinese women, as a large collectivity, finally entered social life and social production. The Communist Party of China (CPC), which governed the country, insisted that 'socialism liberates women'. Gender equality was legitimised by the first constitution of the PRC. Between 1949 and 1978, Chinese women were encouraged by the government to 'do anything a man can do'. Gender sameness was over-emphasised and gender difference was deliberately ignored or even criticised. During this period, the image of the ideal Chinese woman was an 'iron girl [*tie guniang*]', physically strong, mentally determined, wearing a unisex workplace suit similar to her male peers (Croll, 1995). After they were granted the priceless gift of an equal right to education, employment and pay by the CPC (see Li, 1994; Pan, 1988), these 'daughters of the revolution', who were loyal to the CPC, in return poured all their passion and energy into work and the political movement. Domestic issues and family life were marginalised. Chinese women were now reluctant to display affection towards their family, husband and children, for this kind of 'softness' was excluded by the all-pervasive official rhetoric that prescribed correct thought and behaviour in women (Croll, 1995).

China ushered in a new era in 1978. Economic reform started and intellectuals were encouraged by the government to deconstruct Maoism, the dominant ideology during the past three decades. The masculinisation of women, as proof of alienation of human nature resulting from Maoism, was heavily criticised (see Barlow, 1994; Wang, 1997). Both the government and academia agreed that gender difference should not be obliterated or denied. In 1992, the Chinese government formally endorsed the market economy and since then, commercial capital has become the main force advocating gender difference in China in order to pursue greater profit. The mass media have played an important part in creating the new ideal female based on the so-called 'traditional virtues of Chinese women' and consumerism (see Wang, 1997). Although as 'the Party's mouthpiece' the Chinese mass media are still under the strict and strong control of the CPC, most, especially newspapers, have to make a living in the marketplace at the same time. Consequently, the media represent women in a rather fragmentary and inconsistent manner. To satisfy the CPC, the media reinforce the idea that Chinese women should be independent and self-reliant. But in order to pursue profit within the capitalist marketplace, the media try to persuade Chinese women that they are valued only if they are beautiful and feminine. As Wang (1997) notes: '[T]he discourse of femininity has lost its original political edge as a resisting force. Instead, it has been co-opted by increasingly powerful commercial forces' (p. 147). Gu (1997) argues that modern femininity is promoted and presented by the media as a tradable commodity. In this way, the media imply that beauty will bring women wealth (Yang, 2004). Some feminists argue that women's liberation, in fact, has been 'taking the road of regression' (Li, 1994, p. 363) in China since the economic reform started. Jiang (2005) warns that Chinese women today are more likely to become men's 'toys and appendages' than they were in any other period of the history of the PRC. Bao (1995) even argues that gender equality has never been achieved in China, because 'the revolution in China failed to destroy the basis of the oppression of women, and therefore failed to realise the goal of gender equality' (p. 262). Inevitably, the changing discourse of femininity is underpinning media coverage of female athletes in China, which is the main concern of this study.

Media treatment of women's sport and female athletes in China

In China, elite sport fulfils a function very different from that in the West. Modern competitive sport was introduced from the West in the late 1890s and at first was used in the Chinese army as part of military training (Hu, 2002). Initially, it had the goal of 'strengthening the country and the race [*qiangguo qiangzhong*]'; now, this political function is articulated as 'winning glory for the state [*wei guo zheng guang*]' (Wu, 2007). Consequently, Chinese elite athletes who have won glory for the state are typically portrayed as national heroes by the Chinese media.

Between 1949 and 1978, 'the value of a sports news event was that it provided a platform for political propaganda' (Wu, 2007, p. 170). The personal feelings of those involved in reported sports events were not important and a successful athlete was always portrayed as a member of a united and therefore powerful collectivity rather than as an individual. Individual heroism was branded as 'bourgeois' and ruthlessly criticised. However, after the 1978 economic reform, the Chinese media, newspapers in particular, started to employ a new reporting philosophy. Although Chinese elite athletes are still treated within the ideological context of nationalism or patriotism, their individual characteristics and experiences have become the focus of sports news stories (Wu, 2007). From the late 1990s onwards, Chinese elite athletes, especially if they are popular and successful, have been treated as celebrities by the media and their private lives have been under media scrutiny and extensively reported. This new trend – called 'tabloidisation' in sports journalism – has been noticed and discussed by both the media and academia in China (see Guo, 2004; 2005; Sun, 2006). Today, sports superstars like Yao Ming (male, basketball), Liu Xiang (male, athletics) and Guo Jingjing (female, diving) are not only role models but also fashion icons in Chinese society.

In general, women's sport receives much less media coverage than men's sport in contemporary China (see Li, Li and Mi, 2006; Mi and Zhang, 2003; Wu, 2008), but the amount of media coverage of Chinese female athletes did increase appreciably during the Olympics. For example, Wu (2008) found that during the 2004 Athens Olympic Games a typical Chinese daily devoted 34.46 per cent of its sports coverage to female athletes, with men's sport receiving 31.88 per cent. This was a direct result of the reporting policy of 'Chinese gold medal focus' which was employed by the Chinese media during the Olympics. Since 1988 the Chinese female athletes have overtaken their male counterparts in every Olympic Games by winning more gold medals. At the Athens Olympics, the Chinese sportswomen won 19.5 gold medals (including medals in 'mixed' sports), while the Chinese sportsmen won 12.5 gold medals (including medals in 'mixed' sports). However, the media coverage women's sport received during the Athens Olympics was only 1.08 times as large as that of men's sport (Wu, 2008). Thus, the Chinese media still gave preferential treatment to men's sport events during the Olympic Games.

Qualitative studies of how female athletes are portrayed by the Chinese media are few. Through analysing three different newspapers collected between January and April 2002, Yan (2004) found that gender bias was commonly reflected in sports coverage in both 'party organs' and tabloids[1] and further argued that party organs' attitude towards women's sport could be described as 'chauvinistic', while 'tabloids cater to low tastes and focus on female bodies rather than sporting performance of female athletes' (p. 108). Yan (2004) also revealed that while party organs marginalised women's sport by regarding it as less important than men's sport, tabloid newspapers deliberately sexualised female athletes by highlighting their feminine features. Zhang and Ren (2006) analysed the *Football Weekly's* reports on the Chinese women's football team during the 2005 'East Asia Top Four Tournament'.[2] They found that most of the reported speech in the stories was from the male head coach or other male leaders who were in charge of the Chinese women's team. Female footballers, who should have been the reported subjects, were actually left in silence. They argued that this 'silencing' not only revealed 'a heavily biased power relationship between the two genders', but also showed that the newspaper 'holds a negative attitude towards women's salvation and self-reliance'. The real message hidden in the media texts was that 'female footballers have no option but to hope to be liberated and saved by men' (Zhang and Ren, 2006, p. 498). Zhang and Ren (2006) show that Chinese newspapers trivialise female athletes' skill, performance and achievement by emphasising the contributions made by their male coaches and leaders. Niu (2007) examined three sports news programmes on the Sports Channel of the China Central Television Station broadcast between 1 and 9 February 2006 and found that female athletes were treated as objects for the viewers' gaze. The focus was on female athletes' bodies rather than their sporting performance or achievement. Niu (2007) concluded that 'the aesthetic value of a female image seems much more important than the news value of a female athlete's sporting performance' (p. 32). Again, Niu's (2007) findings indicate that the trivialisation and sexualisation of female athletes in media coverage, which are found commonly in the West, are also overt and blatant in China. I now discuss my qualitative study of Chinese newspaper portrayal of female athletes during the Athens Olympic Games.

Data collection and rationale

Two different types of newspaper were chosen for analysis to show a more rounded picture of the sport coverage during the Athens Olympics. The *Titan Sports Weekly* is a market-oriented tabloid, while the

China Sports Daily is a party organ. The *Titan Sports Weekly* is the best-selling and most influential sports-devoted newspaper in China and its weekly circulation has been stable at four million since 2003.[3] Its targeted readership is young males, the majority of whom are university students (Qu,[4] 2006). The *China Sports Daily* is owned by the national governing body of all sports, the General Administration of Sport, and is the most politically prestigious newspaper exclusively devoted to sport in China. It is mainly subscribed by the governmental authorities at different levels of governmental administration. The data were drawn from these two newspapers published from 11 to 30 August 2004.

In this study, media reports on table tennis, diving and weightlifting were analysed. These three sports were chosen because Chinese female athletes enjoyed similar levels of success in these sports at the Athens Olympic Games, winning two gold medals in table tennis, three in diving and three in weightlifting. Accordingly, the media coverage of the Chinese female athletes in these sports was sufficient for textual analysis. More importantly, these three sports are significantly different in respects of athlete's body build, uniform and technical requirements. Chinese female divers are in general petite, while Chinese female weightlifters are muscular and those of >75 kg class are usually well built. Most female table tennis players have a body that is considered neither too slim nor too huge. Female divers wear swimsuits that allow them to show more flesh and curves. Female table tennis players wear T-shirts and shorts and female weightlifters wear tight body suits over a T-shirt similar to male athletes. From a technical point of view, diving is a typical 'artistic' sport and is often referred as 'air ballet'. Table tennis is thought to be an 'intelligent' sport in China and it is not necessary for table tennis players to be especially strong, fast, tall or agile. Weightlifting is a sport typically considered as demanding strength. Through textual analysis of media reports of these three sports, this study attempts to establish whether or not the media treat Chinese female athletes whose body shapes are significantly different from each other in different ways. Furthermore, the study aims to detect which athletes gained preferential treatment from the media and why.

Diving: sexy goddess and love affair

Although four Chinese female divers won gold medals in Athens, almost all the media attention focused on Guo Jingjing, the champion at women's springboard diving and women's synchronised springboard diving. Guo had participated in three consecutive Olympic Games and her superb sporting achievement was definitely an important reason why the media valued her. However, her sporting achievement was clearly not at the core of the media portrayal of her during the Athens Olympics. Both the *China Sports Daily* and the *Titan Sports Weekly* associated her closely with Tian Liang, the leading superstar in men's diving in China, who was reported to be her boyfriend. The media even named them jointly – 'Liang-Jingjing' – a combination of their first names, but also a real Chinese term meaning 'Shining and Twinkling'. In the *China Sports Daily*, the word 'goddess [*nü shen*]' twice featured in the headlines of the Guo-related stories. One read 'Guo Jingjing is like a Goddess', the other 'Beautiful Goddess on the Springboard'. The word 'goddess' was also mentioned in the main texts of the stories as the following examples demonstrate:

> Guo Jingjing kept smiling. Wearing the olive wreath, she looked just like a goddess in Greek fairytales.
>
> (Deng, 15 August 2004, p. 2)

> This is Jingjing, whose dream has finally come true in the third Olympics she attended, who is elegant but not arrogant, who is beautiful and a little bit shy, who is low profile, earnest and not showy. In this evening of victory, she is an ordinary girl, but also a goddess.
>
> (Deng, 27 August 2004, p. 2)

The *Titan Sports Weekly* also portrayed Guo as beautiful and attractive: 'During the training last night, they [Guo Jingjing and Wu Minxia] both wore sexy swimming suits, a red one and a blue one, which made them extremely beautiful and attractive' (Yang, 12 August 2004, p. 8). However, as a market-oriented tabloid, the *Titan Sports Weekly* mainly focused on Guo's alleged love affair with fellow diver Tian Liang. Almost every time Guo was reported, 'Liang-Jingjing' appeared either in the headline or in the main text of the story. On 22 August 2004 two lengthy interviews with Guo and Tian respectively were set on the same page. In fact, neither Guo nor Tian talked about their supposed relationship in the interviews. However, the joint title of the two interviews, 'Xiong Ni[5] Plays Go-Between for Liang-Jingjing', hinted at their love affair in a play on words.

Weightlifting: being beautiful and vulnerable inside

Three Chinese female weightlifters, Chen Yanqing, Liu Chunhong and Tang Gonghong, won gold medals at the Athens Olympic Games.

Although there was considerable coverage of them, their looks were rarely mentioned. Instead, their weight became a major issue. In the lengthy interviews with Chen Yanqing (58 kg class) and Tang Gonghong (>75 kg class) in the *China Sports Daily*, there were two interesting interviews of 'the beauty dilemma faced by female weightlifters'. The first one stated:

> *Interviewer*: Some sports fans discussed online that your facial expression was actually quite beautiful at the moment when you won gold. As far as I am concerned, weightlifting has some negative impact on a girl's figure. Do you feel regretful for all the changes [to your body caused by weightlifting]?
>
> *Chen Yanqing*: Due to strength training, female weightlifters have sturdy arms and legs. However, in general, you will retain your innate and natural figure. The only difference is your muscles will become firmer. We Chinese people do not feel comfortable valuing muscular females, but muscular women are quite fancied in foreign countries.
>
> *Interviewer*: You, actually, still have some prettiness like most Jiangzhe girls.[6]
>
> *Chen Yanqing*: When I went abroad, I was regarded as very strong and very healthy. I think it depends on individual taste of aesthetics. From my point of view, as long as I can improve my sporting performance, I do not care whether I will have to pull on another 10 kg or become ten times uglier.
>
> (Hua'ao, 19 August 2004, p. 7)

The second interview focused even more poignantly on the appearance of the female weightlifter:

> *Interviewer*: I often ask female weightlifters this question: we know that every girl wants to be beautiful. However, female weightlifters of your class have to intentionally keep their weight over 75 kg. So, do you think you show another kind of beauty, i.e. a feisty beauty, which is different from ordinary beauty?
>
> *Tang Gonghong*: I think one is most beautiful only when she is beautiful inside, only after she won a champion title. No matter how physically beautiful you are, you will not be really beautiful if your sporting performance is not good enough.
>
> *Interviewer*: In your free time and outside weightlifting, what do you like to do? Do you have any hobbies?

Tang Gonghong: In my spare time, I like reading books, listening to music and knitting sweaters.

Interviewer: Knitting is painstaking and very different from weightlifting! Do you think knitting could be a kind of training of your patience?

Tang Gonghong: No, I do not think so. I believe knitting is just an appropriate and good thing for females to do in their spare time.

(Hua'ao, 23 August 2004, p. 7)

The *Titan Sports Weekly* did not publish any lengthy interviews with the female weightlifters, nor did it mention the problem of their weight. However, their coverage of these female weightlifters revealed issues of further interest to my analysis:

[Chen Yanqing told the journalists after she won gold] I have two sisters and I am the youngest. However, I think I am better than a boy, because this time I have really glorified my ancestors and family!

(Ge, 17 August 2004, p. 6)

After putting down the weight, Tang Gonghong rushed down the platform and hugged her coach, her voice choked. Li Shunzhu [the coach] patted her and said: 'It is OK now, you have done it.'

(Wang, 22 August 2004, p. 4)

After the medal ceremony, Tang Gonghong came to Yu Guitian, the Minister of Shandong Provincial Administration of Sport, and said: 'Uncle Yu, now I can see you again.' Before she could finish her words, she burst into tears. Before the competition, Yu Guitian and Tang Gonghong made a bet: she would win gold, otherwise she should not see Yu again.[7]

(Ran and Wang, 22 August 2004, p. 4)

I shall return to the issues raised in these quotations in my data analysis section.

Table tennis: sorry and grateful

The media coverage of women's table tennis was largely about Wang Nan and Zhang Yining, who won gold in the women's doubles. Zhang also won gold in the women's singles. Neither the *Titan Sports Weekly* nor the

China Sports Daily reported on the appearances of Wang and Zhang. However, after Wang Nan lost in the quarter-finals of the women's singles, her emotions were described in some detail by both newspapers. In an article in the *China Sports Daily*, Wang Nan told the reporter:

> I burst into tears, because I felt I had let too many people down ... At that moment, I actually did not think too much about myself. I know that too many people hoped that I could win gold at the women's singles ... my coaches and leaders all believed that Wang Nan had the best chance of winning this gold. How could I lose? I have disappointed all of them. I am extremely sorry about this.
>
> (Xia, 2 August 2004, p. 3)

The tone in the *Titan Sports Weekly* was similar:

> Wang left the arena in tears after she lost at the women's singles. She did not want to talk to anybody. Grasping a towel in her right hand, she managed to remain calm when she greeted the audience. As soon as she walked out of the arena, she could not help falling into floods of tears. After she won gold at the women's doubles, she smiled; but her red and swollen eyes were still full of regrets.
>
> (Yan and Zhang, 21 August 2004, p. 4)

After Zhang Yining won gold at the women's singles, the *China Sports Weekly* published a lengthy feature titled 'Zhang Yining's story told by Li Sun'. Li Sun was Zhang's coach and most of the story was written in the first person, with Li telling the story. Some direct quotes from Zhang Yining were attached to the story. For example, at the beginning of the article:

> It is impossible for me to describe in words how grateful I am to Coach Li. When I was growing up, he played all the roles I needed him to play. He is not only my coach, but also my friend and a father figure.
>
> (Xia, 23 August 2004, p. 3)

No interview with Zhang Yining or feature story about her was found in the *Titan Sports Weekly*. Instead, Li Sun gave the newspaper an interview on which a short story about Zhang was based (Wang, 23 August 2004, p. A6). This time, from beginning to end, there was not a single word of direct quote from Zhang Yining.

Data analysis

According to traditional Chinese aesthetics, a beautiful woman should have a dainty figure. Not surprisingly, only the female divers were portrayed by the newspapers as beautiful and sexy among the reported female athletes in the three sports, while the female weightlifters, whose image was similar to the 'iron girl', had to face embarrassing questions about their weight. In both cases, it was the female body rather than the female athlete's sporting achievement that drew media attention. On the one hand, the female diver whose petite body conformed to the hegemonic notions of femininity in China was hailed by the media. The obsession of the media with the 'sexy goddess' could not be better revealed by the *Titan Sports Weekly* headline: 'Perfect Guo Jingjing Makes Everyone Fall for Her' (Li, 27 August 2004, p.A4). On the other hand, the sturdy or outsize body of the female weightlifter was interpreted as a sacrifice made in pursuit of sporting excellence. Although their appearance was not openly criticised or ridiculed by the newspapers, the word 'ugly' was, indeed, ascribed to the female weightlifters. Clearly, the female athletes were being sexualised as objects for the male gaze. Interestingly and intriguingly, while their bodies actually defied the hegemonic notions of femininity, the female weightlifters were still portrayed as conforming to the hegemonic notions of femininity in terms of their demeanour and behaviour. The newspapers deliberately softened the image of the female weightlifters by highlighting that they, just like most ordinary and 'proper' women, liked knitting in their spare time or would readily burst into tears.

Although all the reported female athletes were Olympic gold medallists, their sporting talents and performances were rarely the focus of the news stories. Guo Jingjing won two gold medals at the Athens Olympic Games and was no doubt one of the most accomplished sports heroines in the world. However, she was not reported as a sports heroine at all. Rather, she was pursued and portrayed by the media simply as involved in an alleged love affair. When their sporting performances were reported, the female athletes, despite being at the top of their sports, were deemed incapable of explaining to the media how they had achieved their victories. In most cases, the male coaches appeared to be in charge of all the technical training and tactics. In addition, again and again these male coaches and leaders were reported to have played a decisive role in the female athletes' successes. The reports on Zhang Yining, the gold medallist of women's table tennis singles, clearly revealed the heavily skewed relationship between the male mentor and the female athlete. In both newspapers, the story of the female athlete was told exclusively by the male coach and the only chance the female athlete was given to express her own opinion was to express her gratitude to her male coach. Similarly, the story of Wang Nan, another table tennis player who lost in the quarter-finals of the women's singles, focused on the regret she felt in relation to her male coaches and leaders. It was evident that a female athlete's victory or defeat seemed more important to the male coaches and leaders than to the athlete herself. Ironically, a report on the men's table tennis singles in the *Titan Sports Weekly* revealed the media's trivialisation of sporting achievements of female athletes even more clearly:

> The game is over. The Chinese team have not won all the four gold medals this time. It may not be a bad thing though, in a certain sense. However, they should not have lost the 'heaviest' one [i.e. the most valuable, the men's singles gold medal) among the four. Shame!
>
> (Ge, 24 August 2004, p. 16)

The newspapers further trivialised the achievements of the female athletes by highlighting their vulnerability and, more importantly, by emphasising how they needed the firm support of their male coaches and leaders when they were emotional vulnerable. The story of Tang Gonghong, the champion of the >75 kg class in women's weightlifting, was typical. Although Tang was physically strong, she was reported to have sought consistently for guidance and consolation from her male coach and male leader. When she was in tears, her male coach and male leader tried to calm her down in a rather patronising tone. The male superiors were portrayed as father figures for the female athletes, who appeared more like disconsolate babies than adult women.

Two things are noteworthy here. First, the media should not be held solely responsible for the biased messages of gender relationship. The female athletes themselves were not totally innocent. Rather, they contributed to the creation of these messages too. For example, after becoming the champion of the 58 kg class in women's weightlifting, Chen Yanqing believed she could finally reckon herself better than a boy because she had achieved something normally only men achieved: glorifying her ancestors and family. It is clear that although this female athlete's achievement actually challenged male hegemony, she still subconsciously took the hegemonic notions of masculinity and femininity for granted. Secondly, the female reporters' touch did not significantly differ from that of the male reporters. As a former Chinese sports journalist who used to work for the *Titan Sports Weekly*, the author of this chapter knows all the reporters who covered the stories analysed here. For example, the reporter who wrote 'Zhang Yining's story told by Li Sun' for the *China Sports Daily* is a woman, while the reporter who wrote a short story based on an interview with the same male coach for the *Titan Sports Weekly* is male. However, the two stories are very similar in tone: both focus on the male coach's interpretation of the female athlete's achievement and also highlight the male coach's vital contribution to the female athlete's victory. Sports journalism is an overwhelmingly 'masculine' profession in the West, and this male dominance is argued to be one of the key factors resulting in the media's trivialisation of women's sport and female athletes (e.g. Boyle, 2006; Rowe, 2004). In China, there is greater gender balance among sports journalists than in the West: female sports journalists are definitely not a rare species. However, as revealed in this study, the question of whether or not media treatment of women's sport and female athletes could be significantly improved with more female sports journalists enrolled remains unanswered.

Conclusion

In the West, the development of sport has always been closely related to the notions of masculinity. As Nelson (1994) points out, 'batting, catching, throwing, and jumping are not neutral human activities, but somehow more naturally a male domain' (p. 2). This feminist point of view has been widely accepted in the Western academia. When women actually invade this traditional male domain, the media, which recreate masculine hegemony on a daily basis, not only choose to keep silent about female athletes' sporting achievement, they also reinforce the dominant rhetoric of femininity by focusing on the feminine female body. However, Chinese women's participation in sport has followed a rather different route.

It was after the establishment of the PRC that elite sport started to develop rapidly and systematically. Following the Soviet Union's model, the Chinese government set up its own elite sport system in the 1950s and elite sport has been funded and run by the state ever since (Wu, 2007). The CPC advocates gender equality and Chinese women have always been encouraged by the government to participate in sport. Therefore, Chinese female athletes have not faced overt resistance to sport participation as many Western women have. As I discussed previously, the Chinese media rarely reported on athletes as individuals between 1949 and 1978. The emphasis was always on the political importance of sporting victories rather than personal success or charisma of those who 'won glory for the state'. Simultaneously, gender sameness was advocated during this period. In fact, Chinese female athletes had not been under pressure to look 'properly feminine' until the early 1990s. Even today, the Chinese media rarely criticise the looks of Chinese female athletes. However, media portrayal of female athletes has changed dramatically since the early 1990s, for most of the media have to cater to their audience's tastes in order to survive in the market. Nowadays, when Chinese female athletes' achievements are covered in the media, their feminine traits are commonly the focus of news stories. This study reveals that there is a sharp contrast in media treatment of 'the iron girls' in weightlifting and 'the sexy goddess' in diving. The media eagerly report on the beauty of the female diver with a petite body. At the same time, their portrayal of the female weightlifters as beautiful and feminine on the *inside* is rather hypocritical, because it gives the impression that the female weightlifters were physically unattractive and, therefore, imperfect as feminine women. A feminine body is highly valued by the media and portrayed as an object for the male gaze. The problems in media treatment of female athletes found in this study are similar to those found by Yan (2004) and Niu (2007).

This study also reveals that the sporting achievements of female athletes are trivialised by the media. The female athletes were hardly reported as sporting heroines. Rather, they were portrayed either as happily in love or as emotionally vulnerable. The media depicted the female athletes as rather passive as they appeared to simply follow the guidance of their male coaches and leaders. In the media texts, female athletes were the objects who were advised, guided, encouraged, saved, consoled or even told off by their male coaches and leaders. Female athletes lacked their own voice and seemed incapable of explaining their own success in sport. This finding echoes the problem of 'silencing' the female athletes in the Chinese media, as discussed by Zhang and Ren (2006).

The Chinese women's liberation movement, similar to the media's treatment of women in general and female athletes in particular, has dramatically changed in the last 100 years. However, no matter whether the media advocated gender sameness before 1978 or gender differences now, the deep-rooted male hegemony in Chinese society has always played a determining role in defining 'proper' femininity. From 'iron girls' challenging men to 'sexy goddesses' appealing to men, female athletes have always been portrayed by the media based firmly upon the hegemonic notions of femininity in China.

Notes

1. The Chinese newspapers fall into two main categories: party organ and market-oriented tabloid. All the party organs directly present the Party's interests and employ a conservative and serious reporting policy. Market-oriented tabloids cater to their readers' tastes and please advertisers. Therefore, they employ a relatively liberal and entertaining reporting policy.
2. The *Football Weekly* is one of the best-selling sports newspapers in China; the 'East Asia Top Four Tournament' is a major women's football event in Asia.
3. Data source: the Sina China, the largest gateway website in China. http://finance.sina.com.cn/roll/20030829/1758426671.shtml?bcsi_scan_86 52ED27417F2C25=JjENLna/h2ZpZrLh8KjJXAEAAAB++iwA&bcsi_scan_file-name=1758426671.shtml
4. The author, Qu Youyuan, is the president of the *Titan Sports Weekly* Press.
5. Xiong Ni is a former diving superstar and a household name in China. During the Athens Olympic Games, he worked for the *Titan Sports Weekly* as a guest reporter.
6. *Jiangzhe* means two neighboring provinces, Jiangsu and Zhejiang, in China. In general, young females from these two provinces are regarded as pretty and slim in China.
7. Tang Gonghong comes from Shandong Province in China. In the Chinese administrative system of elite sport, Tang is an athlete directly under the leadership of Yu Guitian, the Minister of the Sporting Authority in the same province.

References

Bao, X. L. (1995) *Xifang nüxing zhuyi yanjiu pingjie* [The Introduction of Western Feminist Research], Shanghai: Sanlian Shudian Press.

Barlow, T. E. (1994). Politics and protocols of funü: (Un)Making national woman. In C. K. Gilmartin, G. Hershatter, L. Rofel and T. White (eds), *Engendering China: Women, Culture, and the State* (pp. 339–59). Cambridge, MA and London: Harvard University Press

Boyle, R. (2006). *Sports Journalism: Context and Issues*. London: Sage.

Croll, E. (1995). *Changing Identities of Chinese Women*. London and New Jersey: Zed Books.

Deng, X. Z. (2004). Guo Jingjing jiu xiang yige nüshen [Guo Jingjing is like a goddess]. *China Sports Daily*, 15 August, p. 2.

Deng, X. Z. (2004). Tiaoban shang meili de nüshen [Beautiful goddess on the springboard]'. *China Sports Daily*, 27 August, p. 2.

Ge, A. P. (2004). Chen Yanqing zhi rang: Wo guang zong yao zu [Chen Yanqing kept shouting: I glorified my ancestors and family]. *Titan Sports Weekly*, 17 August, p. 6.

Ge, A. P. (2004). Wang Hao, shengming zhong buneng chengshou zhi zhong [The unbearable burden in Wang Hao's life]. *Titan Sports Weekly*, 24 August, p. 16.

Gu, Y. (1997). *Nüxing zhuyi zhe yan* [A feminist speech], http://www.feminism.cn/ReadNews.asp?NewsID=307. Accessed 28 August 2007.

Guo, J. Y. (2004). Woguo tiyu dazhong chuanbo de yulehua qingxiang jiqi yihua [Tabloidisation tendency of China's sports journalism and its differentiation].

Shanghai Tiyu Xueyuan Xuebao [Journal of Shanghai Physical Education Institute], 28(6), 30–3.

Guo, S. J. (2005). Tiyu xinwen zheng bei yulehua [Sports news is being tabloidised]. *Chuanmei* [Media], 76 (August), 49.

Hu, X. M. (2002). Xin shiji zhongguo tiyu de lilun chuangxin [New theoretic ideas in Chinese sport of the new century]. *Tiyu* [Physical Education], 10, 11–15.

Hua'ao (2004). Wo congxiao shangshan xiashui you pashu [I was used to climbing mountains, playing in water and climbing trees as a child]. *China Sports Daily*, 19 August, p. 7.

Hua'ao (2004). Neng chi neng lian, ai ting yinyue, zhi maoyi [Good at eating and training, loving music and knitting]. *China Sports Daily*, 23 August, p. 7.

Jiang, H. (2005). Dazhong chuanmei he shehui xingbie [Mass media and gender]. http://www.feminism.cn/ReadNews.asp?NewsID=1092. Accessed 28 August 2007.

Li, S. Z. (2004). Wanmei Guo Jingjing, qingdao suoyou ren [Perfect Guo Jingjing makes everyone fall for her]. *Titan Sports Weekly*, 27 August, p. A4.

Li, W.; Li, J. and Mi, J. (2006). Ye lun baozhi de nüzi tiyu baodao [On female sports report in newspapers]. *Zhonghua Nüzi Xueyuan Xuebao* [Journal of China Women's University], 18(1), 68–72.

Li, X. J. (1988). *Xiawa de tansuo* [Eve's exploration]. Changsha: Hunan Renmin Press.

Li, X. J. (1994). Economic reform and the awakening of Chinese women's collective consciousness. In C. K. Gilmartin, G. Hershatter, L. Rofel, and T. White (eds), *Engendering China: Women, Culture, and the State* (pp. 360–82). Cambridge, MA and London: Harvard University Press.

Mi, J. and Zhang, C. (2003). Baozhi de nüzi tiyu baodao yanjiu [Study on female sports report in newspapers]. *Tianjin Tiyu Xueyuan Xuebao* [Journal of Tianjin Institute of Physical Education], 18(3), 69–71.

Nelson, M. (1994). *The Stronger Women Get, the More Men Love Football: Sexism and the American Culture of Sports*. New York: Harcourt Brace.

Niu, W. H. (2007). Dianshi tiyu baodao zhong de xingbie pianjian yingxiang fenxi [An analysis on the impact of gender bias on TV sports reportage]. *Xinwen Zhishi* [Journalism Knowledge], 6, 32–4.

Pan, S. M. (1988). Fulian yinggai you duli de yizhi (Fulian should have its independent will). *Funu Zuzhi yu Huodong: Yinshua Baokan Ziliao* (Women's organisations and activities: Published press materials reader), 3(44) (published by the People's University).

Qu, Y. Y. (2006). Zhongguo tiyu zhichuanmei ji shouzhong de dutexing [Uniqueness of Chinese sports media and audience]. *Yunmeng Xuekan* [Journal of Yunmeng], 27(1), 154–5.

Ran, X. F. and Wang, Y. Y. (2004). Ouyun 100 jin jingzhong 305 gongjin [The net weight of the 100th Olympic gold medal is 305 kg]. *Titan Sports Weekly*, 22 August, p. 4.

Rowe, D. (2004). *Sport, Culture and the Media*, 2nd edition. Buckingham: Open University Press.

Sun, Y. (2006). Tiyu xinwen baodao de san da wuqu [Three mistakes of Chinese sports journalism]. *Xinwen Qianshao* [Journalism Outpost], 1, 65–6.

Wang, Y. Y. (2004). Tang Gonghong wan de jiushi xintiao [What Tang Gonghong wanted was risk]. *Titan Sports Weekly*, 22 August, p. 4.

Wang, Y. Y. (2004). Shinian de jianzheng [Being a witness for ten years]. *Titan Sports Weekly*, 23 August, p. A6.

Wang, Z. (1997). Maoism, feminism, and the UN conference on women: Women's studies research in contemporary China. *Journal of Women's History*, 8(4), 126–52.

Wu, P. (2007). Co-operation, confrontation and conflict: An investigation of the relationship between the news media and sports administrative organizations in contemporary China. Unpublished PhD thesis, De Montfort University, UK.

Wu, P. (in press). Has Yin got the upper hand of Yang. In T. Bruce, J. Hovden and P. Markula (eds.). *Women in the Olympic Media: A Global Comparison of Newspaper Coverage*, Netherlands and New Zealand: SENSE Publishers and Wilf Malcolm Institute for Educational Research.

Xia, W. (2004). Qinggan shilu: Wang Nan de 17 xiaoshi [Honest account: The 17 hours in Wang Nan's life]. *China Sports Daily*, 21 August, p. 3.

Xia, W. (2004). Ting Li Sun jiang Zhang Yining de gushi [Zhang Yining's story told by Li Sun]. *China Sports Daily*, 23 August, p. 3.

Yan, J. (2004). Tiyu baodao zhong xingbie pianjian [The sexual bias in the sports reports]. *Henan Shehui Kexue* [Journal of Henan Social Sciences], 12(2), 106–9.

Yan, Q. and Zhang, Y. J. (2004). Wang Nan: Shui le yiwan jiu xing le [Wang Nan woke up after only one night's sleep]. *Titan Sports Weekly*, 21 August, p. 4.

Yang, L. (2004). Nüshuang tiaoban: Meng kaishi de difang [Women's synchronized springboard: Where the dream starts]. *Titan Sports Weekly*, 12 August, p. 8.

Yang, Z. (2004). Zhongguo xinwen chuanboxue zhong nüxing zhuyi yanjiu de lishi, xianzhuang yu fazhan [Feminism in the journalism and communication study of China: The History, actuality and evolution], unpublished PhD dissertation, The Huazhong Normal University, China.

Zhang, J. and Ren, X. (2006). Tiyu baodao zhong de nüxing shiyu zheng [On the silence for females in sports news report]. *Hubei Tiyu Keji* [Journal of Hubei Sports Science], 25(5), 497–9.

5
'Acceptable Bodies': Deconstructing the Finnish Media Coverage of the 2004 Olympic Games

Pirkko Markula

Feminist sport studies scholars have examined the ideological construction of feminine identity in the Olympic media by comparing the coverage of women athletes in 'masculine' and 'feminine' sports. Feminist interest in this classification stems from the idea that in the current male-dominated culture of sport, it is more acceptable for women to participate in 'feminine' sports. Female participants in 'masculine' sports will be marginalised in the media coverage because they challenge the existing gender order in sport. At the same time, increased coverage of women in 'masculine' sports indicates resistant change to the ideological construction of sport. In this chapter, I analyse whether feminist research can challenge the current structure behind women's sport media representation through readings of feminine and masculine sports. I use Jacques Derrida's affirmative deconstruction to map the logic of sport classification in feminist sport studies. My discussion is based on two strategies (Patton, 2003): first, I trace the history of the concept of 'acceptable sport' in feminist sport studies; and second, I examine possibilities for changing theoretical understandings of women's sport participation in contemporary society. To illustrate my discussion, I examine the types of sports in which women were represented in a Finnish newspaper during the Athens Olympic Games, 2004.

Deconstruction: an affirmation of feminism

While deconstruction is rare in sport studies (for an exception, see Cole, 1998), several feminist writers have discovered the pertinence of Derrida's thoughts to feminism (e.g. Crosz, 1997; Hekman, 1990; Holland, 1997;

Weedon, 1987). For example, Elizabeth Grosz (1997) argues that Derrida can make feminism 'more aware of necessary conceptual and political investments and the cost of these investments, and thus more effective and more incisive in its struggles than it may have been before or beyond deconstruction' (p. 75). This focus is of particular relevance to this chapter as my aim is to assess the conceptual investment by feminists in the dichotomy of feminine/masculine sports. From my point of view, a deconstruction of this classification can also provide greater insight into the conceptual map of different placements of femininity versus masculinity. Grosz (1997) further asserts that

> [d]econstruction provides a way of rethinking our common conceptions of politics and struggle, power and resistance by insisting that no system, method, or discourse can be as all-encompassing, singular, and monolithic as it represents itself.
>
> (p. 75)

Therefore, not only the structure of sport, but also feminist theory, like any other system, should be open to continual deconstruction, its own undoing. According to Grosz, this undoing should be initiated by the feminists themselves who should acknowledge that feminism does not operate outside of a 'a dominant system' to act as an objective critic that first critiques and then provides alternatives. Susan Hekman (1990) adds that deconstruction enables feminists to reconceptualise femininity in non-dualist terms. This allows researchers to use deconstruction not only as a critique, but also as an interventionist strategy that attacks the root of the problem (the classical dualism) underlying women's oppression and, by designing direct social intervention, aims to displace the system that creates the problem. Therefore, from a Derridean perspective, deconstruction is not conceived as 'a system of critique, of destruction' of feminism, but as a mode of affirmation. This means that feminist sport studies are not positioned outside of the construction of an oppressive 'feminisation' of sport. On the contrary, while the purpose is to critique the structure of sport, feminists, by creating theoretical concepts such as sex-appropriate sports, are always active participants in the process of defining women's sport. For Grosz, engagement in Derridean deconstruction means accepting that critique always embeds the affirmation of the thing that is being critiqued. If this does not mean abandoning the political struggle of feminism, how can deconstruction help eradicate women's oppression through/in sport? According to Grosz, the key is openness to 'internal' critique: a further interrogation of the conceptual binary feminine/masculine (sports) and its impact on perpetuating existing systems of power. To engage in an internal critique, I now trace the history of the concept 'feminine acceptable' sport and its various interpretations. I then apply each interpretation to an analysis of Finnish newspaper coverage during the Athens Olympic Games in 2004 to demonstrate how these concepts have evolved into media analyses.

In this chapter, I analyse the Olympic coverage in a Finnish broadsheet, *Turun Sanomat*. While Finland does not have a 'national' newspaper, *Turun Sanomat*, established in 1905, is the third largest newspaper in Finland with a daily readership of 280,000, making it the most widely read newspaper in south-west Finland. My sample includes all the issues one week before, during and after the Olympic Games (7 August–5 September 2004). An 'Olympic Extra', which discussed the expectation of Finnish success in the Olympics, was included in the analysis. I analysed all articles and photographs devoted to women's sport in this newspaper's coverage (25 articles and 83 photos).

'Acceptable' and 'sex-appropriate sports': a brief theoretical trace

Currently, such concepts as 'feminine' sports, 'acceptable' sports and 'sex-appropriate' sports are often used interchangeably in feminist sport studies despite their different theoretical frameworks. All these terms, nevertheless, can be traced to Eleanor Metheny's groundbreaking research on women's perceptions of sport participation.

Eleanor Metheny: 'acceptable' sports

In 1964 Metheny presented her seminal classification of feminine acceptable sports. Her starting point was to understand the underlying nature of women's exclusion from the Olympics. Radically at her time, Metheny maintained that the culturally formed masculine and feminine images might play a much bigger role than biological differences between men and women in determining why some sports are not considered acceptable for women. Metheny (1965) links the formation of gender images in 1960s America to ancient Greece and notes that the images of Greek goddesses, the feminine role models of their day, were 'almost totally devoid of any suggestions of physical strength' (p. 45). For example, in ancient Greece the virtues of adult women remained those of Demeter (the nurturer and mother earth), Hera (wife and the helpmate of Zeus) and Aphrodite (the goddess of beauty). These images,

Metheny argued, are 'still reflected in the connotations of the words *masculine* and *feminine* as we use them today' (p. 48, emphasis in the original) and the arguments around women's participation in competitive sport 'hinge on those connotations' (p. 48). Similar to many contemporary researchers, Metheny asserts that '[t]oday the image of the feminine athlete is still somewhat blurred, but its modern outlines now seem to be emerging in currently sanctioned patterns of sports competition for women' (p. 48). Metheny also carefully acknowledged that '[t]he socially sanctioned images of femininity and masculinity are always relative. They differ from era to era, from culture to culture, and from group to group within a given social organization' (p. 48). Metheny collected the 'data' to support her argument of longevity of the ancient Greek image of femininity from 'college women in the United States' (p. 49). The details are sketchy, but most of the information appears to come from the University of Illinois and the University of Southern California. How information about their 'attitudes' was collected is unclear, but nevertheless resulted in the memorable classification of sports into:

1. categorically unacceptable to women at the international level;
2. not acceptable to college women at the United States, but may be acceptable to minority groups in college population;
3. individual competition generally acceptable to college women in the United States.[1]

Metheny's classification was based on the amount of force applied to resistance, the space and time the athlete's body had to engage in physical activity and the consequent strength required from the athlete to complete her performance. Generally, sports which require force to overcome heavy resistance (an implement or the opponent's body), and thus necessitate the use of strength, were deemed unacceptable to college women in Metheny's sample.

While grounding her classification on the body's ability to generate strength, Metheny concluded that biology does not provide a logical basis to support such perceptions. Instead, 'in the United States, the image of femininity projected by college women and endorsed by their potential mates is a "double image" – with one aspect identified as "woman at work" and the other identified as "woman at home"' (p. 55). As a working image, Metheny explained, the college women see themselves 'with forces of the universe' but not by using 'sheer muscular force of bodily contact' (p. 55), but by the use of their wits and lightweight equipment that requires dexterity. On the other hand, these women, '[a]s potential wives and mothers', are

> concerned with expressing their femininity in quite different ways. Recognizing their own biologically-based need for dependence on the male wage-earner, they modify their behaviour in ways designed to enhance their own sexual desirability. They may also, on occasion, conceal their own abilities as workers lest the man of their choice might feel belittled by their competence.
>
> (p. 55)

Metheny concluded by noting how college women in the 1960s were able to create a complex image of femininity by combining 'the sexually-based image of Aphrodite, Hera and Demeter with the personal power of Athena, Artemis and Hippolyta, without doing violence to either, within the realm of sports competition' (p. 56). Therefore, Metheny provided evidence of the changing feminine role through women's sport participation and probably would expect us today to continue to examine further changes.

If I followed Metheny's lead faithfully, I would examine what sports Finnish women find acceptable today. However, in a media study I can only conclude that, based on the sports in which Finnish women participated in the Athens Olympics, the feminine role in Finland today appears quite different from the American feminine role in the 1960s. The Finnish Olympic team consisted of 53 athletes, 17 of whom were women. Finnish women competed in archery, badminton, canoeing, sailing, shooting, swimming, and track and field events. The largest women's team was track and field (nine women), of whom three were javelin throwers. In Metheny's America only archery, badminton and swimming were acceptable sports for college women. Javelin, the long jump and shorter foot races (i.e. the 100 and 200 metres), in all of which Finland had an Olympic representative, were acceptable only for lower-class or 'negro' women in America. Canoeing, sailing, the triple jump and shooting did not feature in American college sports. Like the American college women, Finnish elite athletes did not compete in team sports or events requiring body contact. Following Metheny (1965), I could conclude that Finnish women have gone further in combining 'the sexually-based image of Aphrodite, Hera and Demeter with the personal power of Athena, Artemis and Hippolyta, without doing violence to either, within the realm of sports competition' (p. 56) because they participate in a wider variety of sports, but like their

American counterparts have not moved entirely into the realm of physical power of contact and team sports. In this sense, Finnish women's participation in the Olympic Games illustrates the changed image of femininity in the contemporary world. This is a positive finding and, in this sense, Metheny's conceptual schema has helped me to identify a change in sport that is more inclusive of women. Nevertheless, an analysis of 'acceptable sports' fails to explain how and why such a change has taken place. Is the change really a reflection of a changed 'feminine role' or a result of changed economic, political and cultural forces around the Olympic Games, and not of the structure of the Games themselves? In addition, can we assume that college women's ideas about acceptable sports for women reflect the general view of 'acceptable' femininity in society? Other researchers have examined in more detail what is considered 'feminine' and 'masculine' in society. This line of research examines the acceptability of sports for women by attempting to define 'femininity' first.

Bem's gender schema: 'sex-appropriate sports'

While Metheny's concept of 'acceptable' sports is often used interchangeably with 'sex-appropriate' sports, these two concepts have quite different theoretical origins. The notion of 'sex-appropriate' sports draws from Bem's psychologically oriented gender schema theory[2] to examine attitudes towards women's sport. Bem's student Sherri Matteo's (1986) applied the gender schema to determine how sex, sex typing and gender connotations of sport impacted on college women's sport participation. Based on the Bem Sex Role Inventory, Matteo had US students in a first year psychology class rate a list of sports into 30 masculine, 26 neutral and 12 feminine sports and then report which of these 68 sports they had tried at least once. Matteo also determined each student's sex role type (masculine, feminine, androgynous, undifferentiated) through Bem Sex Role inventory. She discovered that men and women had tried an equal number of sports and preferred to participate in neutral sports (e.g. archery, badminton, bowling, diving, golf, swimming, tennis and volleyball), though that their second preference was for sex-appropriate sports. Matteo further suggested that women have a choice of less sex-appropriate activities (only twelve sports were classified as 'feminine' and included, for example, dance, field hockey, figure skating, gymnastics and yoga). Women, however, have more opportunity than men to develop a variety of sport skills because, while they do not prefer masculine sports, they do have the opportunity to choose these sports as well as the feminine sports. Matteo links women's invisibility in the sport media to her findings: the media prefer to air the 'feminine' sports because of the gender biases of the 'sex-typed' producers and viewers.

In my examination of media representations of the Finnish women Olympians, I cannot measure whether the Finns prefer neutral sports or sex-typed females prefer feminine sports. Nor can I focus on the sex typing of the Finnish women Olympians. However, I can detect that the Finnish women Olympians competed in sports that the American undergraduate psychology students classified as neutral (archery, badminton, canoeing, running, sailing, swimming) or masculine (javelin, long jump, skeet) (hammer or heptathlon were not classified). I found that the Finnish women preferred to participate in neutral sports. The newspaper represented women in more different types of masculine sports than in feminine sports. These included beach volleyball, gymnastics and synchronised swimming (which can be considered female-appropriate sports) despite having no Finnish representation in the Olympics, but in general the feminine sports coverage focused on rhythmic (i.e. floor exercises accompanied by music) gymnastics. I asked if women in male-appropriate sport were 'feminised' by frequent comparisons to males or to non-performance-related aspects The femininity of the athletes was not emphasised and only twice were comparisons to men's sports made. Allusions to non-performance aspects were rare and very brief.[3] In this sense, the Finnish newspaper coverage appeared to focus on the masculine sports without much effort to feminise women in these sports. The feminine sports coverage provided some focus on the athletes' appearance, but on the whole, emphasised their performance at the Games. There was, therefore, no specific evidence of emphasised femininity.

Based on these results, one could conclude that, 20 years on, the media are moving towards a gender-aschematic society, as called for by Matteo (1986), who concluded that '[u]nless gender-based stereotypes about activities as well as people are eliminated we will not find ourselves in the gender-aschematic society Bem (1985) prescribed, and our options will remain limited' (p. 431). It is clear that Matteo was measuring attitudes on gender typing in order ultimately to eradicate them. For example, the division of masculine and feminine sports results in differential treatment of women and men involved in sport because of the belief that participating in sport 'masculinises' women: 'the view of the female athlete as aesthetically displeasing, coupled with the belief that women cannot withstand the rigors of competition, has served to (and in some cases completely prevent) access to various sports' (Matteo, 1986, p. 418).

My analysis of sex-appropriate sports expanded my earlier analysis of 'acceptable' sport by providing greater detail on the types of sports women now participate in. In addition, I can link sport to the current conceptions of 'femininity' to reveal that 'neutral' sports are most commonly represented in the Finnish media. The representation of masculine or feminine sports is also neutralised by de-emphasising the femininity of the athletes. I conclude that Finnish newspaper coverage of women in Olympic sports is a step towards more equal treatment of women's sport. However, we must keep in mind that the majority of the Finnish team competed in sports classified as neutral in Matteo's study and thus these articles were excluded from the examination of gender typing as these sport have already moved beyond the limits of gender schema. So, do my results indicate any challenge to the ideological construction of femininity in today's sports? Several more recent studies have used the concepts of 'acceptable' sport and/or 'sex-appropriate' sport to analyse the ideological construction of women's sport representation.

Several researchers (e.g. Borcila, 2003; Harris and Clayton, 2002; Jones, Murrell and Jackson, 1999; Mason and Rail, 2006; Mikosza and Phillips, 1999; Pirinen, 1997) have concluded that identifying the type of sports reported in the media illustrates sportswomen's continued trivialisation and marginalisation in a subtle manner. For example, Mikosza and Phillips (1999) note that '[w]omen who participate in the male domain of sport, an institution constructed by and for men ... and women who compete in sports outside those which confirm traditional notions of "femininity", are often socially marginalized, being chided for appearing too "masculine"' (Mikosza and Phillips, 1999, p. 10). Specific to the media representation of women athletes in the Olympic Games, Borcila (2003) argues

> that the female athlete has arrived on the national media stage in the overdetermined realm of what women studies and media critics call 'feminine sports,' meaning sports such as figure skating and gymnastics, which emphasize grace and beauty over athleticism. If the NBC 1996 Olympics followed recent trends by making women's sports a centrepiece, it also continued the tradition of marginalizing such women's sports as mountain biking, cycling, softball, soccer, and other team-oriented sports.
>
> (p. 132)

Other researchers use Metheny's and/or Matteo's classification as an analytical tool for reading the media texts. For example, Mason and Rail (2006) analysed photographs of athletes in Canadian newspaper coverage of 1999 Pan-American Games by using a combination of Metheny's (1965) and Riemer and Visio's (2003)[4] classification of sports[5] while maintaining that

> feminist cultural studies allows for a greater understanding and deeper interpretation of cultural texts like sports media coverage, in providing a framework wherein the text's possibilities for the promotion of dominant ideologies or the provision of opportunities for resisting them can be identified and deconstructed.
>
> (p. 29)

Mason and Rail (2006) discovered that many photographs pictured women athletes in male appropriate sports. Like Jones, Murrell and Jackson (1999),[6] Mason and Rail found that women participating in male-appropriate sports were 'feminised' to render them less threatening to the traditional notions of masculinity. Maintaining this sexual difference supports male hegemony. 'The underlying message of the media coverage', they conclude, 'is that if sportswomen transgress traditional gender boundaries too much, they will be subject to strategies of "containment", where their power, strength, and size will be diffused in some way' (p. 36). The authors affirm that discrimination continues in more subtle ways that reinforce the stereotype that women who are 'other than men' are also 'less than men' (p. 38). In this sense, the increased women's coverage continued to create 'sexual difference'.

While this research uses the division of masculine/feminine sports to penetrate the ideological construction of women's sport media representation, other feminists in sport studies refer to the liberal feminist premise of both Metheny's and Matteo's projects. Matteo's research, in particular, aligns with the liberal feminist concern with women's equal access and equal opportunity to participate in sport: having to choose gender-'appropriate' sports limits women's sport participation and only by exposing these limitations can all sports become accessible to all women. This liberal feminist approach to women's sport research has received harsh criticism from prominent feminists in sport studies. Consequently, some sport feminists argue that any analysis of masculine/feminine sport does not go beyond liberal feminist agenda.

'Sex-appropriate' sport as a liberal feminist concept

Matteo's (1986) classification of masculine, neutral and feminine sport draws from the same theoretical and methodological path to Bem's sex role typology. The main criticism of sex role research in sport studies is, contra Bem's intention, its continual construction of feminine and masculine sex types. Ann Hall (1981, 1996), for example, argues that it is impossible to create change by using measures that are themselves socially constructed. For example, Bem had individuals arbitrarily classify behavioural characteristics as feminine and masculine and thus reinforced the common social stereotypes by classifying the same individuals into sex roles. In her research findings, sex role stereotypes (of sport) appear as if 'they exist concretely rather than being analytical constructs' (Hall, 1996, p. 21). Furthermore, Hall points out that in Bem's original study, masculine and feminine sex roles appeared as 'independent rather than bipolar dimensions' (p. 19). For example, sport can be easily classified as feminine, masculine or neutral without attending to the ideological construction of sport as a male-dominated space and male sports as more valued. The notion of sex role (and its derivate sex-typed sports), according to Hall, 'focuses attention more on individuals than on social structure and depoliticizes the central questions of power and control in explaining gender inequality' (p. 21). In this sense, sex typing does little to offer women greater access to sports; on the contrary, it hinders attempts to critique and change the current structures of sport (Hall, 1996).

Hall (1996) and other researchers (e.g. Birrell, 1988; Kane, 1995) assign liberal feminist classifications of sex-appropriate sport (Matteo, 1986) or Metheny's (1965) early effort to classify sport as acceptable or unacceptable for women as inadequate in the attempt to create structural change in women's sport. Structural constraints are not overcome by gaining equal access or neutrality of media representation for all sports in which women participate. Kane (1995), for example, argues that a liberal feminist agenda is content to demonstrate that women have access to an expanded range of sports, but does not challenge the fundamental male hegemony that dominates sport. She adds that not only media coverage, but also the research focus on feminine and masculine sports contributes to maintaining male hegemony. To offer an alternative to the dualistic research framework, Kane aims to go beyond the oppositional binary of feminine/masculine (sports).

Beyond the gender schema: sport as a continuum

In her analysis, Kane (1995) not only points to liberal feminism as perpetuating the male hegemonic structures of sport, but also to feminist sport research which tends to reinforce stereotypical notions of binary gender logic. According to Kane, much critical feminist sport research has continued to conceptualise sport as a binary (men's sports/women's sports). Such a frame perpetuates the biological division between the sexes which has been effectively used to place women in an inferior position to men. For example, suggesting 'alternative models of women's sport', demanding the same amount of coverage for women's sports or explaining the inferior position of women's sport merely as a predictable outcome of hegemonic masculinity serves to reinforce conceptions of sport as a bipolar activity divided along gender lines. In this framework, women's sport is always compared to and is competing with superior men's sport. This research continues to 'stress the point that females are biologically different from men' (p. 199) and consequently perpetuates 'the conceptions of gender as a binary that is hierarchically ordered by "othering" the female' (p. 199). Kane affirms that sport research retains the gender binary specifically by typing sports according to highly stereotypical notions of femininity and masculinity, and thus teaches the researcher to read sports dichotomously as men's and women's sports.

To help eradicate the oppressive gender binary, Kane suggests reconceptualising sport as a continuum 'in which many women routinely outperform many men and, in some cases, women outperform most – if not all – men in a variety of sport and physical skills/activities' (p. 193).[7] Such a continuum would reveal that the biological justification for women's inferiority is erased because 'they can possess physical attributes such as strength and speed in greater capacities than do many men' (p. 197). According to Kane, conceptualising sport as a continuum would also ensure that sociological research does not defend, support or reinforce the oppression of women based on biological inferiority. In my newspaper, one article reported that some women weightlifters outperform some male weightlifters even in comparable weight categories. While this article appeared to portray the poor quality of men's weightlifting in Finland, it also supplied some empirical evidence for Kane's theoretical argument.

From Kane's (1995) perspective, however, feminist research, using the classification of some sport as female-appropriate, continues to reinforce the stereotypical notions of bipolar femininity and masculinity and thus perpetuates, and does not erase, the oppression of women. This polarisation assigns women as biologically inferior to men and proves that not only the media, but also the researchers' theoretical framework necessarily contributes to the continual sexual difference in society. Based on Kane's critique, my examination of the Finnish newspaper coverage would necessarily result in finding sexual difference because my theoretical lens is premised on separating the masculine from the feminine through sport reporting. Could Kane's framework, where feminine and masculine are linked as the opposite ends of a continuum, erase differences that oppress sport women? Is it possible to talk about women's sport without conceptual comparisons with men's sport? How do we understand women's sport without reinforcing sexual difference through research? To contest the masculine/feminine binary further, I propose a conceptual framework derived from Derrida's deconstruction.

The double-affirmative: a Derridean redefinition

... the production of reality by trace, by difference.

(Crosz, 1997, p. 84)

Derridean deconstruction has provided tools to critically trace the development of 'feminine-appropriate' sports as a conceptual tool for feminist sport studies. To analyse the limitations of the 'double binary', feminine oppressive sports/masculine liberating sports, further, I shall discuss the role that Derrida assigned feminism in deconstruction. Derrida engaged in an explicit discussion of women or feminism on three occasions.[8] His interview with Christie McDonald, titled 'Choreographies', which makes a direct reference to feminism, is the most pertinent here.

From Derrida's point of view, feminism that is based on a 'homogeneous' view of what constitutes femininity will be rendered useless because it can only work through a goal of homogenous 'liberation'. For example, feminist sport research could be claimed to have adopted a goal of 'homogeneous' definition of feminine as negative and then looked for 'liberation' through a similarly homogeneous 'masculine' media representation. For Derrida, it is impossible to know the truth about sexual difference or 'flow flounder in this same homogenised, sterilised river' in a world where meanings are constantly changing. To long for universal 'liberation' only carries with it the 'metaphysical' dream of autonomy and mastery, which, as many feminists point out, lies at the root of women's oppression. Derrida argues that the idea of homogeneous 'liberation' has resulted in 'reactive' feminism where woman's specific difference, or 'true' femininity, replaces masculine dominance. Such feminism only reappropriates the idea of essential femininity or womanhood: 'The specular reversal of masculine "subjectivity", even in its most self-critical form – that is, where it is nervously jealous both of itself and of its "proper" objects – probably represents only one necessary phase' (Derrida, 2004, p. 143). Feminist sport studies engage in such specular reversal of masculinity, when 'alternative models of women's sport' are suggested to be superior to men's sport (see also Kane, 1995). While radical feminism can be seen as one necessary phase of sport feminism, other feminist perspectives that critique the one-sided 'idealisation' of 'women-centred sports' have not necessarily conquered the formalisation of the 'homogeneous' definition of femininity.

From a deconstructive point of view, formalisation fails because 'typical features' (as fixed meanings) are always unstable, sometimes contradictory and, therefore, undecidable. Any efforts to stabilise these meanings are based on the employment of a binary opposition: 'any break in the movement of reading would settle in a countermeaning, in the meaning which becomes countermeaning. This countermeaning can be more or less naïve or complacent' (Derrida, 2004, p. 145).[9] When sport media analysis links femininity to women's oppression, the only alternative within the binary logic of sexual difference is to attach women's liberation to the 'masculine', the countermeaning of oppressive femininity. This nevertheless locks feminism within the hierarchical binary logic of metaphysics: the meaning of feminine sport continues to be produced through its difference from masculine sport. These binary terms are always interdependent and their difference is necessarily hierarchical. For example, we cannot talk about feminine sport without making some reference to masculinity and masculine sports. Masculine sports, however, remain the desired alternative because women's liberation is fixed at this end of the dichotomy. It is evident that analysing feminine/masculine sports does not erase the hierarchy of sexual difference, but, on the contrary, links tightly with the 'grammar of Western (male) reason' (Cole, 1998, p. 266). In a sense, saying 'no' to the feminine as it trivialises and sexualises women's sport means saying 'yes' to the masculine and an affirmation of male hegemony. Adding a category of 'neutral sports' or connecting femininity and masculinity in a continuum, as suggested by Kane (1995), are still founded on the same binary logic. This means that even when we focus on feminine sport, due to its necessary foundation as 'different from' masculine sport, we always already rely on reinforcing 'masculine' as the superior and foundational structure of sport. To paraphrase Cole (1998): just as deconstructive logic is parasitic on an already given text, terms that are apparently primary to our feminist texts, such as femininity or women's sport, parasitically rely on the term that precedes and opposes it: masculinity or men's sport. This deconstructive critique thus demonstrates that feminist sport media research has not moved as far from the liberal feminist aspirations (which, in Derrida's terms, aim to make women like men) as we would have hoped.

If the first aim of deconstruction is to demonstrate the interdependence of binary terms, the second, deconstructive strategy, is aimed at breaking the binary, hierarchical logic of western reason. In this sense, it should also serve as a feminist strategy for creating research on sport media representation that does not privilege masculine as the primary signifier for sport. Derrida, indeed, believes that a woman can resist and step back from the history that repeatedly inscribes only one meaning for revolution.[10]

First, he suggests that change or displacement (of femininity) is not limited to the poor or fragile (marginalised), but must stem from the individual, from committed singularity. This means that a new conception of femininity should permit the invention of 'another inscription, one very old and very new, displacement of bodies and places, that is quite different' (p. 146). We do not have a 'new concept' of woman yet, because the radicalisation of the problem goes beyond the 'thought' or the concept. Instead of seeking 'difference' before or behind 'sexual difference', we should take off from the current notion of sexual difference (p. 153). Derrida suggests further that no single voice (masculine or feminine) can dominate, but 'a chorus', 'a choreographic text with polysexual signatures', 'multiplicity of sexually marked voices' with 'reciprocal, respective, and respectful excessiveness' should be allowed to enter feminist thought (p. 154). He concludes that we should dissolve the sexual difference without neutralising sexuality:[11]

> This double symmetry goes beyond known or coded marks, beyond grammar and spelling ... beyond sexuality ... this relationship would not be asexual ... but would be sexual otherwise: beyond the binary difference that governs the decorum of all codes, beyond the opposition feminine/masculine ... I would like to believe in the masses, this indeterminable number of blended voices, this mobile of nonidentified sexual marks whose choreography can carry, divide, multiply the body of each 'individual'.
>
> (p. 154)

There are few analyses that make use of Derrida's view of choreography. One relevant example for my research of women's sport is Ann Cooper Albright's (1995) study of dance choreography which recites multiple voices. Dance, she argues, allows changing places without feeling displaced, to move in a way that shifts the meaning of location. Therefore, choreography and dance are about constant displacement. According to Albright, dance is feminine subversion *par excellence* because the feminine realm is not connected to the female body, but serves to signify anything that is outside, although not necessarily unaffected by, dominant structures of power. Dance could thus potentially be subversive or disruptive of that power. Dance can also create a category beyond the dualism of feminine/masculine, because movement slips through sexual difference. Albright illustrates her argument through an analysis of Marie Chouinard's choreography which offers possibilities for a new definition of women and femininity. If dance is a location for deconstruction, why not women's sport, which can also 'slip through sexual difference' when we begin to recognise 'feminine subversion' outside of the masculine/feminine binary? In this chapter, I have demonstrated how the conceptualisation of sport into feminine and masculine actually perpetuates the dominance and superiority of masculine sport. But how do I enter into the next phase of deconstruction which aims to take off from sexual difference to design a choreography of multiple voices that eventually dissolves the current oppressive sexual difference? Thinking beyond the binary of sexual difference is a very demanding undertaking and would require a deeper analysis than is possible in this chapter. However, to illustrate this step of deconstruction to some extent, I suggest some ideas towards 'différance'.

Deconstruction offers an opportunity to replace an analysis of singular 'femininity' with listening to multiple feminine voices in the sport media. My first step towards understanding sexual difference in non-dualistic terms is to recognise that the conditioning of femininity as a polar, yet inferior, opposite to masculine leads also to other binary divisions with a similar hierarchical logic. For example, in my examination of the feminine and masculine sports, such bipolarities as aesthetic/contact sport; technique/strength sports; individual/team sports were fixed with the hierarchical logic of sexual difference: As these polarities affirm femininity as masculinity's inferior other, aesthetic, technical and individual sports tend to devolve into inappropriate, inferior activities compared to contact, strength and team sports. At the same time, strength aspects of 'aesthetics' sport or technical aspects of contact sports are negated. If my feminist research is liberated from the binary of sexual difference, it is also possible to unleash sport to speak with different voices. For example, I could analyse in what sports women were represented and then ask what this says about Finnish (women's) sport. There was coverage of Finnish women who competed in archery, badminton, canoeing, sailing, shooting, swimming, and track and field. If I avoid examining their representation by devaluing certain sports as 'feminine' (and consequently assign feminine as inferior to masculine), I can see that swimming, canoeing and sailing are curious sports to excel in in Finland, where the rivers, lakes and the sea are frozen for several months a year. I also note that many of these sports require equipment, purpose-built indoor facilities and learning a specific technique. In the media text, javelin is constructed as a technique sport compared to, for example, long-distance running. Based on the media texts, it was also evident that it was very difficult for Finnish women to succeed in the Olympic Games as most of them did not qualify for the finals. The highest-placed Finnish athlete was the sailor Sari Multala, who came in fifth place. From this viewpoint, women's sport media representation reflected the global economic situation in terms of wealthy countries having representatives in expensive sports that require equipment, special training facilities and coaching know-how. A small country like Finland finds it increasingly difficult to succeed in international sport competitions, but it would be interesting to explore why these women succeed in these specific sports. Javelin is a 'national' sport in Finland, which explains the good training opportunities for Finnish women, but what can the media text tell us about the other sports?

Another (journalists') voice in many of the women's sport articles spoke about increased drug use: it was dealt with both overtly and covertly in several articles independent of women's sport. This could offer an interesting insight into the discussion of women's sport representation in Finland: why was there such concern about drug use in the Finnish newspaper? This was particularly odd, because of the sports that Finnish women were represented in, only javelin as a field event could generally be considered to benefit from steroid use.

In addition, gymnastics (rhythmic and artistic) were strongly represented, although Finland had no representatives in these sports. Instead of assigning these articles as representing feminine-appropriate sports that trivialise women's sport coverage, I could acknowledge that Finnish women's gymnastics, a form of gymnastics distinct from both rhythmic and artistic (i.e. bar, beam, vault and floor exercise) gymnastics, is the most popular participatory sport among Finnish women and a member of the same national sporting body as the competitive forms of gymnastics. This creates a strong interest in gymnastic disciplines for Finns. Russia's strong tradition in rhythmic gymnastics has also influenced Finland where many high-performance coaches in these disciplines are Russian. What voice did these articles give to women's gymnastics?

Finally, I could ask how I might recognise multiple feminine voices by disconnecting from the essentialism that assigns one femininity to the (woman's) body. For example, instead of automatically treating all blonde, long-haired (Finnish) women in the newspaper photos as sexualised, and thus representing oppressive femininity, how can I open up my analysis to multiple femininities? I first have to note that most of the women in the Finnish Olympic team appeared to be blonde. If I do not fix hair colour to sexualisation, what meanings can I destabilise? All of the represented women athletes were slim. While the rhythmic gymnasts were thinner than the javelin throwers, they also appeared probably the most muscular in the photographs. If I detach muscularity from masculinity and thinness from femininity, I can conclude that athletes need to be slim and muscular to succeed in their sports. What other aspects than body shape can allow a multiplicity of sexually marked voices to become the focus of my analysis? I might analyse why a certain sport is seen to require a certain type of body. For example, if javelin throwing is a skills-based activity, why are drugs a specific concern for this sport? Furthermore, why might a bulky body be required in such a sport? Alternatively, why was the Russian gymnast Khorkina's lanky, long-limbed body deemed (un)suitable for gymnastics? What 'new' concepts of femininity might emerge if no particular type of body is always and necessarily assigned as oppressive or 'resistant'?

Conclusion

Deconstruction has informed this chapter through a dual strategy: along with a critical reading of a conceptual binary underlining feminist media analysis, it has sensitised me to make space for multiple voices. In my analysis, these voices are predominantly sexually marked. Derrida never advocated an erasure of the sexes, but rather demonstrated that the meanings attached to sexed bodies are a result of meanings fixed to a hierarchical binary opposition deriving from western metaphysics. Grosz (1997) endorses Derrida's differance as a strategy for feminism with certain precautions:

> Derrida's dream of a multiplicity of 'sexually marked voices' seems to be worthy of careful consideration, as long as the question of the limits of possibility of each (sexed) body is recognized. Each sex has the capacity to (and frequently does) play with, become, a number of different sexualities; but not to take on the body and sex of the other.
>
> (pp. 94–5)

Derrida's deconstruction forced me to think what it might mean to think 'outside' of a category of feminine/masculine and reach beyond the hierarchical binary structure. This remains a very difficult task and to be exercised to any meaningful extent will require a much more thorough analysis than presented in this chapter. In addition, if feminist theory, albeit unwittingly, endorses the polarisation of sexual difference, the media, embedded in the social structure of binaries, is unlike to embrace multiple voices in its coverage. Regardless, it is important to be open to possibilities for 'subversive' choreography of sport where we can identify voices currently undetected through feminist analyses. While Derrida is not openly credited as an advocate for social change, breaking out from predefined categories of feminine/masculine sport allowed me to link the media representation to its specific cultural context instead of following 'homogenised', binary reading of women's sport.

Notes

1. According to Metheny (1965), college women found sport inappropriate for women if: the resistance of the opponent is overcome by bodily contact; the resistance of a heavy object is overcome by direct application of bodily force; and the body is projected into or through space over a long distance or for extended periods of time. Examples of these sports are wrestling, judo, boxing, weightlifting, hammer throwing, pole vault, the longer (e.g. the 1,500, 5,000 and 10,000 metre) foot races, high hurdles and all forms of team games (except volleyball). In 1964 women were excluded from these events in the Olympic Games.

   Women in 'lower socio-economic' status could engage in sports in Metheny's second category which is characterised by: resistance of an object of moderate weight that was overcome by direct application of bodily forces; a body that was projected into or through space over moderate distances or for relatively short periods of time; and a display of strength needed to control bodily movements. Examples included shot put, discus, javelin, shorter foot races, low hurdles, long jump, gymnastic events and free exercise. Metheny reasons that in the United States 'negro' women are disproportionately represented in track and field events (shot put, discus, javelin, sprint) and this might influence college women's perception of their suitability to some, but not all, women. Moreover, Metheny points out that women of Germanic and Slavic descent in the United States tended to engage in gymnastics at club level in their ethnic communities rather than in colleges, which probably made the college women classify gymnastics as unsuitable for themselves. The current situation in the US is, of course, entirely different and women's gymnastics receive very high media coverage and audience ratings during the Olympic Games. The nature of competitive gymnastics has also changed dramatically since 1960s towards more skill, strength and power. However, with this development the size of gymnasts has diminished and while the actual performance requires great power and the gymnasts look quite muscular, they are referred to as 'little pixies' or little girls due to their stature.

The sports that were wholly appropriate for college women in the US involve: the resistance of a light object that is overcome with a light implement; a body that is projected into or through space in aesthetically pleasing configurations; velocity and manoeuvrability of the body which is increased by the use of a manufactured device; a spatial barrier that prevents bodily contact with the opponent in face-to-face competition.

Sports included in this category are swimming, diving, skiing, figure skating, golf, archery, bowling, fencing, squash, badminton, tennis and volleyball. Metheny notes that some of these sports require considerable amounts of time and money.

2. Bem (1974) aimed to break out from the previous rigid sex-role self-concepts which located masculinity and femininity at the polar ends of a single continuum which resulted in a person always being classified as either masculine or feminine, but not both. Based on empirical research, she developed the Bem Sex Role Inventory (BSRI) which allows validation for a sex-role concept of androgyny; a concept that allowed an individual to engage in both feminine and masculine behaviours. Therefore, Bem's idea was to create research concepts that helped break out from the stereotyped masculine and feminine behaviours in American society. To demonstrate androgyny as a valid self-concept empirically, Bem asked 100 Stanford University undergraduate psychology students to judge 400 personality characteristics as desirable either for a woman or a man in American society. Based on these ratings, she created a list of 40 'items' that characterised a stereotypically feminine or masculine person. In addition, she included a list of 20 items that were 'neutral' (not particular to a feminine or masculine individual). She then tested her scale with 900 students. The results showed that while the majority of the students qualified as sex-typed, many were also classified as androgynous and many individuals were not placed clearly in any of the three categories. Bem concluded that researchers should move away from 'the traditional assumption that it is the sex-typed individual who typifies mental health' (p. 162) and into a more flexible understanding of psychological health. It is fair to point out that Bem actually created her typology to evidence sex-role stereotypes and demonstrate how limiting they are. It appears that sport researchers who use her schema have failed to treat it as an analytical tool. This applies particularly to the line of research that aims to detect the sex types of female athletes in a number of sports. The use of Bem's gender schema to study media representation is rare, but discussions of the sex appropriateness of different sports in media research abound.

3. Following Matteo, I asked if the female-appropriate sport coverage emphasised femininity. Were women in male-appropriate sports 'feminised' by frequent comparisons to males or non-performance-related aspects? The Olympic coverage in this newspaper represented masculine sports (shooting, javelin, football, pole vault, judo, discus, weightlifting, wrestling, basketball) in 15 items (some included pictures only). Two articles compared women's performance to men's performance: one lamented the poor state of Finnish men's weightlifting – the Turkish woman Olympic champion outperformed the Finnish men. The other asked the Russian pole vaulters Elena Isambajeva and Svetlana Feofanova what they thought of Sergei Bubka's comments on women pole vaulting not really being a sport (until women break through the

5 metres barrier). Two athletes' husbands or family were mentioned briefly: a Japanese judo player Ruoko Tani's recent marriage to a Japanese baseball star and Finnish javelin thrower, Taina Kolkkala's plans to have children in the near future. The majority of these articles focused on Finnish javelin throwers' performances including an article that emphasised javelin as a technical rather than a strength sport.

Nine items focused on feminine sports, six of which were on gymnastics or rhythmic gymnastics (in which Finland had no representatives). Only one article focused on an athlete's appearance. The Russian gymnast Svetlana Khorkina was portrayed through her career as a fashion model and her 'un-gymnastics'-like long, thin, lanky body, which, in Russia, draws huge attention from men. Another article discussed the role of rhythmic gymnastics as the ultimate feminine sport in Russia where it is considered an activity that teaches all girls proper femininity. One article focused on arguing that (women's) beach volleyball is a proper Olympic sport.

I also analysed the pictures in the Olympic coverage and discovered that women were pictured in more masculine sports (57) than feminine sports (26). Ten masculine sports were depicted (if track and field is counted as one sport). Javelin was the most pictured sport (seven pictures), but it must be pointed out that the Finnish team also had the most representatives in javelin. Carolina Kluft, the Swedish gold medallist in the heptathlon, had six pictures. There were also five pictures of women's team sports (soccer, softball, two of basketball, European handball) although Finland had no team sport representatives. Women in masculine sports were pictured failing seven times, but again it must be remembered that the Finnish javelin team did not perform as well as expected. In general, women in these sports were not feminised. Two headshots, one of a hammer thrower and one of a javelin thrower, depicted these blonde athletes concentrating before their competitions with make-up on but in their sport uniforms. It was difficult to decide whether these pictures could be claimed to 'feminise' the athletes. Women were pictured in 11 feminine sports, rhythmic gymnastics being the most pictured sport. All pictures were in a performance or competition context, but six portrayed the athlete failing. The most pictured athlete was the sailor Sari Multala who achieved the highest placement of all Finnish athletes (coming fifth). I had difficulty classifying her sport, but currently have placed sailing here within the category of masculine sports. Based on these results, the newspaper pictures did not feminise women's sport in Finland.

4. In their study of 7–12 grade students' attitudes to sport gender typing, Riemer and Visio (2003) acknowledged Hall's and Birrell's critique that researchers reinforce the bipolarity of femininity and masculinity by developing categorisations based on existing cultural norms. They justified their investigation on the basis of the young age of the children who have not developed a sophisticated understanding of multiple meanings attached to gender. They used a classification of sports into masculine, neutral and feminine similar to Matteo (1986). The results indicated that 30 years after Metheny's study, children continued to perceive certain sports as gender-specific, but 'perceptions of the best sports for girls seem to have expanded to include more masculine sports' (p. 203). While women see increased

opportunities to participate in a variety of sports, the feminine sports are still not perceived as acceptable for men. Despite acknowledging the critique, Riemer and Vision do not fundamentally challenge the premise of Bem's gender schema.

5. Mason and Rail (2006) discovered that many photographs pictured women athletes in sports 'that are male-appropriate such as weightlifting and field hockey – sports involving bodily contact or power movements' (p. 34) and less focused on gender-appropriate sports (although gender-appropriate sports like swimming, tennis and gymnastics still remained among the most frequently covered sports). In addition, women were pictured in more sports than men. Like Riemer and Vision (2003) the authors concluded that the media now covers a wider range of women's sports. They noted, however, that Canadian success in rowing, soccer, swimming and basketball increased the coverage of these particular sports. Women's soccer and basketball, in fact, received more photographic coverage than men's soccer and basketball and many pictures contained 'images of intense competition and physical contact' (p. 35). Women's weightlifting was the seventh most pictured women's sport, which could suggest increased acceptance of powerful images of women. However, the authors point out that the photographs tended to picture unsuccessful performances and, in this way, the female athletes 'femininity was carefully reinforced' (p. 36). In addition, women in individual sports received more pictorial coverage than women in team sports.

6. To provide more evidence for Matteo's argument, Jones, Murrell and Jackson (1999) demonstrate that media coverage in the US sex-types sports and thus perpetuates attitudes that certain sports are unsuitable for women. They used Matteo's classification to analyse newspaper coverage of gold medal-winning contests of the US women's basketball, gymnastics, soccer and softball teams during the 1996 Olympics and the US women's ice-hockey team during the 1998 Olympics. They found that female athletes in male-appropriate sports (basketball, soccer, ice hockey) were described by frequent male/female comparisons and comments irrelevant to the athletes' performance. While the reports of female athletes in female sport (gymnastics) focused on their performance, the coverage reinforced female stereotypes. For example, the beauty and grace of the gymnastics team received more emphasis than their actual performance. In addition, women in male-appropriate sports were frequently compared to their male counterparts (see also Pirinen, 1997). The researchers argue that such representation limits women's equal access to sport: 'As a result of beliefs concerning the sex appropriateness of particular sports, women who participate in male-appropriate sports must challenge traditional sex role stereotypes by combating the belief that their participation is less valuable than men's involvement' (p. 184). Therefore, sex typing is likely to be reflected in the media's portrayal of women athletes and thus the media generate and support 'sexist ideologies and beliefs about gender' (p. 184).

7. It is important to note that Bem (1974) actually developed her gender schema to go beyond the limitations of conceptualising gender as a continuum, with femininity and masculinity as polar ends. In this sense, Kane's aim is very similar to Bem's, but returns to the idea of a continuum. However, both aimed to create greater conceptual flexibility to break out

from the rigid classifications of women and men into separate categories which, as both researchers argue, is detrimental to women.

8. J. Derrida (1979) *Spurs/Eperons* (Chicago: University of Chicago Press) focuses on Nietzsche's attitude to women; J. Derrida and D. McDonald (1994) Choreographies. In E. W. Goellner and J. S. Murphy (eds.), *Bodies of the Text: Dance as Theory, Literature as Dance* (New Brunswick, NJ: Rutgers University Press) pp. 141–56, discussed in this chapter; and J. Derrida et al. (1985) Deconstruction in America: An Interview with Jacques Derrida. *Critical Exchange*, 17, 1–33, reiterates the political nature of deconstruction.

9. To deconstruct philosophy, Derrida (2004) focuses on 'the structured genealogy of philosophy's concepts', but at the same time determines 'what this history has been able to dissimulate or forbid, making itself into a history by means of this somewhere motivated repression' (p. 5). He describes this structure as 'logocentric' and its limitations deriving from the model of 'semiology of Saussurian type' (p. 18). Saussure saw the signified (the meaning) of a concept as inseparable from the signifier (the image or sound) of the concept and, therefore, the meaning, once created, is fixed to its material element (the image or sound). Therefore, it is possible to analyse writing and language as a universal structure by determining 'the two-sided unity' of signifier and signified and develop general, metaphysical rules for how language operates. What interested Derrida was to detect a 'general economy' of behind the rules and thus to develop a general strategy of deconstruction (p. 38). To critique the rules of metaphysics, Derrida proposes a new concept of writing that is, instead of structure and sign, based on 'différance' or 'gram'. These concepts also challenge the binary oppositions that constitute a primary element for metaphysical philosophy without simply neutralising or 'residing within the closed field of theses oppositions, thereby confirming it': 'The gram as *différance*, then, is a structure and a movement no longer conceivable on the basis of the opposition presence/absence. *Differance* is the systematic play of differences, of the traces of differences, of the spacing by means of which elements are related to each other. This spacing is the simultaneously active and passive (the *a* as of *différance* indicates this indecision as concerns activity and a possibility, that which cannot be governed by or distributed between the terms of this opposition) production of the intervals without which the "full" terms would not signify, would not function' (Derrida, 2004, p. 24, emphasis in the original).

Differance, therefore, refers to how (what metaphysics calls) the sign (signified/signifier) is produced. It points to the temporal and spatial aspects of the meaning making process. In this process, meanings are not fixed, but constantly produced via the dual strategies of difference and deferral. Derrida observes four characteristics of differance:

1. differance refers to the movement that consists of deferring by means of delay, delegation, reprieve, referral, detour, postponement, reserving;
2. the movement of differance, as that which produces different things, that which differentiates, is the common root of all the oppositional concepts that mark our language;
3. differance is a production of meaning;

4. differance names provisionally this unfolding of difference, in particular, but not only, or first of all, of the ontico-ontological difference (Derrida, 2004, pp. 6–8).

Holland (1997) summarises that Derrida uses differance as a generic tool for deconstructing metaphysical discourse in which foundational concepts are structured in a series of hierarchical oppositions. As a result, Derrida argues that these oppositions have meaning only in relation to each other, not in and of themselves. Readers interested in a more detailed discussion of differance should consult the following texts by Derrida: (2004) *Positions*. London: Continuum; (1978) *Writing and Difference*. Chicago: University of Chicago Press; (1976) *Of Grammatology*. Baltimore, MD: Johns Hopkins University Press.

10. During the interview, McDonald presents the following two-phase programme for a feminist act of deconstruction through a different type of 'writing', 'ecriture' where traditional binary pairing no longer functions by the privilege given to the first term over the second:

   1. a reversal in which the opposed terms would be inverted: woman, as a previously subordinate term, might become the dominant one in relation to man. However, 'because such a scheme of reversal could only repeat the traditional scheme (in which the hierarchy of duality is always reconstituted), it alone could not effect any significant change' (pp. 147–8);
   2. change occurs through a radical phase of deconstruction in which a 'new' concept could be forged simultaneously. 'The motif of difference, as neither a simple "concept" nor a mere "word," has brought us the now familiar constellation of attendant terms: trace, supplement, pharmakon' (p. 147).

   Derrida does not necessarily agree with the notion of two separate phases. He adds that change is not so much a matter of conceptual determinations as 'a transformation or general deformation of logic; such transformations or deformations mark the "logical" element or environment itself, by moving, for example beyond the "positional" (difference determined as opposition), whether or not dialectically' (p. 149). Feminism, he argues, has attempted to 'neutralise' the difference which only privileges the masculine further. This point has proved particularly relevant to the analysis of sport media coverage, where assigning some coverage as 'neutral', privileges the masculine instead of reducing the sexual difference. Derrida further believes that the change in representation would not actually solve anything, because, for him, the question of representation 'seems at once too old and as yet to be born: a kind of old parchment crossed every which way, overloaded with hieroglyphs' (p. 153). While this could be interpreted to mean that deconstruction renders feminist sport media analysis useless, it could also be read as a need for more insightful analyses of media which are not conceptually limited to hierarchical binary oppositions of western metaphysics.

11. Derrida's path out from between the binary necessitates a thought of 'an absolute of unconditioned form (of the concept), where in each case the absolute or unconditioned form of the concept is always paradoxical or impossible' (Patton, 2003, p. 18). The absolute form helps to keep the concept 'open'. For example, thinking of an unconditioned form of sex, while impossible

or abstract, can open avenues to think 'outside' the femininity/masculinity binary. Derrida himself argued for a sexuality more primordial than the binary opposition between the sexes: 'a sexual difference that is neutral with respect to the sexes as they are currently or have been historically represented, a "raw material" out of which, through dispersion and splitting, sexual difference is rendered concrete and specific' (Grosz, 1997, p. 89). This is a sexuality that is ontological but entirely without qualities and attributes. Derrida also distinguished very carefully between sexual opposition and sexual difference: 'between a binary structuring of the relations between the sexes into a model of presence and absence, positive and genitive, and a nonbinarized differential understanding of the relations between the sexes, in which no single model can dictate or provide the terms for the representation, whether negative or positive' (Grosz, 1997, p. 88).

References

Bem, S. L. (1974). The measurement of psychological androgyny. *Journal of Consulting and Clinical Psychology*, 42(2), 155–62.

Birrell, S. (1988). Discourse of the gender/sport relationship: From women in sport to gender relations. *Exercise and Sport Science Reviews*, 16, 459–502.

Borcila, A. (2000). Nationalizing the Olympics around and away from 'vulnerable' bodies of women: The NBC coverage of the 1996 Olympics and some moments after. *Journal of Sport & Social Issues*, 14, 118–47.

Cole, C. L. (1998). Addiction, exercise and cyborgs: Technologies of deviant bodies. In G. Rail (ed.), *Sport and Postmodern Times* (pp. 261–76). Albany, NY: SUNY Press.

Cooper Albright, A. (1994). Incalculable choreographies: The dance practice of Marie Chouinard. In E. W. Goellner and J. S. Murphy (eds.), *Bodies of the Text: Dance as Theory, Literature as Dance* (pp. 157–81). New Brunswick, NJ: Rutgers University Press.

Derrida, J. (1976). *Of Grammatology*. Baltimore, MD: Johns Hopkins University Press.

Derrida, J. (1978). *Writing and Difference*. Chicago: University of Chicago Press.

Derrida, J. (1979). *Spurs/Eperons*. Chicago: University of Chicago Press.

Derrida, J. (2004). *Positions*. London: Continuum.

Derrida, J. and McDonald, C. V. (1994). Choreographies. In E. W. Goellner and J. S. Murphy (eds.), *Bodies of the Text: Dance as Theory, Literature as Dance* (pp. 141–56). New Brunswick, NJ: Rutgers University Press.

Derrida, J. et al. (1985). Deconstruction in America: An interview with Jacques Derrida. *Critical Exchange*, 17, 1–33.

Grosz, E. (1997). Ontology and equivocation: Derrida's politics of sexual difference. In N. J. Holland (ed.), *Feminist Interpretations of Jacques Derrida* (pp. 73–102). University Park, PA: Pennsylvania State University Press.

Hall, M. A. (1981). *Sport, Sex Roles and Sex Identity* (The CRIAW papers/Les Documents de l'ICRAF, No.1). Ottawa, ON: The Canadian Research Institute for the Advancement of Women.

Hall, M. A. (1996). *Feminism and Sporting Bodies*. Champaign, IL: Human Kinetics.

Harris, J. and Clayton, B. (2002). Femininity, masculinity, physicality and the English tabloid press: The case of Anna Kournikova. *International Review for the Sociology of Sport*, 37, 397–413.

Hekman, S. J. (1990). *Gender and Knowledge: Elements of a Postmodern Feminism.* Boston, MA: Northeastern University Press.

Holland, N. J. (1997). Introduction. In N. J. Holland (ed.), *Feminist Interpretations of Jacques Derrida* (pp. 1–22). University Park, PA: Pennsylvania State University Press.

Jones, R., Murrell, A. J. and Jackson, J. (1999). Pretty versus powerful in the sports pages: Print media coverage of U.S. women's Olympic gold medal winning teams. *Journal of Sport & Social Issues,* 23, 183–92.

Kane, M. J. (1995). Resistance/transformation of the oppositional binary: Exposing sport as a continuum. *Journal of Sport & Social Issues,* 19, 191–218.

Mason, F. and Rail, G. (2006). The creation of sexual difference in Canadian newspaper photographs of the Pan-American Games. *Women in Sport and Physical Activity Journal,* 15, 28–41.

Matteo, S. (1986). The effect of sex and gender-schematic processing on sport participation. *Sex Roles,* 15(7/8), 417–32.

Metheny, E. (1965). *Connotations of Movement in Sport and Dance.* Dubuque, IA: Wm. C. Brown.

Mikosza, J. M. and Phillips, M. G. (1999). Gender, sport and the body politic: Framing femininity in the golden girls of sport calendar and the Atlanta dream. *International Review for the Sociology of Sport,* 34, 5–16.

Patton, P. (2003). Future politics. In P. Patton and J. Protevi (eds.), *Between Deleuze & Derrida* (pp. 15–29). London and New York: Continuum.

Pirinen, R. M. (1997). The construction of women's positions in sport: A textual analysis of articles on female athletes in Finnish women's magazines. *Sociology of Sport Journal,* 14, 290–301.

Riemer, B. A. and Visio, M. E. (2003). Gender typing in sports: An investigation of Metheny's classification. *Research Quarterly for Exercise and Sport,* 74(2), 193–204.

Weedon, C. (1987). *Feminist Practice & Poststructuralist Theory.* Oxford, Basil Blackwell.

6
Double Trouble: Kelly Holmes, Intersectionality and Unstable Narratives of Olympic Heroism in the British Media

Laura Hills and Eileen Kennedy

In the run-up to the Athens Olympic Games the British daily newspaper the *Guardian* produced a booklet entitled 'Olympics 2004' which provided a guide to the events and highlighted promising athletes from Britain and elsewhere. Kelly Holmes was not counted as one of the 'Ten of the Best' British stars of the Games. Neither was she mentioned in their identification of potential 'Showstoppers' or 'Other Brits to watch' for the day of the women's 800 metres. Holmes was considered one of the 'Brits to watch' on the day of the women's 1500 metres, but in a way that did not concede much hope of victory. She was described as one of two 'stalwarts of British athletics' competing that day, who would 'be hoping for a bang rather than a farewell whimper this evening' (p. 78). In fact, Holmes resoundingly exceeded all expectations. She won both the 800 metres and the 1500 metres, becoming the first British female track athlete to win two Olympic gold medals and the first British double gold medallist at the same Games since 1920.

Rowe (2004, p. 38) suggests that by paying attention to the practices of sports journalism, 'it is possible to "de-naturalize" media sports texts and so to understand that they are particular creations and constructions arising from the complex, contradictory forces that make culture'. Rowe argues that the production of media sports involves 'many decisions, calculations, dilemmas and disputes' (2004, p. 39). Whannel's (2002) examination of the repeating characteristics of sports biographies indicates that sports writers draw on pre-existing formulaic narratives to mould the raw material of the sports world into stories designed to appeal to their readers. The 'punishing, stressful deadlines' (Rowe 2004,

p. 43) of the sports press are likely to exacerbate journalists' reliance on culturally prescribed framing techniques to produce dramatic stories at a moment's notice. When the unexpected happens, journalists need to work fast to transform the surprise event into a fully formed narrative. In this chapter, we explore the narratives constructed in the British press the day after Holmes won her second gold medal. To do this, we first show how narratives constructed by journalists attempted to locate Holmes within existing discourses of sport and femininity. However, we argue that facets of Holmes' background, personality and lifestyle presented a challenge to the production of a coherent storyline. The eventual disjointed press articles were threaded through with discourses of class, gender, sexuality, race and national identity, but, as a black, working-class, British woman *and* a double Olympic champion, Holmes resisted easy incorporation into journalistic conventions. The chapter concludes by arguing that Holmes' untypical background and social identity succeeded in productively troubling the category of sports hero.

Narratology and the sports hero

Whannel (1992, p. 121) has observed that 'star performers are characters within a set of narratives'. The media reconstruct the sporting contest as a story, identifying heroes and villains and creating drama and interest. Narrative is, therefore, a way of making sense of events. It does not simply reflect what happens, but it constructs possibilities for what can happen, generating and interpreting sporting moments as meaningful elements within a meaningful whole. Considered in this way, analysis of narratives in cultural texts can illuminate values and discourses within specific cultures.

Whannel (1992; 2002) argues that narratives in the sport media involve the 'recomposition of space, place and time' (Whannel, 2002, p. 54). As Prince (1980) observed, the order of events in a narrative can take many forms: events can be recounted in the order they happen or in a different order; an important happening can be repeatedly mentioned or not mentioned explicitly at all. The way the story is told has consequences for how we come to know the central character, the hero (or villain).

Whannel (2002) suggested that there is a relationship between heroes, heroism and the heroic and the society which creates them as such. He argued that statements about heroes 'carry a marked positionality, inscribing the perspective from which they are made and the frame through which we should perceive society' (2002, p. 40). Considering a multitude of biographies of sports Whannel (2002) identified repeating narrative formulae used to reconstruct the events of a star's life. Moreover, Whannel (2002) suggests that sports star biographies are constantly retold throughout their lives, often in accordance with changing social values, so that different narratives are used to make sense of the same events. Using this approach, Whannel (2002) was able to identify sets of narrative functions in the narrativisation of sports stars' careers.

Star biographies, according to Whannel, are composed according to pre-existing narratives structures which conceal or highlight events in the star's career. For example, the 'golden success story' is produced soon after a star's early triumphs, marginalising any setbacks and failures that may have occurred. By contrast, the 'ups and downs story' is a narrative produced towards the end of a career, where early success is followed by a repeating sequence of failure and success. Another variant, the 'rise and fall narrative', is applied to sports stars who have encountered problems such as ill-disciplined personal lives, where early successes are followed by a cycle of setbacks and failures.

Whannel's (2002) analysis is insightful in pointing to the existing narrative scripts used to frame the events of a sport star's career. The media use already constructed narratives to make sense of events in sports stars' lives even at the moment they are occurring. For example, as a gold medal is won, a newspaper story is being written that draws on formulaic narratives used many times before. However, Whannel's (2002) focus was on narratives surrounding male sport stars, and it is possible to see that gender is a critical dimension within the narrativisation of the sports hero. This chapter considers how Kelly Holmes as a female champion was located within press narratives of sports heroism.

Gender and narrative

The film theorist Mulvey (1993) pointed to the necessity of gendering the character of the hero. Because marriage to the princess is an important aspect of conventional narrative closure, this function demands that the hero be male. When female characters are introduced as central to a story, another kind of narrative needs to be produced. Research on the representation of women in the sport media has indicated that the framing of sportswomen is very different from sportsmen. The representation of sporting women in the media continues to reflect the perceived need to balance depictions of sporting embodiment and cultural configurations of femininity (Bernstein, 2002; Billings and Eastman, 2002;

Cooky, 2006; Daddario, 1998; Duncan and Messner, 1998; Jones, Murrell, and Jackson, 1999; Kane and Lenskyj, 1998; Spencer, 2003). The reluctance of the media to move away from traditional constructions of heroes and femininity arguably relates to anxiety around changing configurations of power in society. This can be seen in the continuing need to ensure that femininity and masculinity can be distinguished despite the increasing evidence of great overlaps in men's and women's capabilities. Sporting women force the issues through their displays of skill, strength, competitiveness, courage and tenacity.

Kane and Greendorfer (1994), for example, have shown that sports media consistently under-represent sportswomen, resulting in their symbolic annihilation, and when they are shown, coverage is characterised by techniques which sexualise and trivialise women's sport. Other commentators such as Duncan, Messner, Williams and Jensen (1994) have pointed to the less frequent use of power descriptors in describing women's sport when compared to men's sport. The consistent use of the thematic device of infantilisation has been observed within women's sport: in different contexts, Daddario (1994), Duncan et al. (1994) and Kennedy (2001) have all noted the media portrayal of sportswomen as daughters or little sisters.

Kennedy (2001) analysed the media narratives surrounding the Wimbledon Ladies Singles finalists from 1996. Focusing on two pre-recorded television sequences prior to the match, Kennedy (2001) observed the complex narrative elements that the media used to make sense of the finalists, Steffi Graf and Arantxa Sanchez Vicario. Elaborate combinations of gender signifiers circulated around each player. The sequence about Steffi Graf, for example, began by portraying her as strong and determined, evoked by the soundtrack, 'I want to be a sledgehammer ...' and the images, rapid cuts between shots of her on one side of the court then the other, making it look as if she was in competition with herself. This was followed by references to her as a queen, as a child dominated by her father, as susceptible to injury, and as responding to a marriage proposal from a member of the crowd. The sequence ended by positioning her as a western film hero, accompanied by the theme tune of the film, *The Magnificent Seven*.

The unevenness of this narrative indicates the challenge that sporting femininity presents to the media – the demands of the heroic narrative conflict with the cultural narratives of femininity as infantilised, vulnerable, heterosexually attractive and dependent on men. Yet, despite the ambivalence of this representation, the sequence achieved a level of narrative coherence by compartmentalising femininity and athleticism.

The associations with strength, power and heroism were separated from the other aspects of Graf's life, which provided the basis of the narrative of 'correct' femininity. The attempt to partition sport and femininity within narratives surrounding sportswomen indicates the disruptive potential of female athletic identity to discourses of gender. The media attempts to ease this tension by trying to keep sport and femininity as separate elements in the narrative. When this proves impossible, as was the case of Holmes, sporting femininity cannot avoid troubling conventional gender categories.

The trouble with sportswomen

Butler (1998) asserted that the sporting woman represents a challenge to our understandings of the meaning of gender and a forced dislodging of our assumptions about the potentiality of female embodiment. She argued:

> That reconsideration of what we claim to know or imagine as gendered life can take place only by passing through an unstable and troubled terrain, a crisis of knowledge, a situation of not-knowing; at that moment there is a risking of gender itself, an instability that exposes our knowledge about gender as tenuous, contested and ungrounded in a thorough and productively disturbing sense.
>
> (para. 25)

For Butler, instability or trouble must occur in order for change to take place. Women and sport is a terrain that demonstrates some of the instabilities of gender and provides opportunities for social change. The disruption of hero narratives and the uneven coverage of sporting women therefore can be perceived as productive of new understandings of gender and generative of the possibilities of transformation.

The Olympics represents one of few sporting events where women do receive substantial media coverage (Messner, Duncan and Cooky, 2003; Vincent, 2004; Vincent, Imwold, Masemann and Johnson, 2002). Messner, Duncan and Cooky (2003) found that tennis was the most frequently broadcast women's sport followed by Olympic track and field stories, which accounted for 16 per cent of all of the sports stories about women on American television within the timeframe of their study. In this international event some women manage to achieve celebrity status due to their success. Rojek (2001) states: 'achieved celebrity derives from the perceived accomplishments of the individual in open competition. In the public realm they are recognized as individuals who possess rare talents or skills' (p 18). Medals won by men or women can symbolise the success of the nation, and the inherent newsworthiness of Olympic success can result in a more even spread of media coverage by gender (Vincent, Imwold, Masemann and Johnson, 2002). The Olympics, therefore, represent an opportunity for the mass mediation of exceptional sporting female bodies with the potential to contest preconceived understandings of gender and identity.

Intersectionality

Sporting bodies, however, are never only gendered, they are infused with meanings relating to multiple intersecting relations of power. As Birrell and MacDonald (2000) asserted:

> The methodology of 'reading' sport – that is, of finding the cultural meanings that circulate within narratives of particular incidents of celebrities – also requires critical attention to the ways that sexuality, race, gender, and class privileges are articulated in those accounts.
>
> (p. 11)

Holmes is a woman from a working-class background, whose white, English mother is separated from her black, Jamaican father, and whose relationship status is equivocal. As such, she resists easy categorisation in terms of social stratification and identity. Our reading of the intersections of power relations become more complex when we attempt to move beyond binary conceptualisations of identity in terms of black and white or working and middle classes. Instead, we need to acknowledge the abundant differences within particular groups and the possibility for complex layers of (dis)identifications among group members. These changing configurations and their subsequent representations within the media create possibilities for new ways of conceptualising and defining ourselves, disrupting understandings of particular social identities as representative of homogenous groups (Rojek, 2001).

Collins (2005) suggests that representations of black women evidence a space for the production of new understandings of identity:

> representations of black women athletes in the mass media also replicate and contest power relations of race, class, gender, and sexuality.

> Because aggressiveness is needed to win, Black female athletes have more leeway in reclaiming assertiveness without enduring the ridicule routinely targeted toward the bitch.
>
> (p. 134)

Collins discusses the ways that the tennis players Venus and Serena Williams have resisted tennis norms and desisted from creating themselves within the confines of middle-class white tennis traditions. She suggests that the sports domain presents a space where assertive black femininity can be understood as a partial requirement of sporting endeavours. This potentially positive image of assertiveness provides a different way of reading black femininity and the infusion of working-class, black culture within the tennis world challenges the cultural imagination of the 'typical' tennis player.

There is, however, a specificity to the configuration of race, class and gender within different national contexts. In Britain, the legacy of imperial masculine dominance over differently gendered, classed and raced bodies at home and abroad has 'helped Britain define itself by processes of disidentification' (Puwar, 2004, p. 35). The figure of the amateur sporting gentleman as authentically British restricts the possibilities for the kinds of bodies that are able to represent the nation in terms of sport. Britishness is imagined to be white and male with the habitus of the upper middle classes (Puwar, 2004).

Skeggs (2004) has explored the ways that representations of class serve to attribute value and create boundaries between the middle and working classes. In Britain and elsewhere, class is not a simple category to define. Class membership can be mobile and unstable in ways that differ from other classifications such as gender and race. Anthias (2005) observed that in the case of class 'movement in or out is seen as a product of individual capacities. In the case of race/ethnicity and gender, there can be no movement in and out in terms of capacity. The capacity is written into the very classification' (p. 29). As a result, boundary maintenance is constantly under threat, not from 'dangerous others' but from 'proximate strangers' (Skeggs, 2004, p. 164), making it difficult to put people confidently in their place. This anxiety suffuses the media's representation of the working class as culturally distinct from the middle class. Skeggs (2004) identifies a number of ways that working classes are 'Othered' in the media: 'as excess, as waste, as authenticating, as entertainment, as lacking in taste, as unmodern, as escapist, as dangerous, as unruly, and without shame, and always as spacialised' (p. 99). In a different national context, Stoloff (2000) argues that the spectacle surrounding the antagonism between ice skaters Tonya Harding and Nancy Kerrigan was framed in class terms: 'Harding satisfied the stereotypes of the undisciplined lower classes, the lack of bodily containment and control' (pp. 237–8). Themes of bodily control have also been a feature of the British sport media framing of sports stars in class terms (Kennedy, 2004).

The media narration of Kelly Holmes involves intersecting discourses of gender, sexuality, race, class and nation. To analyse how Holmes' identity was constructed in the media, we collected the British national press coverage of her double Olympic victory the day after her second gold medal on Sunday, 29 August 2004. We used media discourse analysis to explore images and text within four newspapers, *The Sunday Times*, the *Observer*, the *Sunday Mirror* and the *News of the World*. In selecting these papers, we aimed to incorporate both the populist 'tabloid' as well as the 'quality' press, and include papers from both right- and left-of-centre political perspectives. We employed media discourse analysis to explore intersectionality in the media framing of Holmes as an unexpected British Olympic champion.

Gobsmacked – the shock of Holmes' gold medal(s)

The unexpectedness of Holmes emerging as a hero of the 2004 Olympics was evident in the way that surprise was a consistent theme across the press coverage. The *News of the World* followed their backpage headline 'Kelly's All Goold' [substituting Olympic medals for the 'o's'] with 'Double has her gobsmacked' (Harrison, 2004, p. 104), referencing her own words after the race. In the *Sunday Mirror* a photograph of Holmes holding 'her head in her hands, unable to take it all in', with the headline 'I can't believe it ...' (Boniface and Eady, 2004, p. 3). *The Sunday Times* sport section ran a headline that read: 'WAKE ME UP, IT'S A DREAM SAYS KELLY' (Hughes, 2004, pp. 14–15). Steve Ovett in the *Observer* maintained that Holmes' triumph was 'what the Olympics are really about: unpredictability, not world records' (2004, p. 27).

The narratives that appeared in the media were in the context of this unpredicted and significant event. The press responded to the task of constructing Holmes as an instant national hero(ine) with a host of multiple and changeable storylines. This inconsistency was exemplified by two articles in *The Sunday Times*. A lengthy written profile of Holmes was included in the paper's 'Comment' section (which contains editorial comment and debate on leading current affairs issues). The profile was accompanied by a line-drawn cartoon head-and-shoulders image of Holmes grinning broadly, with arched eyebrows and staring eyes, giving her a slightly crazed look. Departing from both 'golden success' and 'ups and downs' narratives, the headline constructs a different kind of story: 'Bad luck finally runs out for our golden girl' ('Comment', 2004, p. 15). Beginning with a negative and ending with a familial embrace of Holmes as 'our golden girl', there is no dramatic rise referenced at all, merely the end of a long, drawn-out fall. The mood of the headline continued into the first paragraph of the profile:

> Kelly was a broken figure. Defeated, humiliated and hobbling on crutches outside Atlanta's Olympic stadium in 1996, she concluded that if athletics could be so cruel she didn't need it. In an act of renunciation, she threw her spikes into a dustbin.

It is unusual to begin celebrating a momentous event involving one of Britain's greatest Olympic athletes with an almost sadistic interest in the low points of her career. This atypical narrative of stardom changed abruptly in the second paragraph with an allusion to a better-known tale, that of Cinderella:

> That was the poisoned apple moment in the fairy tale. The happy ending seemed chalked in for last Monday night, when Holmes surfaced from years as the forlorn 'bridesmaid' of British athletics to find Lord Coe, her childhood hero, gently removing her spikes in an act of homage to her stunning victory in the women's 800 m at the Athens Games.

The quotation marks around 'bridesmaid' referenced the use of the words by Holmes herself in an interview which appeared to form the basis of the article. However, this emphasis adds to an overall lack of believability in this romantic storyline. The next paragraph underscored this with another change of narrative direction: 'the former army sergeant was not simply going to the ball: the golden coach was heading for her coronation'. As an army sergeant, Holmes is neither a convincing bridesmaid nor fairytale princess. A few lines further into the article, the profile mentioned that her Olympic achievements have in fact surpassed those of Sebastian Coe, her figurative Prince Charming, thereby puncturing further the cohesion of the Cinderella narrative. The text then characterised her as a 'geriatic' (aged 34) and suggested her injuries were so numerous they would 'condemn a horse to the knackers' yard' (for the slaughtering of worn-out livestock). This distinctly unromantic storyline gave way to another: 'she could destroy the world's fastest runners with searing bursts of speed'.

The unevenness of the narrative in the profile typified the press coverage of Holmes' victories. Multiple storylines were arranged around her, without any appearing to be a good fit. Holmes was not easily incorporated into any of the existing narratives of athleticism, heroism or female stardom.

A double-page spread inside the front cover of *The Sunday Times*, under the title 'Holmes charges into front rank of the Olympic greats' (Lewis and Munro, 2004, pp. 2–3) compared her victories to those of her predecessors. The text began by comparing Holmes' two gold medals with other 'great Olympic women champions' which produced a confusing narrative that sought to identify Holmes as, most importantly, a female athlete and then a British athlete. The images that accompanied the story included a large, aesthetically pleasing action shot of Mary Rand (British medallist from 1964) in mid-long jump. Before discussing Rand's achievements, the text referred to her as Mick Jagger's dream date. Next to the picture of Rand, were two images of male athletes in action: the British middle-distance runners Albert Hill (the only other athlete who had won gold in both events) and Sebastian Coe. The text below switched from the comparison of Holmes with other women athletes to a comparison with British male athletes. The narrative was full of stops and starts, with few of the athletes mentioned providing a direct comparison with Holmes. Holmes is female but not as glamorous as Rand. She is British but not male like Hill and Coe. Her story is not one of the evolution of British athletics. As the headline read, she broke the ranks of previous winners by charging in front. Holmes disrupted narratives of British athletic heroism by outdoing her male counterparts.

Holmes and intersectionality

Holmes was an unprecedented heroic figure both by virtue of both her massive achievement and the particular intersection of race, class and gender that make up her social identity. The photograph of Holmes on the cover of *The Sunday Times* showed her smiling and giving a 'thumbs up' sign while holding a Union Flag round her shoulders. The caption underneath praised her as 'the most successful British middle-distance runner of modern times' ('Golden joy': Kelly's historic double, 2004, p. 1). The accompanying article, however, qualified this by pointing to her gender – 'the most successful female runner this country has ever produced' – reinforcing perhaps the inability of a woman to embody the national heroic without question. Press coverage of Holmes was characterised by this uneven marking of gender – *The Sunday Times* cover story described her (perhaps tellingly) as the 'nearly-woman of British athletics', while inside, Coe was quoted as saying, 'She ran with great confidence and massive authority ... when it came to flat-out speed she could beat anybody' (p. 3). Far from trivialising her sporting achievement, the language used to describe her performance emphasised qualities previously associated with masculinity: skill, strength, speed, power, tactics. *The News of the World* used both 'Focus' (Harrison, 2004, p. 104) and 'Strength' (Sabey and Bhatia, 2004, p. 6) as headers, and quoted her saying: 'I used all my guts and strength' (p. 6). *The Sunday Mirror* described her characteristics as 'Keep on going. Guts. Tunnel vision' and said she 'powered over the line' (Clavane, 2004, p. 84).

However, while Holmes was considered as strong and determined, there were suggestions that these qualities also permeated her personal life. *The Sunday Times* profile discussed her relationship with the runner Maria Mutola as formerly 'one of the closest' in athletics, but now in a 'glacial phase' (p. 15). Hughes, in the *Sport* section, described her attitude as one of 'cold, calculated determination', and suggested that 'when she cruised round the finalists yesterday, there was an eerie lack of camaraderie, an initial lack of human response to her' (2004, p. 14). Smith in the *Observer* quoted her former coach, Arnold, 'She can be very aggressive, and very, very determined' and described her 'ascetic lifestyle' which means 'no drinking and few nights out' (2004, p. 3). In the *News of the World*, Sabey and Bhatia revealed 'the secret that drove Kelly to win a second gold medal – Alicia Keys' song If I Ain't Got You playing over and over in her mind'. This love song was interpreted by Holmes as being 'about my gold medal' they explained (2004, p. 6), giving an indication of Holmes' personal priorities.

This kind of attitude departs from traditional images of femininity. Nor does her naked ambition accord with the upper-middle-class, amateur gentleman legacy of British sport culture, which devalues trying too hard. Yet, her discipline and self-control do not match the typical media portrayals of the British working class as excessive and unrestrained either (Skeggs, 2004). Nevertheless, the press coverage invoked previous framing devices for sportswomen and working-class Britons, combining infantilising strategies with a focus on an ill-disciplined and turbulent home life. An inset on the front page of the *Sunday Mirror* previewed a story inside the paper with 'Golden Kelly's Secret Dad' against an image of Holmes at the moment of victory and a smaller photograph of a smiling black man with greying hair.

A double-page spread was given over to this story, with the headline: 'KELLY'S REAL DAD TALKS FOR THE FIRST TIME' (Stretch, 2004, pp. 4–5). Another headline taking up a third of the first page of the article provided a quote from Derrick Holmes: 'I wish I could hug my little girl again ... but she doesn't want to know me' (p. 4). The photograph of Derrick Holmes presented him in a light-hearted pose, playfully jabbing the air, and was captioned: 'LADIES' MAN But Derrick is desperate for a reconciliation' (p. 5). The article's reference to Derrick Holmes as an 'emotional', 'happy-go-lucky' 'ladies' man', inhabiting a 'down-at-heel' area, someone who 'struggles financially', 'touting for work door-to-door' or 'in some pub with a pint in one hand and a young lady in the other', evoked the media stereotype of dissolute, working-class behaviour patterns.

The emphasis on Holmes' childhood and family background was not restricted to tabloid coverage, however. The *Observer* employed a version of the 'rags to riches' storyline to emphasise disturbance in her upbringing: 'Like some of our other Olympic winners, Holmes is a success story from a broken home' (Smith, 2004, p. 3). The article combined reports of a happy home life with references to 'domestic flux' and lack of contact with 'her biological father'. Mention of her mother's lack of a passport (and therefore non-attendance at the Games) subtly indicated her parochial background, in contrast to the regular international travellers among the typical Observer readership. As Skeggs observed, a 'way of signifying unmodernity is through spatial fixity, through not being mobile' (2004, p. 112).

Yet Holmes herself has none of the characteristics that the newspapers associate with her parents. This narrative of uncontrolled and turbulent working-class origins contrasted with other reports of her self-discipline and work ethic. Similarly, she is globally travelled, having lived with Mutola in South Africa, a long way from her mother's house in the village of Hildenborough, and competed all over the world. The attempt to construct her as somebody's daughter is contradicted by her reported lack of interest in her 'biological father' and her mother's statement: 'I was never out for saying you have to do this or that; Kelly's done it for herself' (cited in Smith, 2004, p. 3). It is equally difficult to conceive of her simultaneously as a 'geriatric' and a 'little girl'.

Both The *Observer* and *The Sunday Times* discuss 'speculation' (Hughes, 2004, p. 15; Smith, 2004. p. 3) about her relationship with Mutola. Both papers carefully avoided an outright suggestion of the existence of anything more than a training partnership or friendship between them, but talked about 'gossip' (Hughes, 2004, p. 15; Smith,

2004, p. 3). The spectre of a lesbian relationship made it difficult for the papers to fit her into a narrative of heterosexual femininity. Interestingly, the tabloids made no attempt to do so, while the *Observer* quoted 'Holmes' childhood sweetheart, Simon Wixen, now a 34-year old computer analyst' (Smith, 2004, p. 3), who apparently could not be drawn on the question of Holmes' sexual orientation.

A very British heroine?

The headline accompanying the feature article in the *Observer* read: 'Victory for a very modern heroine' (Smith, 2004, p. 3). Images next to it, underneath the caption 'The long road to glory', showed Holmes after her success, raising the British Union Flag above her head, with three smaller insets: a photograph of Holmes as a child in the back garden of a typical working-class house with a white boy and a dog (the boy was her 'childhood sweetheart'); a picture of Holmes as a young woman smiling in her army uniform; and an image of Holmes and her mother, posing with an honour she received from the Queen for her service to the armed forces. The unusual (almost anachronistic) expressions 'modern' and 'heroine' signified a lack of ease within the narrative constructed in words and images around Holmes. 'Modern' could be interpreted as code for troubling on a number of levels. Holmes' success, as indicated earlier, was framed in power descriptors associated far more with a sports hero than a heroine, and the *News of the World* anticipated that she would 'receive a hero's welcome when she returns home' (Sabey and Bhatia, 2004, p. 6). The array of colour photographs showed her as disrupting many categories: nation (a black woman against the Union Flag); sexuality (the absence of a current romantic partner); gender (the army career); ethnicity (the picture of a white mother with a black daughter); class (the ordinary garden, the ordinary attire, the extraordinary feat). Holmes' relationship with Britishness was not depicted as straightforward: the text described her as achieving her dreams 'despite – or thanks to – the state of modern Britain' (Smith, 2004, p. 3). This confusing sentiment was echoed in *The Sunday Times*. Hughes appeared to struggle to find a coherent narrative to account for her:

> Her story is not one of being a minority, the only child in a family of five who is black, the recipient of genes from a Jamaican father and an English mother. Nor is it specifically about being one of the few mixed-race children growing up on a council estate in Kent. But

it is a fusion of those things, and a response in life to being a more driven individual than her siblings, and a remarkable obsession to push herself towards that podium.

(2004, p. 14)

The article also reproduced two of the same images as the *Observer* feature (the army picture and photograph with her mother) along with others including one showing her as a small child with two white siblings, and another flexing her biceps. The intersection of questionable national and racial identifiers (Jamaican/English/black/white) are combined in this portrait with Holmes' unfeminine and non-working-class personality traits. Indicating a level of fascination with her background, Hughes returned later in the article to the same theme, describing her as 'a talent made in England, of a Caribbean father who drifted apart from her teenaged mother when Kelly was two years old' (p. 15).

Broken body

Running throughout the press coverage of Holmes' performance was a dual emphasis on the uniqueness of her triumph and the injuries she had overcome. Daley Thompson (the former British decathlete) described her as 'the greatest middle-distance runner in the world' whose 'easy victory in the 1500 m merely underlines her dominance here' (Thompson, 2004, p. 83). Clavane in the same paper pointed to the physical problems she experienced after the 800 metre medal: 'on the verge of collapse as she came over to the press ... a doctor treated her for stomach cramps' (2004, p. 84). He described her career as 'injury ravaged' and suggested that many 'would have given up. Not Holmes'. The press narratives construct Holmes as almost superhuman, both in her capacity to have persevered despite injuries and setbacks and to have achieved her victories at 34. In addition, articles returned again and again to her injuries, describing them in graphic, visceral ways. For example, *The Sunday Times* Sport section includes these references to Holmes' pain and injury:

> the agonies of waiting have been so long, often so painful, it has felt like the nation sharing her tearing of tendons and sinews.
> ... her Achilles tendon ruptured ... accumulated wear and tear.
> The look in the dark eyes told you that she would strive beyond doubt, as she often has beyond pain.

(Hughes, 2004, pp. 14–15)

Holmes' body, despite being in peak physical condition, is regularly referred to as damaged: 'Guts and willpower have pushed her body beyond its limits' (Hughes, 2004, p. 15); 'Victory belied the years suffered in pain, on crutches or plunged into depression as her body failed her' (Smith, 2004, p. 3). Hughes uses Holmes' own words to point to her muscular physique, illustrated by the accompanying image of her flexing her biceps: ' "It wasn't until I came out of the Army six years ago that I realised how big I had become in the arms and upper body" ... it was bulk, achieved in part by heavy weight lifting, and the raised veins in her legs a legacy ...' (Hughes, 2004, p. 14). References to Holmes as an animal or an inanimate object are also littered throughout the coverage:

> it was like telling a dog not to bark
>
> (Hughes, 2004, p. 15)

> her pace akin to a Ferrari
>
> (Hughes, 2004, p. 15)

> enough injuries to condemn a horse to the knackers' yard
>
> ('Comment', 2004, p. 15)

In these ways, Holmes is depicted as departing from normative embodiment, and in so doing she encapsulates Shildrick's (2002) notion of the monstrous. The extreme depiction of her pain, injury and suffering coupled with the glorification of the results of her endeavours arguably confuses a number of categories. Male sports heroes are typically represented as possessing idealised bodies, at the height of physical condition. Holmes' feminine, excessively muscular, animalistic, objectified, damaged, worn-out body challenges not only the gender of the hero but the association of sport with health, beauty and fitness. Yet, it is this damaged body that has come to stand for the national body in the press narratives, as Holmes is appropriated as Britain's Olympic hero. As Shildrick stated:

> so long as the monstrous remains the absolute other in its corporeal difference it poses few problems; in other words, it is so distanced in its difference that it can clearly be put into an oppositional category of not-me. Once, however, it begins to resemble those of us who lay claim to the primary term of identity ... then its indeterminate status – neither wholly self or wholly other – becomes deeply disturbing.
>
> (Shildrick, 2002, p. 2)

Holmes' race, class and gender identity may mark her out as the 'not-me' of Britishness, yet her sporting accomplishments have given her the status of national hero. Puwar (2004, p. 11) observes that 'a muted sense of terror and threat underlies the reception of racialised minorities and women in predominantly white and masculine domains'. Arguably, this is the feeling that runs through Holmes' press coverage.

Kelly Holmes since Athens

Soon after her Olympic achievements, Holmes appeared on the cover of the celebrity news magazine *Hello!* A photograph of Holmes was the main cover image, taking up two-thirds of the space, with three smaller images running vertically along the side: the Olympic medal winning rower Matthew Pinsent and his wife; the American actress Cybill Shepherd; and the British soap opera actress Shobna Gulati. The text placed next to the photograph of Holmes read 'EXCLUSIVE GOLDEN GIRL KELLY HOLMES AS YOU'VE NEVER SEEN HER BEFORE' with 'All I ever wanted was to get my medals' further down the page. The image of Holmes presented her face onto the camera with a rather stiff smile, her long hair styled in a plaited bun on top of her head and trailing over her right shoulder. She was wearing a sparkly, white, shoulder-less evening dress, with her two gold medals around her neck. Inside the magazine, three double-page spreads depicted Holmes in a number of different evening gowns in the leafy grounds of what appeared to be a stately home. In one of the photographs, she is shown standing on a garden swing, shoeless, with a dress split to the thigh ending in a fish-tail train. In another, she is seated by a lake, wearing a sleeveless dress covered in multicoloured sequins, again split on the thigh, revealing her legs.

Underneath one of the photographs is a quote from Holmes, 'I never wear dresses. I'm much more comfortable in a track suit and trainers' (*Hello!* 14 September, 2004, p. 75) and Holmes did look awkward in the poses. The background to the shots bore no relation to Holmes or her family and succeeded in dislocating her totally from her background and claim to fame – her sport. The ease with which the other celebrities on the cover presented themselves to the camera underscored the tension within Holmes' self-presentation. For example, Pinsent was shown sitting at home with his glamorous wife in a relaxed pose with a glass of champagne, exuding upper-middle-class poise and self-assurance. Both female actresses adopted flirtatious poses indicating their familiarity with the celebrity press. These codes of heterosexuality and femininity were absent from Holmes' images, and she appeared 'dressed up' and out of place.

The attempts by sectors of the media to transform Holmes into a conventional celebrity attracted comment themselves. Referencing an attempt by the ITV breakfast show *GMTV* to make over Holmes prior to her appearance at the Woman of the Year lunch, Alison Kervin in *The Times* criticised the glamourising of sportswomen, arguing that 'No one would take a male athlete and dress him up so that he could "be more masculine". Indeed it would be deeply offensive to question a man's masculinity, whatever his occupation' (2004. p. 63). Similarly, Clare Balding, the BBC Sports presenter, suggested that the 'clothes thing has become a subject of debate. Kelly does not really "do" clothes. She is a professional athlete who spends her life in tracksuit and trainers' (2004, para. 10).

After announcing her retirement from athletics, Holmes appeared in the ITV reality TV programme *Dancing on Ice*, in which celebrities learn how to ice dance with professional ice skating partners, signalling, perhaps, an attempt to transform herself into a mainstream celebrity. Holmes' physicality and gender identity appeared once more to trouble the conventions of the media. On the second show in the series, Jason Gardiner, one of the judges, commented: 'You have such an amazing physical body, it's so muscular and it's great but because you dance so hard, you run the risk of almost looking like a man in drag' (*Dancing on Ice*, 21 January 2006, ITV1).

Nevertheless, Holmes has become part of the British cultural establishment. In the New Year's Honours List of 2005, Holmes was made a Dame Commander of the Order of the British Empire, one of the highest honours made personally by the Queen (the feminine version of a knighthood). On 1 February 2006, Holmes was named by the British government as the first National School Sport Champion, charged with getting more British schoolchildren interested in sport and physical education. Holmes has been associated with the London 2012 Olympics campaign and subsequent preparations, launching an initiative to get girls involved in sport in connection with the Games in November 2006.

Conclusions

The Sunday Times profile concluded that despite Holmes' broken body, advanced age and history of setbacks, her triumph positioned her as 'eclipsing her childhood hero Sebastian Coe' ('Comment', 2004, p. 15). This chapter has explored the ways the press constructed the story of an unexpected sporting hero. We have argued that the multiple and competing narrative strands that were used to frame Holmes and her double gold medal-winning performance belied the challenge she presented to conventional understandings of sporting heroism. The troubling representations surrounding Kelly Holmes indicates the inability of the media to configure her in traditional narrative formations. The intersections of gender, class, race, sexuality, age and nationhood Holmes embodies disrupt prevailing discourses surrounding Olympic heroism in the British press. The framing of Holmes also departs from the stereotypical depiction of sportswomen in the media, as identified in previous feminist research. The analysis presented in this chapter extends existing work by pointing to the changing representations of gender in the media. Despite the trouble they cause, some female sporting triumphs cannot be ignored, particularly when they represent the nation. As a result, media portrayals of sportswomen continue to have a particular capacity to disturb definitions of gendered embodiment. While elements of traditional narrative frameworks were apparent in the press coverage of Holmes' victories, the instabilities and discontinuities within the media texts can also be read as productive of new understandings of gender.

References

Anthias, F. (2005). Social stratification and social inequality: Models of intersectionality and identity. In F. Devine, M. Savage, J. Scott and R. Crompton (eds.), *Rethinking Class: Culture, Identities and Lifestyles* (pp. 24–45). Basingstoke: Palgrave Macmillan.

Balding, C. (2004). *Home Girl.* http://observer.guardian.co.uk/sport/story/0,,1372165,00.html. Retrieved 6 November 2007.

Bernstein, A. (2002). Is it time for a victory lap? Changes in the media coverage of women in sport. *International Review for the Sociology of Sport*, 37(3), 415–28.

Billings, A. C. and Eastman, S. T. (2002). Selective representation of gender, ethnicity, and nationality in American television coverage of the 2000 summer Olympics. *International Review for the Sociology of Sport*, 37(3–4), 351–70.

Birrell, S. and McDonald, M. (2000). Reading sport, articulating power lines: An introduction. In S. Birrell and M. G. McDonald (eds.), *Reading Sport: Critical Essays on Power and Representation* (pp. 3–13). Boston, MA: Northeastern University Press.

Boniface, S. and Eady, P. (2004,). I can't believe it ... *Sunday Mirror*, 29 August, p. 3.

Butler, J. (1998). Athletic genders: hyperbolic instance and/or the overcoming of sexual binarism. *Stanford Humanities Review*, 6.2. http://www.stanford.edu/group/SHR/6-2/html/butler.html. Retrieved 6 November 2007.

Clavane, A. (2004). Heaven for Kel. *Sunday Mirror Sport*, 29 August, pp. 84–5.

Collins, P. H. (2005). *Black Sexual Politics: African Americans, Gender and the New Racism.* London: Routledge.

'Comment'. (2004). *The Sunday Times*, 29 August, p. 15.

Cooky, C. (2006). Strong enough to be a man, but made a woman: Discourses on sport and femininity. In *Sports Illustrated for Women*. In L. K. Fuller (ed.), *Sport, Rhetoric and Gender: Historical Perspectives and Media Representations* (pp. 97–106). Basingstoke: Palgrave Macmillan.

Daddario, G. (1994). Chilly scenes of the 1992 winter games: The mass media and the marginalization of the female athlete. *Sociology of Sport Journal*, 11, 275–88.

Daddario, G. (1998). *Women's Sport and Spectacle: Gendered Television Coverage and the Olympic Games*. London: Praeger.

Duncan, M. C., Messner, M., Williams, L. and Jensen, K. (1994). Gender stereotyping in televised sports. In S. Birrell and C. L. Cole (eds.), *Women, Sport and Culture* (pp. 249–72). Champaign, IL: Human Kinetics.

Duncan, M. C. and Messner, M. A. (1998). The media image of sport and gender. In L. A. Wenner (ed.). *MediaSport* (pp. 170–85). London and New York: Routledge.

First exclusive interview. Double Olympic gold medallist. Kelly Holmes (2004). *Hello!* 14 September, pp. 70–7.

Gardiner, J. (2006). *Dancing on Ice*. 21 January London: ITV 1.

Golden joy: Kelly's historic double (2004). *The Sunday Times*, 29 August, p. 1.

Holmes charges into front rank of Olympic greats (2004). *The Sunday Times*, 29 August, pp. 2–3.

Harrison, D. (2004). Kelly's all goold. *News of the World*, 29 August, p. 104.

Hughes. R. (2004). Wake me up it's a dream says Kelly. *Sunday Times Sport*, 29 August, pp. 14–15.

Kane, M. J. and Greendorfer, S. (1994). The media's role in accommodating and resisting stereotyped images of women in sport. In P. Creedon (ed.), *Women, Media and Sport* (pp. 28–44). London: Sage.

Kane, M. J. and Lenskyj, H. J. (1998). Media treatment of female athletes: Issues of gender and sexualities. In L. A. Wenner (ed.), *Mediasport* (pp. 186–201). London and New York: Routledge.

Kennedy, E. (2001). She wants to be a sledgehammer? Tennis femininities on British television. *Journal of Sport & Social Issues*, 25(1), 56–72.

Kennedy, E. (2004). Bodies laid bare: Sport and the spectacle of masculinity. In E. Kennedy and A. Thornton (eds.), *Leisure, Media and Visual Culture: Representations and Contestations* (pp. 21–40). Eastbourne: Leisure Studies Association

Kervin, A. (2004). Women don't need to keep up appearances. *The Times*, 12 October, p. 63.

Jones, R., Murrell, A. and Jackson, J. (1999). Pretty versus powerful in the sports pages: Print media coverage of U.S. women's Olympic gold medal winning teams. *Journal of Sport & Social Issues*, 23(2), 183–92.

Messner, M. A., Duncan, M. C. and Cooky, C. (2003). Silence, sports bras, and wrestling porn: Women in televised sports news and highlights shows. *Journal of Sport & Social Issues*, 27(1), 38-51.

Mulvey, L. (1993). Afterthoughts on 'Visual Pleasure in Narrative Cinema' inspired by King Vidor's *Duel in the Sun* (1946). In A. Easthope (ed.), *Contemporary Film Theory* (pp. 111–24). London: Longman.

Olympics 2004 (2004) *Guardian*.

Ovett, S. (2004). Why we do it. *The Observer*, 29 August, p. 27.

Prince, G. (1980). Aspects of a grammar of narrative. *Poetics Today*, 3(1), 49–63.

Puwar, N. (2004). *Space Invaders: Race, Gender and Bodies out of Place*. Oxford: Berg.

Rojek, C. (2001). *Celebrity*. London: Reaktion Books.

Rowe, D. (2004). *Sport, Media and Culture*, 2nd edition. Maidenhead: Open University Press.

Sabey, R. and Bhatia, S. (2004). Kelly does old won 2. *News of the World*, 29 August, pp. 6–7.

Skeggs, B. (2004). *Class, Self, Culture*. London: Routledge.

Shildrick, M. (2002). *Embodying the Monster*. London: Sage.

Smith, D. (2004). Victory for a very modern heroine. *The Observer*, 29 August, p. 3.

Spencer, N. E. (2003). America's sweetheart and 'Czech-mate': A discursive analysis of the Evert–Navratilova rivalry. *Journal of Sport & Social Issues*, 27(1), 18–37.

Stoloff, S. (2000). Tonya Harding, Nancy Kerrigan, and the bodily configurations of social class. In S. Birrell and M. G. MacDonald (eds.), *Reading Sport: Critical Essays on Power and Representation* (pp. 234–50). Boston, MA: Northeastern University Press.

Stretch, E. (2004). I wish I could hug my little girl again but she doesn't want to know me. *Sunday Mirror*, 29 August, p. 6.

Thompson, D. (2004). Dame Game. *Sunday Mirror Sport*, 29 August, p. 83.

Vincent, J. (2004). Game, sex, and match: The construction of gender in British newspaper coverage of the 2000 Wimbledon championships. *Sociology of Sport Journal*, 21, 435–56.

Urquhard, J. and Crossman, J. (1999). *The Globe* and *The Mail* coverage of the winter Olympic Games: a cold place for women athletes. *Journal of Sport & Social Issues*, 23(2), 193–202.

Vincent, J., Imwold, C., Masemann, V. and Johnson, J. T. (2002). A comparison of selected 'serious' and 'popular' British, Canadian, and United States newspaper coverage of female and male athletes competing in the centennial Olympic Games: Did female athletes receive equitable coverage in the 'games of the women'? *International Review for the Sociology of Sport*, 37(3–4), 319–35.

Whannel, G. (2002). *Media Sports Stars*. London: Routledge.

Whannel, G. (1992). *Fields of Vision: Televised Sport and Cultural Transformation*. London: Routledge.

7
Different Shades of Orange?
Media Representations of Dutch
Women Medallists

Agnes Elling and Roelien Luijt

In this chapter we discuss, from a critical cultural studies perspective, how individual female Dutch medal winners at the Athens Olympics 2004 from different ethnic backgrounds were portrayed in two national newspapers: *Het Algemeen Dagblad* and *NRC Handelsblad*. Our main focus is on three athletes with different ethnic-racial backgrounds: the white, ethnically Dutch swimmer Inge de Bruijn (one gold, one silver and two bronze medals), the black Surinam-Dutch judoka Deborah Gravenstijn (bronze) and the black Indonesian-Dutch badminton player Mia Audina (silver). We analysed the photo representations of Audina, Bruijn and Gravenstijn to examine the intersections of nationalistic, gendered and racial-ethnic subtexts in their portrayal. To do this, we first present our critical analytic framework, followed by our methodological approach. Then we present and discuss the media representations of the three women Olympic medallists and finish with some concluding remarks.

Critical media studies perspective to studying Dutch media content

In this study we acknowledge that societies in general and social practices like sports and the media are structured around unequal, interrelated positions of gender, age, class, ethnicity and sexuality (e.g. Acker, 2006; Bourdieu, 1984; Butler, 1993; Kellner, 1995). The most dominant groups in these status relations (men, higher social classes, white non-migrants, heterosexuals) have more resources and power to determine dominant meanings and ideologies or, in other words, construct hegemonic discourse, with respect to social and cultural practices and the legitimacy of unequal status positions. However, power hierarchies are never fixed and status positions and dominant social images are constantly reconstructed and challenged. For example, social inequalities and their underlying power relations play an important role in the (re)construction, confirmation and challenging of existing stereotypes, for example racial and gender stereotypes (MacDonald, 2003; Van Dijk, 1993). Stereotyping and discrimination derive from the anxiety created by the constantly challenged position of dominant groups. When the established hierarchy diminishes due to processes of emancipation and empowerment, stereotypes are created and (re)used to create social distance between the dominant and non-dominant groups. We acknowledge that power inequalities influence the life choices and chances of groups of people (including within sport) and their representation in dominant communication structures like the (sports) media. However, like Giddens (1987) and Hall (1991), we also acknowledge that dominant ideologies and their institutionalised structures never entirely determine individuals' possibilities or interpretations of, for example, media texts. There is always some degree of subjective freedom and negotiation in making sense and taking action (*agency*). Texts and images can be written and read from a variety of interpretive frameworks (e.g. Hall, 1980). For example, not only do the editors and (photo) journalists mediate the image presentation of athletes, but the athletes themselves and the public too are actively negotiating the writing and reading of different gendered images. In this chapter, however, we focus on reading media images created by journalists rather than eliciting interpretation from the public or athletes.

Western sport journalists are mainly white men (Claringbould, Knoppers and Elling, 2004; Kinkema and Harris, 1998) and may (subconsciously) *encode* their texts by using dominant, stereotyped discourses about women in general or women belonging to specific ethnic-racial groups (e.g. Surinam/black or Indonesian/Asian). Sports media products can be characterised as straight reporting in which personal struggles, social conflicts and competition instead of social processes are underlined (Fiske, 1987). In addition, the sport sections of newspapers tend to be directed towards a male erotic gaze (Davis, 1997; Duncan, 1990; Knoppers and Elling, 2004). Such heterosexist reporting reflects the genre preferred by white male media sport consumers (Rose and Friedman, 1997) who read media texts and photo images encoded by the white male journalists. In any case, while most regular and Olympic coverage is devoted to male athletes (Duncan and Messner, 1998), we are interested in the meanings attached to the representation of Dutch female athletes. Generally, in the sport media both men and women athletes are represented as competent and physically strong (Birrell and Theberge, 1994; Knoppers and Elling, 1999, 2001b; Van der Lippe, 2002; Luijt and Elling, 2007). However, compared to men, female athletes are more often portrayed as dependent on men (coaches, husbands, fathers), emotionally unstable and (heterosexually) attractive. Some researchers argue that such representation provides ambivalent readings of women athletes: even when they are given ample attention, their achievements are trivialised, for example, by emphasising emotional weakness (Billings and Eastman, 2002; Birrell and Theberge, 1994; Knoppers and Elling, 1999; 2001b). These images are further based on specific types of sport (masculine- versus feminine-defined sports) and on the specific type of media (e.g. more intellectual versus popular mass media). Moreover, most sport media research has focused on white (male) athletes (for notable exceptions, see Bruce and Hallinan, 2001; Douglas, 2002; Elder, Pratt and Ellis, 2006; Spencer, 2004). Therefore, we are interested in the portrayal of women athletes of different racial and ethnic backgrounds in the Dutch media.

As already established, women athletes tend to be marginalised and trivialised in the sport media coverage. In addition, athletes from different ethnic backgrounds are often portrayed in (slightly) different ways in the sport media. For example, Duncan and Messner (1998) showed that men's basketball matches were broadcast differently compared to women's matches. The men's play was constructed as more exciting and more historically important than the women's, which featured less detail on players, statistics and slow motions. Other research showed that success by white athletes is commonly ascribed to mental acumen, whereas the achievements of black athletes are more often ascribed to natural talent (Billings and Eastman, 2002; McCarthy and Jones, 1997; Sabo et al., 1996). Such a portrayal reinforces the existing colonial ideologies that position blacks as closer to nature and lower in the societal status hierarchy compared to white men. This structural emphasis on certain characteristics may lead to confirmation of existing stereotypes that contribute to nationalism, sexism and ethnocentrism. At the same time, media images are the results of encoding and decoding processes in which dominance and resistance are negotiated. For example, the sport media often present explicit counter-images so that some women athletes are celebrated as strong women (Knoppers and Elling, 1999, 2001a; Wilson, 1997) and some black athletes, like Michael Jordan

(Jackson, Andrews and Cole, 1998), are represented as 'good blacks'. Athletes from marginalised groups may also function as role-models that simultaneously challenge and conform to the dominant stereotypes. On the other hand, such images can be regarded as false representations of a society in which all people, regardless of gender or race/ethnicity, are equal. The fact that women's and ethnic minority athletes' successes are celebrated in the sports media may disguise general unequal and stereotypical media representations by gender and race/ethnicity and mask inequality and injustice in society (Coakley, 2007; Knoppers and Elling, 2001b). Because the sports media often communicate contradictory and ambivalent social meanings, we are particularly interested in meanings attached to the ethnicity of the female athletes in the Dutch Olympic coverage. In addition, the representation of female athletes in the context of Olympics is often deeply embedded in nationalism.

Kinkema and Harris (1998) have argued that international tournaments like the Olympic Games provide prominent representations of national ideology. These international competitions reinforce 'us' versus 'them' attitudes, which are often strengthened by the particular focus of national media on athletes from their own country (Billings and Eastman, 2002; Jackson, Andrews and Cole, 1998). Furthermore, successful athletes of the home country are likely to be regarded as national heroes, while their opponents, who represent other national and cultural values and norms, may be depicted in more stereotypical ways. This nationalist ideology might influence the interrelated representations with respect to gender, race/ethnicity and sexuality (Billings and Eastman, 2003; Hills, 2007; Wensing and Bruce, 2003). Earlier, we conducted a quantitative analysis of the photo coverage of the 2004 Athens Olympics in two Dutch national newspapers to locate some connections between nationalism and ethnicity.

In our study we found that the Dutch media representations of the Athens Olympics are highly influenced by nationalistic and ethnocentric ideology: 62 per cent of all photos pictured Dutch athletes and all Dutch medal winners, regardless of gender and race/ethnicity, were represented as national heroes (Luijt and Elling, 2007). Pictured non-Dutch athletes were mainly medal winners, but according to the total medal position of the different countries, athletes from more cultural-proximate countries like Germany and England were over-represented compared to countries like China, Russia and Japan. These results indicate that photos are selected according to nationalistic and ethnocentric biases of cultural proximity. Since nationality may overrule gender and race/ethnicity as identity markers in media representations of international sporting competitions, social differences regarding gender and race/ethnicity among Dutch athletes appears less significant.

Previous research of Olympic media coverage confirms that female athletes feature relatively prominently in Olympic coverage (Knoppers and Elling, 1999; 2001b), although men and women of different ages and ethnic backgrounds are unevenly represented in the sports media outside of the Olympics. Our previous quantitative research showed that men received somewhat more coverage (53 per cent) than women (43 per cent) (Luijt and Elling, 2007). Compared to gender participation ratios of the Olympic athletes (a general female/male ratio of 35/65 and 40/60 for the Dutch Olympic team) women were even slightly over-represented. This rather surprising finding can be explained by the fact that women won more of the Dutch medals (13 of 22), possibly combined with production criteria based on the male gaze of the printed sports media (Duncan, 1990; Knoppers and Elling, 2004; Rose and Friedman, 1997). Although female athletes are seldom explicitly sexualised as pin-ups in Dutch sports media, the portrayal of athletes is gendered in several ways. For example, our results confirmed that the Dutch female athletes were more often portrayed as emotionally unstable and dependent on men than male athletes (Luijt and Elling, 2007; see also Knoppers and Elling, 1999). However, the portrayal of Dutch athletes was less gendered and less negatively racialised than non-Dutch athletes (Luijt and Elling, 2007). Especially non-Dutch black female Olympic athletes were represented in more stereotypical feminine ways (emotional, passive and inferior) compared to other groups. These findings are remarkable because previous research generally states that the othering of female athletes (e.g. non-white; non-heterosexual) occurs through masculinisation (Birrell and Theberge, 1994; Douglas, 2002; Spencer, 2004). Within the hegemonic nationalistic framework, however, both medal-winning men and women athletes may be ascribed by hegemonic masculine characteristics that are commonly attached to physical prowess and sporting heroes (Lines, 2001; Vande Berg, 1998). Earlier research by Knoppers and Elling (1999) and Sterkenburg and Knoppers (2004) also provides examples of stereotypical racialised images (e.g. animalistic, aggressive black athletes; see also Hoberman, 1997) in the Dutch sports media. Where gender and race/ethnicity may have traditionally been positioned in binary and hierarchical categories as strong men versus weak women and good whites versus bad blacks, in contemporary, postmodern, multicultural societies media images are more complex, especially when they interact with other identities such as nationality and sexuality. Jackson, Andrews and Cole (1998) argue that nationalistic frameworks may make the binary racial categories, like gender and sexuality (Billings and Eastman, 2002; Hills, 2007), more diffuse. New intra-gender and intra-racial/ethnic categories like good blacks and bad blacks (Wilson, 1997) that underline the fluidity and instability of contemporary celebrity-hood (Andrews and Jackson, 2001, p. 2) are likely to appear. Simultaneously, such a diffuse and hybrid media portrayal aligns with (more implicit) stereotypically gendered and racialised media coverage, which reproduces hegemonic ideologies and social inequalities. Few previous studies, however, have focused on intersections of nationality, gender and ethnicity. Our analysis, therefore, aims to reconstruct the complexly layered images of the white Dutch swimmer Inge de Bruijn who won several medals, the non-white Indonesian-Dutch silver medallist winner in badminton Mia Audina, and the black bronze medallist judoka Deborah Gravestijn, who is of Surinam descent, to look for interrelations of gender, race/ethnicity, class, and sexuality in the Dutch media coverage.[1]

Methods

In this chapter we use data collected for our earlier research on the photo representation for gender, ethnicity and nationality in the Dutch sports media (Luijt, 2005; see also Luijt and Elling, 2007). A total of 649 photos, including accompanying headlines/subscription representing athletes and coaches who participated in the Athens 2004 Summer Olympics, were analysed. All photos were printed in two Dutch national daily newspapers, *Algemeen Dagblad* (AD) and *NRC Handelsblad* (NRC). AD can be characterised as a more popular type of newspaper with a strong focus on sports (it has a special sports supplement), while NRC is directed more towards the intellectual elite. Since AD published more pictures (567) compared to NRC (82), the results mainly reflect the more populist media representation in the Netherlands. For this chapter, we selected photos representing de Bruijn (swimming), Audina (badminton) and Gravenstijn (judo).

Inge de Bruijn was born in 1973 in Barendrecht, the Netherlands and made her Olympic debut as a swimmer in 1992 where she finished 8th in the 100 metre freestyle. Shortly before the 1996 Olympics in Atlanta begun, de Bruijns' swimming career seemed to come to a dramatic halt after she broke with her coach and was dropped from the Dutch team due to her lack of motivation and for being too demanding. She moved to the United States to train with the drill coach Paul Bergen. In 1999, de Bruijn set a world record in the 50 metre butterfly and won the 50 metre freestyle at the European Championships. In the months preceding the centennial Olympic Games in Sydney, she was unbeatable and broke several world records. In Sydney she became the queen of the swimming pool by winning three gold medals – the 50 metre and 100 metre freestyle, and 100 metre butterfly – and setting world records in all three events. In addition, she won a silver medal with the 4 × 100 metre freestyle relay team. She was nicknamed Invincible Inky. At the 2001 World Championships, de Bruijn also won titles in three events and *Swimming World* named her Female World Swimmer of the Year in 2000 and 2001. At the 2003 World Championships de Bruijn defended her 50 metre freestyle and butterfly titles. At the 2004 Summer Olympics in Athens she retained her gold medal in the 50 metre freestyle and also took one silver (100 metre freestyle) and two bronze (100 metre butterfly and 4 × 100 metre freestyle). With this medal harvest de Bruijn became the most successful performing Dutch athlete in Olympic history. In March 2007, she announced her retirement from competitive swimming.

Mia Audina (born 1979) was a professional badminton player born in the former Dutch colony of Indonesia. She started competing internationally for Indonesia in 1993 and won the world title with the Indonesian team in 1994 when she was only 14 years old. At the 1996 Olympics in Atlanta, Audina won a silver medal for Indonesia. For the next few years she cared for her sick mother, who died in 1999. After marrying a Dutchman she gained Dutch nationality and started competing for the Netherlands in 2000. Audina won several medals at the European and World championships. She reached the quarter-finals in the 2000 Olympics in Sydney, and four years later in the Athens Olympics she won a silver medal in the women's singles. In the quarter- and semi-finals, Audina had a fairly easy victory over her British and Chinese opponents in two sets. In the finals Audina lost in three sets to Zhang Ning from China. In August 2006, Audina announced her retirement from professional badminton.

Deborah Gravenstijn was born in the Netherlands in 1974. Her parents (Hindustani mother, Creole father) grew up in the multicultural, former Dutch colony of Surinam. Gravenstijn has always had Dutch nationality and works as a physiotherapist for the Royal Dutch Air Force. Gravenstijn won three bronze medals in the women's 57 kg weight class at the European Championships of 1998, 1999 and 2000. At the 2000 Olympics in Sydney, Gravenstijn participated in the women's 52 kg category and came in fifth. In 2001, she won a silver medal (52 kg) at the

European and World Championships. At the 2004 Olympics in Athens Gravenstijn received a bronze medal in the women's 57 kg class after a difficult period during which she was injured frequently, lost her sister and her mother was diagnosed with cancer.

We found 27 photos representing de Bruijn, eleven photos representing Audina and seven photos representing Gravenstijn. In our analysis of the intersection of gendered, national and ethnic-racial subtexts in the portrayal of these athletes we focused on five features related to gendered and racial representations (e.g. Duncan, 1990; Knoppers and Elling, 1999; Philips and Hardy, 2002):

- Activity refers to the extent in which bodies are pictured as physically active (e.g. athlete in action versus medal ceremony).
- Emotion refers to joyful, tense, sad/disappointed or neutral emotions.
- Camera position refers to the way athletes are made symbolically superior (looking up to the subject) or inferior (looking down to the subject).
- Erotic content refers to whether photos explicitly focus on certain body parts with erotic connotations (breasts or buttocks) or show athletes in a provocative pose.
- Tone refers to the total context in which the photo is placed, such as the photo caption or header and/or the header and textual content of the accompanying article.

Apart from describing these photographic dimensions regarding the representations of three female Dutch medal winners, we discuss the ways these characteristics and the accompanying text headers are framed within hegemonic and alternative discourses relating to gender, race/ethnicity and nationality. Since Olympic media representations are strongly framed by a nationalistic discourse, it can be expected that images of both white and non-white female medal winners are (re)constructed to better fit them as typically Dutch winners (e.g. Wensing and Bruce, 2003).

Results and discussion

Typically, the Dutch media focused on medal winners: the four Dutch gold medal winners (three females and one male) received most attention (all more than 25 photos) and were all depicted as hero(in)es with supernatural powers. One of these gold medal winners was white swimmer Inge de Bruijn.

Sexy model: representations of Inge de Bruijn

The portrayal of multi-medallist de Bruijn was filled with ambivalence. In addition to being extremely talented and competent, she was pictured relatively more often in passive, sexualised poses (seven out of 27 photos) compared to the other female (gold) medal winners. Notably, also six out of 31 photos of her male counterpart Pieter van den Hoogenband (gold and multi-medallist in swimming) had erotic connotations. Only in two pictures is de Bruijn portrayed in an active sports position. Three photos are taken from a camera position below eye-level; the rest are neutral. Passive portrayal and sexual objectification may be partly related specifically to swimming as a sport. It is difficult to identify swimmers in the pool, yet it is possible that the physique of the swimmers draws more attention outside of the pool compared to other sports. The two other female gold winners – Anky van Grunsven (equestrian) and Leontien van Moorsel (road cycling) – were hardly depicted in poses with an erotic undertone (only one photo of Van Moorsel); nor were Mia Audina and Deborah Gravestijn. De Bruijn seems complicit in this (hetero)sexualised representation when pictured modelling in sexy bikinis, coiffured hair, make-up and sunglasses. Although years of intensive training have made her body extremely muscular and flat-chested, her physique was more than once described as perfect (The ideal body – Who draws her outlines, should recognize a waterdrop [AD, 12 August 2004] and Inky: The Body [AD, 12 August 2004]).

Moreover, de Bruijn's (heterosexual) femininity was underlined by frequent reference to her American male coach and by a portrayal of her as an emotional diva. When her male counterpart Van den Hoogenband lost the 200 metre freestyle final he was represented as a sportsmanlike loser. For example: Thorpe wins the battle of the titans – Van den Hoogenband: I have no need to feel ashamed (AD, 17 August, 2004) and VDH: Nonetheless not (AD, 17 August, 2004). De Bruijn's defeat, however, was more harshly judged when she was represented as a disgruntled drama queen after losing the 100 metre freestyle final: Inge de Bruijn not yet a real hero (NRC, 20 August, 2004); and De Bruijn longing for heroine status (NRC, 20 August, 2004). However, the accompanying picture shows a smiling de Bruijn congratulating the Australian winner Jodie Henry, and not looking disappointed about not winning gold.

The extreme focus on heterosexual femininity in the media portrayal of Olympic gold medallist de Bruijn is at odds with the results of the quantitative analysis that in general non-Dutch women were more stereotypically gendered compared to Dutch medal winners (Luijt and

Elling, 2007). We argued that only by showing masculine characteristics similar to male winners' (physical strength, perseverance and mental resilience) while remaining feminine can women athletes be truly regarded as heroes. But, although her medals were celebrated, de Bruijn was not portrayed as a typical Dutch sports heroine (a talented and hard-working, no-nonsense girl next door), but more as a celebrity (Andrews and Jackson, 2001; Vande Berg, 1998) with an attitude, a portrayal that might be more associated with the music industry or with some black sports stars. The rather ambivalent portrayal of de Bruijn as a spoiled, glamorous diva (Elling, 2008) was combined with her relative invisibility during her training in the US with her American coach. The ambiguous gendered media portrayal of de Bruijn shows that whiteness alone does not guarantee unproblematic recognition of Olympic champions as our hero(i)nes. On the other hand, the images of non-white Dutch medal winners were often infused with nationalism.

Integrated but different: Mia Audina

In the eleven analysed photos and headers, Mia Audina is portrayed as an immigrant and serious athlete. Audina is mainly represented in a positive context, in an active position concentrating on her sport performance (seven photos). Compared to de Bruijn she was relatively often portrayed from a camera position below or above eye-level. Three out of eleven photos placed her in a superior position and in two photos she was looked down upon. None of the photographs could be regarded as sexually suggestive. Compared to all other Dutch medal winners, the balance in activity/passivity is most skewed in the direction of activity. The emotional portrayal, however, distinguished her most clearly from the other medal winners, who were pictured mostly as happy or neutral. She is seldom portrayed looking happy despite having quite easily won five matches on different dates before being awarded the silver medal. Only in two out of a total of 14 photos was Audina pictured smiling.

Audina's sport achievements were celebrated, but on several occasions accompanying headlines in AD also stressed her successful assimilation into Dutch society. For example, AD provided the headline: Also happy with a heart of gold – Mia Audina after winning silver: foreigners are not always evil-minded (20 August 2004). Even though Audina's personality may be more introverted and serious compared to the athletes that are mainly represented by joyful emotions, this presentation might reflect a more stereotypical representation of Asian athletes as robotic, hard-working and emotionless (e.g. Coakley, 2007). The active and serious presentation of Audina could also be read as masculinising her in relation to other typically white, female Dutch medal winners, since Asian features do not fit hegemonic western femininity (e.g. Douglas, 2002). Emphasising her otherness through a less feminine physicality and attitude and by explicitly framing her as an immigrant, although well integrated, results in a somewhat ambiguous representation of Audina as a Dutch champion. Her silver medal is celebrated as a Dutch victory, but she is not represented as a typical, white Dutch woman. Her recent immigration status was especially emphasised in the header: Question 8: What is a patatje oorlog? – Integration test for the new Dutch Olympians (AD, 12 August 2004). In the accompanying article, the newspaper gave the results of an integration test with eight new Dutch athletes; athletes who had fairly recently been naturalised as a Dutch citizen. This underlining of Audina's ethnic/racial otherness reflects the much debated issue of immigration, integration and nationalist loyalty in the Netherlands, which has resulted in stricter laws and policies. One recently introduced law is a compulsory integration test, or a more specific citizenship test (inburgeringstest). Although probably meant as a humorous example, the question 'What is a patatje oorlog?' not only refers to a typical Dutch snack, but ironically also to Dutch colonialisation of Indonesia. Patatje oorlog literally means fries at war and the snack consists of French fries with mayonnaise and sateh sauce, the latter being an imported Indonesian product to the Dutch kitchen.

Strong and innocent blackness: Deborah Gravenstijn

Bronze medal judoka Deborah Gravenstijn was mostly pictured in a positive context and expressing positive emotions. Gravenstijn was most often portrayed in active positions, usually while training or just before or after a match. In contrast to white female athletes like de Bruijn and the cyclist Leontien van Moorsel, Gravenstijn was not represented actively in other activities. For example, de Bruijn was photographed juggling balls at her birthday party in Athens and van Moorsel was shown in the Olympic village on a reclining bike. Gravenstijn was most often shown after her matches or during a medal ceremony celebrating, unlike Audina, who was depicted concentrating on her play. Two of the photos were taken from below eye-level, looking up at her and one from above, looking down on her.

The journal articles presented Gravenstijn as a young woman focusing on judo and overcoming a difficult period beset with injuries and illness in her immediate family. Her overcoming of these difficulties in life was often emphasised in the accompanying headings. For example: Never write off Deborah – Judo player wins bronze medal after frequent injury distress (AD, 17 August 2004), Bronze reflects resilience of judo player Deborah Gravenstijn (NRC, 17 August 2004) and Judo player's bronze for sick mother (AD, 17 August 2004). This general photographic and textual representation of Gravenstijn does not correspond to such stereotypical images as black (female) athletes having above all physical talent (power, speed), being aggressive or being egocentric and arrogant (e.g. Billings and Eastman, 2002; Davis and Harris, 1998; Douglas, 2002). This is interesting, because a display of a powerful and aggressive physicality would also fit her masculine sport, exemplified by several pictures of the other Dutch medal winners in judo (one woman and two men) who were portrayed more often as physically strong and in active fighting positions. While presented as physically and mentally strong, Gravestijn is foremost characterised as a very kind and friendly person. Her embodied blackness is not emphasised as dangerous or erotic as in hegemonic racial discourse (Hoberman, 1997; Spencer, 2004); rather it is made invisible by focusing, for example, on her non-threatening, friendly, smiling face (e.g. Wensing and Bruce, 2003). For example, one picture in AD that captured Gravestijn after she was awarded the bronze medal creates a particular image of innocence. In this photo, Gravenstijn is portrayed during the medal ceremony with a typical Lady Di look: innocently looking up. This expression of the girl next door, combined with a general portrayal of physical and mental strength, could be read as whitening her to fit better with privileged, White femininity (Knoppers and Elling, 2001) and to typical Dutch (sport) celebrity-hood (Giesen, 2007).

In conclusion: different shades of orange

Comparing the general images of the three selected female Dutch medal winners with each other and with other medallists shows several similarities, but also clear differences, which illustrate the ambiguity or instability of Olympic heroism narratives (e.g. Andrews and Jackson, 2001; Hills, 2007). All three athletes are accommodated in a nationalist framework representing true Dutch medal winners, but are simultaneously othered by gendered and ethnic-racial discourses. Compared to the media portrayal of the white multi-medal swimmer de Bruijn and the Indonesion immigrant Audina (silver in badminton), the media representation of black Surinam-Dutch Gravenstijn (bronze medallist in judo) was accommodated most often with a nationalist framework of (sporting) heroes and privileged femininity.

In general the two non-white female medal winners Audina (badminton) and Gravenstijn (judo) are pictured in a positive light: like white male and female medal winners they are depicted as modest, but physically and mentally strong athletes. A closer look, however, could acknowledge different gender and racial/ethnic subtexts although these are complexly layered constructions, interacting with types of sport and personality. Although both Indonesia and Surinam are former Dutch colonies, there are differences in cultural proximity. Contemporary Surinam gained independence in 1969, but is culturally and politically more closely associated with Dutch society than Indonesia, which gained independence after the Second World War after a bloody war and is the biggest Muslim country in the world (although Audina is a Christian). In addition to their different ethnic origins, Audina's and Gravenstijn's different immigrant histories, combined with a political and cultural decline in immigration tolerance in Netherlands, may have an even greater impact on their different portrayal. Although she identifies more strongly with her Surinamese ethnicity, Gravenstijn was born in the Netherlands (Van den Brink, 2006). Audina, however, had only been a naturalised Dutch citizen for four years when she competed in Athens in 2004. Therefore, their success was constructed as Dutch success through very different portrayal of gender and race/ethnicity. Such a representation, however, was no doubt also influenced by the different personal characteristics, such as appearance and mentality, of the two athletes. Black Gravenstijn appeared to be whitened and naturalised as typically Dutch through feminisation and softening of the stereotypical masculine image of black women as strong, aggressive and arrogant. Underlining winning characteristics such as perseverance and physical and mental strength but at the same time emphasising the girl next door-like approachability and ordinariness, constructed Gravenstijn as a typical Dutch winner despite her gender or race/ethnicity. Audina received photo coverage similar to most male athletes: she was most often pictured in active positions, showing concentration. Audina's silver, however, was celebrated through emphasis on her ethnic-racial otherness constructed partly through de-feminisation of her portrayal (e.g. Douglas, 2002; Hills, 2007).

As one of the (expected) most successful Dutch athletes, the white medal winner de Bruijn received a lot of attention and was celebrated for her (near-) victories. But her media portrayal was also peppered with gendered ambivalence that trivialised her athletic performances and infantilised her as an athlete (Birrell and Theberge, 1994; Knoppers and Elling, 2001b) through erotic portrayal and depiction of her as an emotional diva dependent on her male American coach. Compared to all other Dutch medal winners – male and female of different ethnicities – her portrayal most typically revealed encoded meanings that privilege the (white) male subject position (Davis, 1997; Knoppers and Elling, 2004). In certain ways, de Bruijn's presentation also resembled the rather negative portrayal of black female American athletes. This othering of de Bruijn might be a result of her leaving the Netherlands to train with an American coach. Nor has de Bruijn adopted the traditional Dutch mentality of remaining ordinary (Giesen, 2007). Although the media crowned Dutch winners as kings/queens and god(esse)s, Dutch athletes, let alone (white) Dutch women, are not supposed to behave like conceited celebrities. This paradoxical construction of heroes in contemporary Dutch society might have led to a clear incorporation of the black bronze medal winner Gravenstijn as an ordinary Dutch woman and a simultaneous othering of the white mult-imedal winning diva de Bruijn.

In conclusion, de Bruijn, Audina and Gravenstijn were portrayed quite differently from one another. Gender construction played a role in both incorporating and othering athletes as typical Dutch female champions. The portrayal of the success of these three women athletes illustrated the growing ambiguity in nationalist, gendered and racial/ethnic portrayal in the Dutch media and thus added more shades of orange.

Note

1. The Netherlands is a small, prosperous, densely populated country (16.4 million inhabitants with a density of 480 per square kilometre), located in north-western Europe. Ten per cent are of the population are of non-western ethnic origin (SCP, 2007a). The largest ethnic minority groups are first- and second-generation immigrants from Surinam, Turkey and Morocco, most of whom live in the four main cities. Two-thirds of the population practise sport on a monthly basis and half the population at least once a week (this includes recreational physical activities such as swimming, walking and cycling). Whereas many people practise sports individually or in commercial organisations (i.e. fitness clubs, gyms), traditional sport clubs still form the core of organised sports, with a total of 27,000 voluntarily associations.

    Mainly due to a well-organised competitive club sports system, a substantial number of male and female athletes have won medals in various sports throughout modern Olympic sports history. Apart from conquering dangerous waters (most of the country lies below sea level) by constructing dykes, canals and ships, the Dutch have also won many competitions in the Olympic swimming pools and on the ice rink (speed skating). Especially in speed skating and football, international competitions are attended by large crowds, often wearing orange, the traditional colour of the dynasty (the national flag is red, white and blue); the fans are referred to as the orange army. Although many inhabitants are proud of their (historic) sport champions, a strong sense of patriotism, celebrity culture and a competing-to-win mentality are not typical of contemporary Dutch society. On the contrary, the eighteenth-century Enlightenment (*Verlichting*) introduced a political and cultural egalitarian philosophy aimed at the development of society at large and not at individual excellence (Giesen, 2007). This egalitarian and non-hierarchical culture became even stronger during the 1960s and 1970s. The expression 'behaving normally is crazy enough' exemplifies this dominant normative value, which also fits within the dominant Calvinist ideology of working hard and living soberly. However, hegemonic cultural values and norms are not static and may be ambiguously related to concrete social practices. In recent years, critical voices from different social sectors (politics, education, culture, sports) have spoken out against the 'ordinary is enough' mentality, and they call for excellence to be encouraged and celebrated instead of being downplayed. Tolerance has historically been another distinguishing characteristic of Dutch society (Halman, Luijkx and Zundert, 2006). This general tolerance towards (ethnic) minority groups and alternative lifestyles (e.g. use of soft drugs, same sex-marriage) is accompanied by progressive equity and anti-discrimination laws. Nonetheless, the employment rate of women in the Netherlands is quite low and women and minorities are largely under-represented in leadership positions in academia and the business sector (SCP, 2007b). Moreover, immigration and integration policies have become stricter (e.g. through compulsory citizenship tests [*inburgeringstest*]), accompanied by a growing public intolerance of otherness and stronger call for cultural assimilation.

References

Acker, J. (2006) Inequality regimes. Gender, class and race in organizations. *Gender & Society*, (20)4, 441–64.

Andrews, D. L. and Jackson, S. J. (2001). Introduction. Sport celebrities, public culture, and private experiences. In D. L. Andrews and D. L. Jackson (Eds.), *Sport Stars: The Cultural Politics of Sporting Celebrity* (pp. 1–19). London: Routledge.

Billings, A. C. and Eastman, S. (2002). Selective representation of gender, ethnicity, and nationality in American television coverage of the 2000 Summer Olympics. *International Review for the Sociology of Sport*, (37)3–4, 351–70.

Birrell, S. and Theberge, N. (1994). Ideological control of women in sport. In D. M. Costa and S. R. Guthrie (eds.), *Women and Sport: Interdisciplinary Perspectives*. Champaign, IL: Human Kinetics, pp. 341–59

Bourdieu, P. (1984). *Distinction. A Social Critique of the Judgement of Taste.* Cambridge, MA: Harvard University Press.

Brink, C. van den (2006). Deborah Gravenstijn.In dit judopak zit een Surinaams meisje dat trots is op haar afkomst. In E. Wieldraaijer, C. van den Brink and

Th. Stevens (eds.), *Hinderlijk buitenspel. Sport als motor van integratie* (pp.12–22). Deventer: ... daM.

Bruce, T. and Hallinan, C. (2001). Cathy Freeman: The quest for Australian identity. In D. L. Andrews and S. J. Jackson (eds.). *Sport Stars: The Cultural Politics of Sporting Celebrity* (pp. 257–70). London: Routledge.

Butler, J. (1993) *Bodies that Matter. On the Discursive Limits of Sex.* New York: Routledge.

Claringbould, I., Knoppers, A. and Elling, A. (2004). Exclusionary practices in sport journalism. *Sex Roles* (51)11–12, 709–18.

Coakley, J. J. (2007). *Sport in Society, Issues and Controversies,* 7th edition. Boston, MA: McGraw-Hill.

Davis, L. R. and Harris, O. (1998). Race and ethnicity in U.S. sports media. In L. Wenner (ed.), *MediaSport* (pp. 154–69). London: Routledge.

Davis, L. (1997). *The Swimsuit Issue and Sport: Hegemonic Masculinity in Sports Illustrated.* New York: SUNY Press.

Dijk, T. A., van, (1993). *Elite Discourse and Racism.* Newbury Park, CA: Sage.

Duncan, M. C. (1990). Sports photographs and sexual difference: Images of women and men in the 1984 and 1988 Olympic Games. *Sociology of Sport Journal,* 10, 353–72.

Duncan, M. C. and Messner, M. (1998). The media image of sport and gender. In L. Wenner (ed.), *MediaSport* (pp. 170–85). London: Routledge.

Douglas, D. D. (2002). To be young, gifted, black and female: A meditation of the cultural politics at play in representations of Venus and Serena Williams. *Sociology of Sport Online* 5/2, http://physed.otago.ac.nz/sosol/v5i2/v5i2_3.html.

Elder, C., Pratt, A. and Ellis, C. (2006). Running race: Reconciliation, nationalism and the Sydney 2000 Olympic Games. *International Review for the Sociology of Sport,* 41(2), 181–200.

Elling, A. (2008). Van afgeschreven supertalent tot Olympisch zwemkoningin. Tussen startblok en catwalk: nog ééenmaal de allerbeste. In W. van Buuren (ed.), *Hollands Goud.* Amsterdam: J. M. Meulenhoff.

Fiske, J. (1987). *Television Culture.* London: Methuen.

Giddens, A. (1987). *Social Theory and Modern Sociology.* Cambridge: Polity Press.

Giesen, P. (2007). Land van verdachte strebers. *De Volkskrant,* Kennisbijlage, 15 September, 1.

Hall, S. (1980). Encoding/decoding. In *Working Papers in Cultural Studies, 1972–1979. Culture, Media, Language* (pp. 129–38). London: Hutchinson.

Hall, S. (1991 [1980–89]). *Het minimale zelf en andere opstellen.* Amsterdam: Sua.

Halman, L. Luijkx, R. and Zundert, M. van (2006). *Atlas of European Values.* Leiden and Boston, MA: Brill Academic Publishers.

Hills, L. (2007). Double trouble: Kelly Holmes, intersectionality and unstable narratives of Olympic heroïsm. Paper presented at the World Congress of the International Sociology of Sport Association (ISSA) and International Society for the History of Physical Education and Sport (ISPHES), 31 July–5 August, Copenhagen.

Hoberman, J. (1997). *Darwin's Athletes: How Sport has Damaged Black America and Preserved the Myth of Race.* Boston, MA: Houghton Mifflin.

Jackson , S. J., Andrews, D. L., and Cole, C.L. (1998). Race, nation and authenticity: A comparative analysis – The Everywhere Man (Michael Jordan) and the Nowhere Man (Ben Johnson). *Journal of Immigrants and Minorities,* 17(1), 82–102.

Kellner, D. (1995). *Media Culture: Cultural Studies, Identity and Politics between the Modern and the Postmodern*. Londen: Routledge.

Kinkema, K. M. and Harris, J. C. (1998). Media sport studies: Key research and emerging issues. In L. Wenner (ed.). *MediaSport* (pp. 27–54). London: Routledge.

Knoppers, A. and Elling, A. (1999) *Gender, etniciteit en de sportmedia. Een inventarisatie vanreguliere en Olympische berichtgeving*. Utrecht: CBM (UU)/ Tilburg: Vrijetijdswetenschappen (KUB).

Knoppers, A. and Elling, A. (2001a). *Gender, etniciteit en de sportmedia: selectie en interpretatie*. Arnhem: NOC*NSF.

Knoppers, A. and Elling, A. (2001b). Sport and the media: Race and gender in the representation of athletes and events. In J. Steenbergen, P. De Knop and A. Elling (eds.), *Values & Norms in Sport* (pp. 281–300). Oxford: Meyer & Meyer Sport.

Knoppers, A. and Elling, A. (2004). We do not engage in promotional journalism: Discursive strategies used by sport journalists to describe the selection process. *International Review for the Sociology of Sport*, 39, 57–73.

Lines, G. (2001). Villains, fools or heroes? Sport stars as role models for young people. *Leisure Studies*, 20, 285–303.

Lippe, G., van der (2002). Media image: Sport, gender and national identities in five European countries. *International Review for the Sociology of Sport*, 37(3–4), 351–70.

Luijt, R. B. (2005). Worstelen met het stereotype: een onderzoek naar de weergave van Olympische sporters in Nederlandse kranten. Unpublished MA thesis, Universiteit Utrecht, the Netherlands.

Luijt, R. B. and Elling, A. H. F. (2007). Oranje sporthelden zijn niet zwart of wit. Een onderzoek naar de weergave van Olympische sporters in Nederlandse kranten. *Vrijetijdstudies*, 24(1), 31–45.

Macdonald, M. (2003). *Exploring Media Discourse*. London: Arnold.

McCarthy, D. and Jones, R. L. (1997). Speed, aggression, strength, and tactical naïveté: The portrayal of the black soccer player on television. *Journal of Sport & Social Issues*, 21, 348–62.

Philips, N. and Hardy, C. (2002). *Discourse Analysis: Investing Processes of Social Construction*. London and New Delhi: Sage.

Rose, A. and Friedman, J. (1997). Television sports as mas(s)culine cult of distraction. In A. Baker and T. Boyd (eds.), *Out of Bounds: Sports, Media, and the Politics of Identity* (pp. 1–15). Bloomington, IN: Indiana University Press.

Sabo, D., Curry, T., Jansen, S., Tate, D., Duncan, M. C. and Leggett, S. (1996). Televising international sport: Race, ethnicity, and international bias. *Journal of Sport &Social Issues*, 20(1), 7–21.

SCP (2007a). *Sport in the Netherlands*. Den Haag: Sociaal en Planbureau.

SCP (2007b). *De sociale staat van Nederland*. Den Haag: Sociaal en Cultureel Planbureau.

Spencer, N. E. (2004). Sister Act VI: Venus and Serena Williams at Indian Wells: Sincere fictions and white racism. *Journal of Sport & Social Issues*, 28(2), 115–35.

Sterkenburg, J. and Knoppers, A. (2004). Dominant discourses about race /ethnicity and gender in sport practice and performance. *International Review for the Sociology of Sport*, 39(3), 301–21.

Vande Berg, L. R. (1998). The sports hero meets celebrity hood. In L. Wenner (ed.), *MediaSport* (pp. 135–53). London: Routledge.

Wensing, E. H. and Bruce, T. (2003). Bending the rules: Media representations of gender during an international sporting event. *International Review for the Sociology of Sport*, 38(4), 387–96.

Wilson, B. (1997). Good blacks and bad blacks: Media constructions of African-American athletes in Canadian basketball. *International Review for the Sociology of Sport*, 32(2), 177–89.

8
Winning Space in Sport: The Olympics in the New Zealand Sports Media

Toni Bruce

Introduction

In this chapter, I draw on feminist cultural studies theorising to explore the ways in which the Olympic Games may become a site where female athletes claim centre stage in the media and public imagination. The analysis is underpinned by Proctor's (2004) argument that cultural studies research involves 'exposing the relations of power that exist within society at any given moment in order to consider how marginal, or subordinate groups might secure or win, however temporarily, cultural space from the dominant group' (p. 2). Thus, the focus is on a rare moment when sportswomen, a marginal group within the broader culture of sport, are able temporarily to win space for themselves in the mainstream media. While newspaper coverage of New Zealand's three female medallists at the 2004 Olympic Games is the empirical basis for the analysis, my focus is on exploring the articulations and relations of power that create the opportunity for such visibility.

Feminist cultural studies

Feminist theoretical contributions to cultural studies have ensured that gender relations are integral to the broader cultural studies focus on culture and power relations. Indeed, Stuart Hall has argued that 'a theory of culture which cannot account for patriarchal structures of domination and oppression is, in the wake of feminism, a non-starter' (1980, p. 39). However, it is clear that feminism's *entrée* into cultural studies was not always smooth. Instead, feminism has played a disruptive and consistently challenging role within broader cultural studies theorising (Brunsdon, 1996; Franklin, Lury and Stacey, 1991; Hall, 1996): feminism 'interrupts cultural studies at every turn' (Pollock, 2003, p. 128). Feminism entered cultural studies 'with the firm resolve to legitimise the "feminine" ' (Parameswaran, 2005, p. 197; Zelizer, 2004), an approach which led to a focus on entertainment genres such as dance, romance novels, soap opera and other 'light' or 'lowbrow' entertainment associated with women or femininity (e.g. Modleski, 1984; McRobbie, 1978; Radway, 1984). This approach meant challenging the central position of journalism and news media which were associated with 'privileged masculine forms of address' (Parameswaran, 2005, p. 199). As a result, Parameswaran (2005) argues, since the 1980s journalism has seldom received adequate attention from cultural studies scholars. The analysis on which this chapter is based is located in the area of feminist cultural studies that is 'concerned with textual meaning ... and issues of representation' (McRobbie, 1997, p. 171). However, unlike much feminist cultural studies research which focuses on how 'female' popular culture informs the cultural construction of female identity, it takes as its target one of the most male-dominated areas of news media – sports journalism. It assumes that because 'those who control the media control a society's discourses about itself' (Denzin, 1996, p. 319), the study of media representations is a key element in understanding how gender relations operate in specific cultural and historical contexts. Given that the mass media generally construct narratives told from white, male, middle-class, heterosexual perspectives (Bell, 2004; Denzin, 1991), there is little doubt that media representations, like gender relations, are inherently relations of power. Further, this analysis is grounded in the cultural studies understanding that rather than expressing an existing reality, media representations are 'instead actively constitutive of reality' (McRobbie, 1997, p. 172). It assumes that media stories have the potential to structure our consciousness in ways that have both social and political consequences (Bennett, 1982). Rather than directly affecting our behaviour, media stories slowly transform what appear to be 'the most plausible frameworks we have of telling ourselves a certain story about the world' (Hall, 1984, p. 8).

At the same time, cultural studies theorising insists that there is no direct relationship between media texts and how audiences (readers, listeners, viewers) make sense of them. Indeed, research on a variety of popular media texts such as televised women's basketball or men's rugby, romance novels, movies and prime-time drama clearly demonstrates that people – particularly marginalised groups who are represented as the 'other' – are able to reject or ignore elements of texts, and interpret them in completely different ways than appear possible based on analysis of the preferred meanings encoded in them (e.g. Bruce, 1998; Morley, 1980; Radway, 1984; Star, 1992). However, challenges or reintepretations of media texts are most likely to come from groups or individuals with local knowledge of the experience being represented or for whom the dominant representations do not reflect their own experiences or reality such as fans of women's sport (Bruce, 1998).

In this chapter, I am not concerned with the 'truth' or 'adequacy' of representations of New Zealand female athletes. Instead, I use this case study of Olympics media coverage to think through 'relations of difference' (McRobbie, 1997, p. 175) that are reflective of the imaginings of sports media workers and their understandings of females in sport. In this case female athletes, like women more generally, are not just talked about (or ignored as they usually are) but are envisaged and defined by a variety of competing and opposing interest groups who have more or less power to have their vision activated in the mainstream press (McRobbie, 1997). I attempt to follow McRobbie's argument that feminist cultural studies analyses must consider 'these circulating definitions in all their complexity' (1997, p. 180) as I demonstrate how 'sportswoman' becomes a convenient image that stands in for broader cultural shifts and tensions. The key consideration in my analysis is the process of articulation. According to Hall, 'a theory of articulation is both a way of understanding how ideological elements come, under certain conditions, to cohere together within a discourse, and a way of asking how they do or do not become articulated, at specific conjunctures' (in Grossberg, 1996, pp. 141–2). Thus, for Hall, the key question is to ask 'under what circumstances can a connection be forged or made?' (in Grossberg, 1996, p. 141). A key point is that there is no necessary correspondence between such elements; no matter how strong the linkages may appear, they are always 'connected through a specific linkage, that can be broken' (Hall, cited in Grossberg, 1996, p. 141).

In taking a feminist cultural studies approach, I argue that gender is a key factor in determining women's and men's understandings and experiences of the world. This does not mean that all women's experiences are the same – clearly they are not. Because women's experiences differ along many axes of difference, such as race, ethnicity, age, disability, class, religion, sexuality and nation, it is important to temper the focus on gender relations by rejecting totalising, essentialist or universalising theories and narratives (Bordo, 1990). However, although it is important not to privilege gender as the only or necessarily the most important form of oppression, there is little doubt that in sporting contexts, women are generally subordinated to men and that gender/power relations privilege males. In short, the articulation of sport (and sports media) with masculinity is particularly potent.

Sport and sports media as ideologically masculine

Feminist researchers have long argued that sport is permeated with ideologies of male dominance and female subordination, based on apparently incontrovertible evidence of superior male power, physical strength and aggression. The articulation of sport and masculinity has a long history and, as Hall argues about other cultural forms, it constitutes 'magnetic lines of tendency which are very difficult to disrupt' (Grossberg, 1996, p. 142). At the same time, cultural studies theorising reminds us of the need to investigate the gender/power relations operating in the local sites we research rather than assuming, for example, that women are always subordinate to men (see also Mac an Ghaill and Haywood, 2007). However, Cameron and Kerr (2007) recently argued that in New Zealand sport 'women's place generally is subordinate, inferior, invisible, or at best, marginal' (p. 339; see also Thompson, 2003).

Existing research in New Zealand and internationally identifies sports journalism as an overwhelmingly male domain in which male sports media workers produce media coverage about males for a predominantly male audience (Duncan, Messner and Willms, 2005; Ferkins, 1992; Knoppers and Elling, 2004). Duncan et al. (2005), for example, identified an 'almost unbroken chorus of men's voices' in Californian televised sports news which, combined with an almost exclusive focus on men's sports, served to 'buttress the myth that sports is an exclusive male realm' (p. 22). However, although individual sports media workers may produce words and images that reinforce dominant cultural assumptions, this production is the result of their location in a culture that sees such beliefs as self-evident. In Hall's (1995) terms, media workers 'speak through ideological discourses that are already active in society and that provide us/them with the 'means of 'making sense' of social relations and our place in them' (p. 19). Therefore, although the sports media may systematically reinforce gender ideologies, it is not necessarily because sports media workers are active sexists. It is through the sets of practices and discourses by which knowledge is constructed in the sports media that ideologies that reinforce existing gender relations continue to be recreated. Thus, the sports media generally reflect dominant cultural assumptions that female sport is less interesting or exciting than men's sport, and that female athletes are less capable than men. Further, decisions about who and what sport gains coverage tend to be made on the basis of intuition, anecdotal evidence, historical precedent and taken-for-granted beliefs about what the public wants (Ferkins, 1992; Fountaine and McGregor, 1999; Knoppers and Elling, 2004; Lowes, 1999). These assumptions tend to result in coverage that either ignores females (Bruce, 2008; Bruce, Falcous and Thorpe, 2007; Ferkins, 1992; Fountaine and McGregor, 1999; McGregor, 2000) or reinforces gendered cultural discourses. Indeed, such findings should not surprise us. As David Papke argues, if sports culture 'is sexist and overwhelmingly gendered, we shouldn't be at all surprised that the overall edifice of sports journalism is also sexist and gendered' (cited in Seib, 2002, p. 66).

The strength of the articulation between men and sport appears so powerful in New Zealand that some male journalists feel no need to justify it – the linkage is, for them, 'natural' (e.g. McGregor, 2000; McGregor and Fountaine, 1999). In just one recent example, rather than reflect on such inequalities, an influential media executive unapologetically told a packed crowd of women's sport fans that he ignored research on gender differences in sports coverage (B. Cox, personal communication, 8 July 2007).

Given this broad context, what interests me is the 2004 Olympic Games; a site at which the articulation between sport and masculinity appeared to be interrupted by narratives which highlighted rather than denigrated female sporting achievement.

Newspaper sources

The textual analysis (see McKee, 2001; Turner, 1997) on which this research is based draws on articles published in four major daily newspapers, the largest circulation Sunday newspaper and five smaller regional newspapers. Articles were accessed by a Newztext database search of Fairfax newspapers and the *New Zealand Herald*, the nation's largest circulation daily newspaper and the only one in the study not owned by the Australian-based Fairfax Media group. Fairfax sent selected journalists and photographers to the Games and shared stories and photographs across the newspapers (M. Donaldson, personal communication, 17 August 2005). At the 2004 Games, New Zealand women represented 45 per cent of the national team and won two of the country's five medals. They also won the first two medals of the Games; a gold by the rowers Caroline and Georgina Evers-Swindell in the women's double sculls, followed the next day by the cyclist Sarah Ulmer, who twice broke her own world record on the way to winning gold in the 3000 metre individual pursuit. In part because the newspaper coverage overwhelmingly focused on these three women, the analysis was limited to stories and images about them.

Mapping the articulations that lead to sportswomen's visibility

In the following sections I map some key articulations that appear to have led to the visibility of these three women at the 2004 Games. More specifically, I make the case that the opportunity for sportswomen to win space in the sports media is the result of a complex articulation of cultural forces relating to 1) tensions around strong women capable of success in a patriarchal society; 2) the strength of the articulation of sport to national identity, which is amplified by a national insecurity about New Zealand's place in the world; and 3) the continuing importance placed on values traditionally associated with the amateur model of sport such as self-sacrifice and humility. At the same time, I want to complicate the growing belief that such temporary visibility is linked, in any straightforward way, to nationalism. As Jorid Hovden points out, nationalism is always gendered, and feminist researchers should remain wary of falling into the trap of uncritically celebrating the increased coverage and visibility of female athletes during the Olympics (Hovden and Markula, 2007).

Tensions around gender equality

When considering how Olympic media coverage might articulate to discourses of gender, it is important to note the strength of the 'myth' of gender equality in New Zealand. New Zealand prides itself on being the first self-governing nation to give all women the vote and it has been led by consecutive female prime ministers for more than a decade. Other powerful political appointments such as the Queen's representative (the Governor-General), Minister of Finance and Attorney General have been held by women in recent years. New Zealand also has the lowest gender gap in median earnings for full-time workers among the OECD countries (Dixon, 2000; OECD, 2006). In this context, one might conclude there would be few barriers to the acceptance and celebration of female athletes who compete at any level, both within and beyond the borders of the nation. However, this real shift in power relations has engendered some backlash against women's political success and criticism of the apparent feminisation of the nation; a backlash which feminist researchers have argued may 'harm the terrain of gender relations in New Zealand' (Fountaine, 2005, p. 3). In addition, despite women's success in sport and the realms of political power, popular imaginings of the nation continue to be defined in masculine and Pakeha[1] terms (see Bell, 2003; Cosgrove and Bruce, 2005; Hokowhitu, 2004; Phillips, 1996). Since the emergence of New Zealand as a 'nation' in the mid-1800s, the nation and national character have been defined primarily through an idealised white masculinity. As Cooper (1999) has argued, New Zealanders equate 'masculinity with New Zealandness and New Zealandness with masculinity. ... The heroic ... is written in the masculine' (p. 97). In sport, although women have long enjoyed access to many kinds of physical recreation, they have also had to struggle 'against ideological beliefs defining sport as extremely highly valued male terrain' (Thompson, 2003, p. 253). For example, athletic women were not only directed into sports considered suitable for females (e.g. netball and field hockey) but also rejected and resisted when they expressed interest in sports strongly associated with masculinity (Thompson, 2003).

Although uncommon, the 2004 Olympics coverage revealed some examples of the broader cultural uncertainty around perceived female power. While most often presented by male sportswriters in tongue-in-cheek fashion, the way in which Olympic success and gender were mentioned suggests that female sporting success poses some kind of 'problem' for sport or, at the very least, for some males' understandings of normality within sport. For example, the media commentator Gordon McLauchlan described the women's gold medal success as having 'heaped humiliation on the ordinary Kiwi bloke already cringing with emotional and intellectual inferiority' (McLauchlan, 2004, np.). The journalist Tony Smith referred to an 'outbreak of "girl power" in Athens' (Smith, 2004b, p. 1). Another male journalist expressed relief when men finally won some medals: 'Things were getting a tad embarrassing for us blokes, with the female brigade leading the way in the medal hunt' (Hills, 2004, p. 15). Implicit in these comments are that men should – in the natural order of things – be leading the way in sport. In addition, the taken-for-granted nature of this articulation was recognised by a female letter writer in response to a letter mentioning only male athletes: 'I am saddened by the omission of the name of any female athlete. ... What is also sad is that this sexism is almost certainly unintended but is so ingrained as to be completely unwitting' (Lest we, 2004, p. 4).

Thus, although rare within overall coverage that embraced female success, these examples highlight tensions over changing gender relations in New Zealand society and point to contestations over who and what counts in sport.

Disrupting usual discourses of gender and sport

International research suggests that the gendered discourses are less prominent in media coverage of sportswomen whose success becomes articulated to national identity (Wensing and Bruce, 2003). In such cases, gender may not be the overriding signifier of identity and the articulation between 'female athlete' and 'discourses of femininity' may weaken significantly. Indeed, it appears that in order for female success to be articulated to nationalism, the more common forms of female representation must be set aside in favour of descriptions that are more usually associated with male athletes. In the 2004 Olympics coverage, newspapers seldom emphasised New Zealand women as sex objects, in heterosexual roles or via stereotypically feminine characteristics such as physical or emotional weakness. Only rarely were Ulmer or the Evers-Swindells described in ways that articulated with traditional conceptions of femininity such as being represented as 'pin-up girls', 'bubbly', 'effervescent' or 'blonde' or through a focus on appearance or family/relationships. Although this latter discourse did occur in the case of Ulmer's partner Brendan Cameron and Georgina Evers-Swindell's boyfriend Sam Earl, the men were often discussed in relation to their sporting connections to the athletes: Cameron as Ulmer's coach and Earl as an injured rower working in a support capacity for the New Zealand team. In only one other instance was heterosexuality addressed specifically, in quotes from an interview with the Evers-Swindells' father, who stated that his daughters began rowing 'because they thought it was a good way to meet boys' (McLoughlin, 2004, p. 1). Yet at the same time, a response in the *Southland Times* disrupted the usual power relations by suggesting it would be difficult to predict whether the rowers' success 'will prompt more girls to show up at rowing clubs or more boys hoping to draw the eye of athletes like the twins' (And didn't, 2004, p. 4).

Although such references – to family, to heterosexual relationships, emotions and appearance – have tended to be interpreted as examples of ambivalence or as reinforcing dominant ideologies about femininity, further analysis of coverage of all New Zealand's gold medallists suggests that the picture is more complex. New Zealand's only male gold medallist, the triathlete Hamish Carter, was represented in ways that, had they been written about a female, would fit neatly into notions of the feminine, such as emphasising a heterosexual identity, reliance on the opposite gender and focusing on displays of emotion. For example, several stories discussed how Carter took advice from his wife and Sarah Ulmer before the race. After winning, he was described as losing it, 'leaping, screaming and crying with joy', punching the air in delight and being so emotional he was unable to speak (Bingham, 2004; Carter finally, 2004; Cooper, 2004a, p. 24; Leggatt, 2004). Further, in an article discussing the post-Games marketing opportunities for medallists, Carter, Ulmer and the Evers-Swindells were described in substantially similar ways, with a focus on their good looks and personalities. Thus, a comparative approach which considered both male and female representations pointed towards more broadly circulating discourses that may transcend gender.

Articulating (women in) sport to national identity

In this section, I argue that the ability of female athletes to capture media space is strongly tied to the importance of sport in New Zealand's visions of itself. Although far from unique in its articulation of sport to nationalism, this linkage has greater resonance in New Zealand because sport is perceived to be one of the few areas of culture in which this small nation of four million people can shine on the world stage. As a result, patriotism is embedded in sporting discourse around international competition: 'nationalistic fervour and patriotic pride are taken for granted in all ... coverage of international sport' (Bassett, 1984, p. 19; see also Wensing, 2003, Wensing, Bruce and Pope, 2004). As one journalist wrote during the 2004 Games, 'Athens will be full of genuine champions – athletes who achieve Olympic honour purely through sacrifice and hard work. We'll applaud their successes – *and in the case of our own New Zealand team* – bask in the reflected glory' (Martin, 2004, p. 22, emphasis added).

In the 2004 Games, those meanings became strongly articulated to female athletes, and throughout the newspaper coverage Ulmer and the Evers-Swindells were represented as a credit to the nation. For example, 'The nation's hopes now ride ... on the broad shoulders of rowers Caroline and Georgina Evers-Swindell ... and in the fast-twitch fibres of Sarah Ulmer's legs' (Smith, 2004a, p. 3). After they won, another newspaper wrote: 'With captivating grace and potency, three young women have in recent days stood on the mountain top to join the pantheon of truly great sporting New Zealanders' (And didn't, 2004, p. 4).

While it could be argued that the highlighting of sport and national identity by the media, politicians and researchers does not necessarily reflect the broader public view, there exists a wide variety of expressions of popular support for sport which demonstrate the strength of this articulation. For example, New Zealanders not only ranked sport as the most important element of culture for their sense of national identity in a 1991 international survey, but were also first equal in the importance they gave to sport (Evans and Kelley, 2002). Government decisions to invest in New Zealand sporting teams are usually positively received, and athletes are regularly selected for reality television shows, often winning those in which public voting plays a role. Athletes have also dominated the annual *Readers' Digest* 'most trusted' survey, occupying almost 90 per cent of the top ten positions since 2004.

In relation to gender, a growing number of international studies over recent years have, implicitly if not explicitly, pointed to the importance of nationalism in disrupting gender narratives. Although women have not historically been seen as carriers of national identity, any athlete or team has the potential to become a symbol of nationalism (von der Lippe, 2003). During major events like the Olympics, the media tend to focus on athletes who represent the nation regardless of gender (e.g. Jorgensen, 2002; Wensing, 2003). For example, during the 2002 Commonwealth Games, New Zealand women received more photographs and stories than New Zealand men, leading Wensing (2003) to conclude that 'these figures indicate that media images of women in sport at this international event may be just as, if not more valued and interesting than those of men' (p. 67). Wensing attributed this extraordinary finding to the fact that New Zealand women won more medals than men. Winning appeared to be the key element in media interest: 'the most frequently photographed New Zealand athletes all won gold or silver medals' (Wensing, 2003, p. 95).

This trend was also evident during the 2004 Olympic Games, in which the three most photographed and discussed female athletes were Ulmer and the Evers-Swindells. They were regularly described in ways that reinforced a connection to winning, and the clichéd used of the term 'golden' was ever-present (e.g. 'golden girl', 'golden girls', 'our golden girls', 'Olympic golden girls'). Thus, during the Olympics, nationalistic fervour and pride appeared easily articulated to female athletes. The articulation of their wins to nationalism was widely evident, as journalists described the women's gold medals as 'the two that New Zealanders wanted most' (Finally some, 2004, p. 9), and claimed 'we shouted and applauded back home, and our hearts swelled with pride' (Anthem Stirs, 2004, p. 4; All eyes, 2004). Several articles highlighted the expectation that Ulmer's race was important enough for most people to make an effort to watch, with one article comparing her race to the sport most strongly articulated to national identity: 'A nation that once set its alarm clock to rise in the wee small hours to watch live television coverage of All Black rugby tests should be rolling out of the pit to see Ulmer's 3000m pursuit race at 2.45am on Monday' (Up against, 2004, p. 1). The media also highlighted quotes from members of the public, such as the mother of a male cyclist who described Ulmer's gold medal ride as 'awesome, electrifying and made you proud to be a Kiwi' (Treasured experience, 2004, p. 5). Along with the male gold medallist Hamish Carter, the women were described as having 'captured the hearts of a nation in winning gold' (Bidwell, 2004, p. 2). Both 'hardened hacks' and Ulmer's former coach were reported as being moved to tears by her race (Marshall, 2004; Smith, 2004c). Success was articulated as allowing the women to experience 'the same enduring fame as the past great champions' (All eyes, 2004, p. 10).

However, winners who can be articulated to discourses of nationalism must demonstrate characteristics that have historically been coded as masculine, such as power, strength, determination and physical and mental control. Thus, if Ulmer and the Evers-Swindells were to successfully be represented as national heroines, media descriptions would be expected to highlight such attributes. And indeed, this is what they did. All three women, and in particular Ulmer, were described in ways that emphasised physical power, strength and domination. These were evident in a wide range of descriptions of Ulmer's performances. Her dominance of the event was characterised by one journalist in the following way: 'Ulmer did not so much reclaim the record as grab it, pack it up and tell anyone who wanted it to go take a hike' (Smith, 2004b, p. 1). Terms such as scorching, crushing, blistering, slashing, sizzling, shattering, overpowering, incredible, sensational, phenomenal, staggering, shimmering, gobsmacking, brilliant, remarkable, exceptional, stunning, stirring and inspirational were used to describe her riding, world record and gold medal. She was represented as having slashed, blitzed, powered, smashed, conquered, carved up, crushed and thrashed her opponents, the record or the gold medal race. Ulmer herself was described as indomitable, a perfectionist, world class, cool and calculating, in absolute control, meticulous, composed, at the top of her game, relaxed and focused, and as having ridden virtually flawlessly. Although fewer in number, media discourses around the Evers-Swindell 'turbo twins' (Cleaver, 2004a, p. 1) followed a similar format. They were described as magnificent, confident, convincing, powering through, showing absolute commitment and competing with blinkered focus, cool heads and an intimidating aura. With 'even more

Teutonic efficiency than the fast-finishing Germans' (Cleaver, 2004b, p. 22), and their 'bodies and blades working in machine-like unison' (Cooper, 2004b, p. 1), they beat off 'a determined challenge' with 'their own sweat and determination' (McLoughlin, 2004, p. 1). The images that accompanied the stories were primarily representative of the athletes as winners, with medals, smiling, on the podium or immediately after the race. Many showed them in their black and silver uniform with the words New Zealand or the stylised silver fern design that is the acknowledged symbol of New Zealand's sporting teams. The headlines and captions that accompanied the photographs highlighted gold, glory, medals, winners and victory.

However, it is not just any woman who can avail herself of such visibility. Success alone is insufficient: 'Instead, it is the manner in which success is celebrated that plays an even larger role in whether or not an individual is taken up as representative of the nation' (Cosgrove and Bruce, 2005, p. 345). Ironically, the popularity and visibility of these New Zealand sportswomen may reflect their primarily amateur sport status which more easily permits an articulation to historically valued 'national' personality characteristics such as humility, modesty and sacrifice for the nation. Both Ulmer and the Evers-Swindells were represented as typical Kiwis – down-to-earth, modest, humble and reluctant to put themselves above others. This discourse was particularly evident in articles discussing the refusal of New Zealand's medallists to take up an airline offer to travel home in business class: 'Georgina Evers-Swindell may be an Olympic champion but she wasn't above sleeping on the floor of her plane on the way home ... [saying] it "wasn't fair" to the rest of the team' (Hopkins, 2004, p. 1; NZ medallists, 2004). Another article explained that all three women had 'made New Zealand proud' and showed 'they not only know how to win, but how success should be celebrated. They showed that pride and passion are part of the winning formula, but that winners can also show humility' (Finally some, 2004, p. 9). This trend towards valuing female athletes for their stronger connection to traditional sporting values is already apparent in the high number of female athletes, including Ulmer and the Evers-Swindells, who have appeared on recent annual *Readers' Digest* 'most trusted' surveys; a poll in which the most trusted individuals are seen as sharing 'the common trait of humility' (Sir Ed, 2005, para. 5).

Tensions over professional sport

Linked to the discourse of humility is the perceived accessibility of many female and Olympic athletes, who are seen as 'everyday' people who have to struggle along like the rest of us. New Zealand's small population means that many 'star' athletes live in 'our' towns, shop at 'our' supermarkets and hold down 'ordinary' jobs to fund their sporting aspirations (Harris and Monaghan, 2000). This perception is, however, increasingly less true for rugby union players since the sport turned professional in 1995. Over time, rugby has become articulated to discourses of individualism and self-interest which go against the traditional discourses around national character.

Thus, another articulation which may open up spaces for female visibility is New Zealand's uneasy relationship with professional sport (Phillips, 2000; Wensing et al., 2004). New Zealand has not made an easy transition to a commercialised and globalised sporting environment. Ongoing concerns about the 'effect' of professionalism on male rugby players' commitment to the nation are regularly expressed in the media via letters to the editor and calls to talkback radio (see Phillips, 2000), and demonstrate an unwillingness to give up historically 'amateur' notions of self-sacrifice and competing for something that is greater than the self (Wensing et al., 2004). As Phillips (2000) describes it:

> Many brought up with the old cultural expectations about sport have not found the revolution easy. The lure of money, the apparent rejection of local and patriotic sentiment, the acceptance of sport as a job and a business, the behaviour of extrovert stars who flaunt their sensational lifestyles rather than accept their responsibility as moral exemplars – all this comes hard to generations brought up in the old order. Hence the anger of the letter writers and columnists ...
>
> (p. 331)

Similarly, the shift of free-to-air live television coverage of rugby to subscription satellite television in the 1990s 'infuriated many pundits, fans, and politicians, and triggered pleas for legislation that protected live coverage of All Blacks test matches in the name of national interest' (Scherer, Falcous and Jackson, 2008, p. 53). In another example, the America's Cup sailor Russell Coutts, who left 'Team New Zealand' to lead a Swiss syndicate to victory in the 2003 America's Cup, was widely criticised and even received death threats for deserting the nation and putting financial considerations ahead of the nation, despite the reality that he was making an intelligent financial choice as a professional sailor (see Phillips, 2000; Wensing et al., 2004). Thus, being seen as sacrificing and competing *for* the nation is a key element in any athlete being able to win space in the media and public consciousness (Cosgrove and Bruce, 2005).

Conclusion

If we accept that the sports media, like sport itself, is a site where gender relations are not merely reflected but are accentuated, then all analyses of sports media can provide insights into the current state of gender relations. Further, if we accept that there is no necessary 'belonging-ness' between sport and masculinity, no matter how strong the linkage appears to be, then we can begin to consider moments or sites during which such articulations can be disrupted, however temporarily, in ways that allow subordinate groups such as sportswomen to win cultural space. In the twenty-first century, female athletes are carving out new spaces for themselves (Heywood and Dworkin, 2003; Thorpe, 2008). These spaces and the female subjectivities that accompany them may offer the possibilities for new articulations that substantially weaken the ideologies that have sustained male dominance of sport and the sports media.

Circling back to Stuart Hall's question of under which circumstances particular articulations can occur, this analysis suggests that the histori-cally potent linkage between sport and masculinity may weaken when the success of female athletes can be articulated to changing understand-ings of gender, including significant shifts in sporting girl culture (see Heywood and Dworkin, 2003; Thorpe, 2008), and to the nationalistic project. Further, if sportswomen can take advantage of their primarily amateur or semi-professional status to mobilise a public and media already uncomfortable with rugby's shift away from valued traditional sporting values, the spaces for coverage also open up. While taking heed of Jorid Hovden's warning that feminist researchers should remain wary of uncritically celebrating increased coverage during the Olympic Games, it seems clear that analysing the specific conjuncture under which the usual subordination of female athletes was overturned provides impor-tant insights into a series of articulations that might prove fruitful for future political strategies aimed at changing the routine practices of sports journalists.

Note

1. Pakeha is an indigenous Maori term used to describe New Zealanders of non-Maori heritage, primarily those of British or European white heritage. At the time of the Olympics, the country was dominated by Pakeha (approximately 80 per cent of the population), followed by indigenous Maori (approximately 15 per cent) and growing numbers of citizens of Pacific and Asian heritage (Demographic Trends, 2005).

References

All eyes on Athens (2004). *Christchurch Press*, 14 August, p. 10.

And didn't it feel good (2004). *Southland Times*, 24 August, p. 4.

Anthem stirs the heart. (2004). *Timaru Herald*, 24 August, p. 4.

Bassett, G. (1984). Screen-play and real-play: Manufacturing sport on television. *Sites*, 9, 5–31.

Bell, C. (2004). Kiwiana revisited. In C. Bell and S. Matthewman (eds.), *Cultural Studies in Aotearoa New Zealand: Identity, Space and Place* (pp. 175–87). South Melbourne, Victoria: Oxford University Press.

Bell, M. (2003). 'Another kind of life': Adventure racing and epic adventures. In R. Rinehart and S. Sydnor (eds.), *To the Extreme: Alternative Sports, Inside and Out* (pp. 219–53). Albany, NY: SUNY Press.

Bennett, T. (1982). Theories of media, theories of society. In. M. Gurevitch, T. Bennett, J. Curran and J. Woollacott (eds.), *Culture, Society and the Media*. London: Methuen.

Bidwell, P. (2004). Some NZ sports still need work. *Dominion Post*, 3 September, p. 2.

Bingham, E. (2004). Triathlon: This is all I ever wanted, says champ. *New Zealand Herald*, 27 August, np.

Bordo, S. (1990). Feminism, postmodernism, and gender-scepticism. In L. J. Nicholson (ed.), *Feminism/Postmodernism* (pp. 133–56). New York: Routledge.

Bruce, T. (2008). Women, sport and the media: A complex terrain. In C. Obel and T. Bruce and S. Thompson (eds.), *Outstanding: Research about Women and Sport in New Zealand*. Hamilton: Wilf Malcolm Institute for Educational Research.

Bruce, T. (1998). Audience resistance: Women fans confront televised women's basketball. *Journal of Sport and Social Issues*, 22(4), 373–97.

Bruce, T., Falcous, M. and Thorpe, H. (2007). The mass media and sport. In C. Collins and S. Jackson (eds.). *Sport in Aotearoa/New Zealand Society*, 2nd edition (pp. 147–69). Auckland: Thomson.

Brunsdon, C. (1996). A thief in the night: Stories of feminism in the 1970s at CCCS. In D. Morley and K-H. Chen (eds.), *Stuart Hall: Critical Dialogues in Cultural Studies* (pp. 276–86). London: Routledge.

Cameron, J. and Kerr, R. (2007). The issue of women in sport: 'No bloody room for sheilas'. In C. Collins and S. Jackson (eds.), *Sport in Aotearoa/New Zealand Society* (pp. 335–54). Auckland: Thomson.

Carter finally gets his gold. (2004). *Dominion Post*, 27 August, p. 12.

Cleaver, D. (2004a). Turbo twins lead from go to whoa! *Sunday Star Times*, 22 August, p. 1.

Cleaver, D. (2004b). Marvels and misfits. *Sunday Star Times*, 29 August, p. 22.

Cooper, A. (1999). Nation of heroes, nation of men: Masculinity in Maurice Shadbolt's *Once on Chanuk Bair*. In R. Law, H. Campbell and J. Dolan (eds.), *Masculinities in Aotearoa/New Zealand* (pp. 84–103). Palmerston North: Dunmore Press.

Cooper, T. (2004a). Quinella the perfect result. *Waikato Times*, 27 August, p. 24.

Cooper, T. (2004b). Ulmer triumphs in sizzling ride. *Southland Times*, 23 August, p. 1.

Cosgrove, A. and Bruce, T. (2005). 'The way New Zealanders would like to see themselves': Reading white masculinity via media coverage of the death of Sir Peter Blake. *Sociology of Sport Journal*, 22, 336–55.

Demographic Trends 2004 (2005). *Statistics New Zealand/Te Tari Tatau,* Wellington, New Zealand.

Denzin, N. K. (1996). More rare air: Michael Jordan on Michael Jordan. *Sociology of Sport Journal,* 13, 319–42.

Denzin, N. K. (1991). *Images of Postmodern Society: Social Theory and Contemporary Cinema.* London: Sage.

Dixon, S. (2000). Pay inequality between men and women in New Zealand. *Occasional Paper 2000/1.* Wellington: New Zealand Department of Labour, Labour Market Policy Group. http://www.dol.govt.nz/PDFs/op2000-1main.pdf. Accessed 29 March 2007.

Duncan, M. C., Messner, M. A. and Willms, N. (2005). *Gender in Televised Sports: News and Highlights Shows, 1989–2004.* Los Angeles: Amateur Athletic Foundation of Los Angeles.

Evans, M. D. R. and Kelley, J. (2002). National pride in the developed world: Survey data from 24 nations. *International Journal of Public Opinion Research,* 14(3), 303–38.

Ferkins. L. R. (1992). New Zealand Women in Sport: An Untapped Media Resource. Unpublished MA thesis. Wellington: Victoria University of Wellington.

Finally some gold (2004). *Nelson Mail,* 23 August, p. 9.

Fountaine, S. (2005). Who's the boss? The girl power frame in New Zealand newspapers. *Occasional Paper 11.* Belfast: Queen's University Centre for Advancement of Women in Politics.

Fountaine, S. and McGregor, J. (1999). The loneliness of the long distance gender researcher: Are journalists right about the coverage of women's sport? *Australian Journalism Review,* 21(3), 113–26.

Franklin, S., Lury, C. and Stacey, J. (1991). *Off-centre: Feminism and Cultural Studies.* New York: HarperCollinsAcademic.

Grossberg, L. (1996). On postmodernism and articulation: An interview with Stuart Hall. In D. Morley and K-H. Chen (eds.), *Stuart Hall: Critical Dialogues in Cultural Studies* (pp. 131–50). London: Routledge.

Hall, S. (1980). Cultural studies and the Centre: Some problematics and problems. In S. Hall, D. Hobson, A. Love and P. Willis (eds.), *Culture, Media, Language* (pp. 15–47). London: Hutchinson.

Hall, S. (1984). The narrative construction of reality. *Southern Review,* 17, 3–17.

Hall, S. (1995). The whites of their eyes: Racist ideologies and the media. In G. Dines and J. M. Humer (eds.), *Gender, Race and Class in Media: A Text-reader* (pp. 18–22). Thousand Oaks, CA: Sage.

Hall, S. (1996). Cultural studies and its theoretical legacies. In D. Morley and K-H. Chen (eds.), *Stuart Hall: Critical Dialogues in Cultural Studies* (pp. 262–75). London: Routledge.

Harris, J. and Monaghan, J. (producers) (2000). *The Price of Fame* (documentary). Auckland: Greenstone Pictures Limited.

Heywood, L. and Dworkin, S. L. (2003). *Built to Win: The Female Athlete as Cultural Icon.* Minneapolis: University of Minnesota Press.

Hills, M. (2004). Saved from being up a creek without a paddle. *Taranaki Daily News,* 28 August, p. 15.

Hokowhitu, B. (2004). Tackling Maori masculinity: A colonial genealogy of savagery and sport. *The Contemporary Pacific,* 16(2), Autumn, 259–84.

Hopkins, S. (2004). Medallists in class of their own, *Waikato Times,* 1 September, p. 1.

Hovden, J. and Markula, P. (2007). *Sari and Siren: Gender and National Identity in Women's Sailing*. Paper presented at the International Sociology of Sport Association annual conference, July, Copenhagen.

Jorgensen, S. S. (2002). Sports journalism favours stars, is uncritical of financial interests, trans. S. Watts. *Monday Morning* (special print: Industry or Independence? Survey of the Scandinavian Sports Press), November, pp. 1–8.

Knoppers, A. and Elling, A. (2004). 'We do not engage in promotional journalism': Discursive strategies used by sport journalists to describe the selection process. *International Review for the Sociology of Sport*, 39(1), 57–73.

Leggatt, D. (2004). Triathlon: Veteran Carter leads Docherty to double Olympic glory. *New Zealand Herald*, 27 August, np.

Lest we forget the women (2004). Letters to the Editor. *Dominion Post*, 1 September, p. 4.

Lowes, M. D. (1999). *Inside the Sports Pages: Work Routines, Professional Ideologies, and the Manufacture of Sports News*. Toronto: University of Toronto Press.

Mac an Ghaill, M. and Haywood, C. (2007). *Gender, Culture and Society: Contemporary Femininities and Masculinities*. Basingstoke: Palgrave Macmillan.

Martin, W. (2004). Kenyan boxer suffers TKO without throwing a punch. *The Nelson Mail*, 14 August, p. 22.

McGregor, J. (2000). The mass media and sport. In C. Collins (ed.), *Sport in New Zealand Society* (pp. 187–200). Palmerston North: Dunmore Press.

McKee, A. (2001). A beginner's guide to textual analysis. *Metro, 127/128*, 138–49.

McLauchlan, G. (2004). Shopping is for the birds. *New Zealand Herald*, 28 August, np.

McLoughlin, D. (2004). It's been their life, says dad. *Dominion Post*, 23 August, p. 1.

McRobbie, A. (1997). The Es and the Anti-Es: New questions for feminism and cultural studies. In M. Ferguson and P. Golding (eds.), *Cultural Studies in Question* (pp. 170–86). London: Sage.

McRobbie, A. (1978). Working-class girls and the culture of femininity. In Women's Studies Group, Centre for Contemporary Cultural Studies, *Women Take Issue*. London: Hutchinson.

Marshall, J. (2004). Old coach moved to tears. *Christchurch Press*, 24 August, p. 11.

Modleski, T. (1984). *Loving with a Vengeance*. London: Methuen.

Morley, D. (1980). *The Nationwide Audience: Structure and Decoding*. London: BFI Monograph 11.

NZ medallists decline business-class offer (2004). *Christchurch Press*, 31 August, p. 2.

OECD (2006). *Women and Men in OECD Countries*. Paris: Organisation for Economic Co-operation and Development Publications. http://www.oecd.org/dataoecd/45/37/37964069.pdf. Accessed 29 March 2007.

Parameswaran, R. (2005). Journalism and feminist cultural studies: Retrieving the missing citizen lost in the female audience. *Popular Communication*, 3(3), 195–207.

Phillips, J. (1996). *A Man's Country? The Image of the Pakeha Male – A History*, 2nd edition. Auckland: Penguin Books.

Phillips, J. (2000). Epilogue: Sport and future Australasian culture. In J. A. Mangan and J. Nauright (eds.), *Sport in Australasian Society: Past and Present* (pp. 323–32). London: Frank Cass.

Pollock, G. (2003). Becoming cultural studies: The daydream of the political. In. P. Bowman (ed.), *Interrogating Cultural Studies: Theory, Politics and Practice* (pp. 125–41). London: Pluto Press.

Proctor, J. (2004). *Stuart Hall*. Routledge Critical Thinkers. London: Routledge.

Radway, J. A. (1984). *Reading the Romance: Women, Patriarchy, and Popular Literature*. Chapel Hill, NC: University of North Carolina.

Scherer, J., Falcous, M. and Jackson, S. (2008). The media sports cultural complex: Local–global disjuncture in New Zealand/Aotearoa. *Journal of Sport & Social Issues*, 32(1), 48–71.

Seib, P. M. (ed.) (2002). *Winning and Losing: The Ethics of Sports Journalism*. Milwaukee, WI: Marquette University.

Sir Ed tops NZ's most trusted list (2005). *One News: National*. Television New Zealand, 1 July, Available: http://tvnz.co.nz/view/page/423466/595189.

Smith, T. (2004a). Maybe medals will come our way ... for best moaning. *Christchurch Press*, 19 August, p. 3.

Smith, T. (2004b). No headline. *Christchurch Press*, 23 August, p. 1.

Smith, T. (2004c). 'Cambridge cyclone' gets tears flowing. *Waikato Times*, 24 August, p. 28.

Star, L. (1992). Undying love, resisting pleasures: Women watch telerugby. In R. DuPlessis (ed.), *Feminist Voices: Women's Studies Texts for Aotearoa/ New Zealand* (pp. 124–40). Auckland: Oxford University Press.

Thompson, S. M. (2003). Women and sport in New Zealand. In I. Hartmann-Tews and G. Pfister (eds.), *Sport and Women: Social Issues in International Perspective* (pp. 252–65). London: Routledge.

Thorpe, H. (2008). Feminism for a new generation: A case study of women in the snowboarding culture. In C. Obel, T. Bruce and S. Thompson (eds.), *Outstanding: Research about Women and Sport in New Zealand* (pp. 7–30). Hamilton: Wilf Malcolm Institute for Educational Research.

Treasured experience for Ryans (2004). *Timaru Herald*, 4 September, p. 5.

Turner, G. (1997). Media texts and messages. In S. Cunningham and G. Turner (eds.) *The Media in Australia: Industries, Texts, Audiences*, 2nd edition (pp. 381–93). St Leonards, NSW: Allen & Unwin.

Up against the world. (2004). *Dominion Post*, 21 August, p. 1.

Von der Lippe, G. (2003). Media images: Sport, gender and national identities in five European countries. *International Review for the Sociology of Sport*, 37(3/4), 351–70.

Wensing, E. H. (2003). Print Media Constructions of New Zealand National Identity at the 2002 Commonwealth Games. Unpublished MA thesis, School of Education, University of Waikato, Hamilton.

Wensing, E. H. and Bruce, T. (2003). Bending the rules: Media representations of gender during an international sporting event. *International Review for the Sociology of Sport*, 38(4), 387–96.

Wensing, E. H., Bruce, T. and Pope, C. (2004). Playing to win or trying your best: Media representations of national anxieties over the role of sport participation during the 2002 Commonwealth Games. *Waikato Journal of Education*, 10, 203–19.

Zelizer, B. (2004). When facts, truth, and reality are God-terms: On journalism's uneasy place in cultural studies. *Communication and Critical/Cultural Studies*, 1(1), 100–19.

9
Heroes, Sisters and Beauties: Korean Printed Media Representation of Sport Women in the 2004 Olympics

Eunha Koh

This chapter examines how sportswomen were represented in a Korean newspaper, *Donga Ilbo*, during the 2004 Olympic Games in Athens. To locate this discussion within a cultural context, a brief introduction to the media's role in Korean society is provided. Second, previous feminist research regarding sports media reports in Korea is presented. Finally, before embarking on the ideological content of the newspaper representation, the method is detailed.

Sport, media and Korean society

Modern sports were first introduced in Korea at the beginning of twentieth century after the the nation's gate to the world were first opened in 1876 (Na, 2001). After the establishment of the Korean government in 1948 and the end of the Korean War in 1953, the South Korean government concentrated on re-establishing physical education in schools with the assistance from the United States. Competitive sport also began to develop at the national level. Media coverage of sports during this period was in an incipient stage and the technology used by the printed and broadcasting media was elementary.

The full development of Korean sports at the national level took place in the 1960s when sports began to serve a role in Korean politics. The regime of President Chung-hee Park in the 1960s and the 1970s was characterised by national reconstruction, economic development and modernisation. A strong sports policy was first set up to unify the nation, to spread the nation's resolve abroad and to confirm the legitimacy of the ruling political power. During this period, the mass media, by publishing or releasing sports reports, often served as a means to reinforce nationalism and thus to confirm the legitimation of the authoritarian government. Victories at international sport competitions, such as professional wrestling and professional boxing, international sports championships and the Olympics were covered extensively while the country was under reconstruction following the Korean War. This was during the Cold War when victory in sport was often regarded as a way of proving national superiority (Koh, 2004; Korea Sports Council, 1990). Two other military regimes, led by Jun Doo-hwan Jun and Tae-woo Roh, continued to give strong support to sport in the 1980s and created the basis for South Korea's current sports policy. In addition, the 1988 Seoul Olympic Games, which are often mentioned as the watershed in the history of Korean sport, and the launch of professional sports leagues, such as the Korean professional soccer league (now known as the K-League) and Korean professional base-ball league, triggered a sharp growth in Korean sport (Ha and Mangan, 2003).

Throughout the 1980s and 1990s, both participation in and specta-torship of sporting events diversified due to increased leisure time and the consequent demand for daily sports activities. At the same time, Korea has become a strong player in world sports, ranking in the medal tables of the Summer Olympics and gaining success in interna-tional championships in several sports. In addition, Korea has been awarded further international mega-sport events such as 2002 FIFA Soccer World Cup and 2011 IAAF World Athletics Championships. Although the recent growth of Korean sports has been influenced by a combination of sociocultural factors and the effective promotion of sports, the mass media have performed a pivotal role in bringing sport to people's daily lives as well as in gaining world recognition for Korean sport. Broadcasting international sporting events, in which Korean athletes featured with the national flag on their uniforms, the mass media not only reinforced nationalism but introduced postwar Korea to the world.

Women's sports in the Korean media

Feminist researchers from such fields as sports sociology and media research have focused on how ideologies such as sexism, racism and nationalism are reproduced through print media. In Korea research on sport media reports from a feminist perspective began in earnest in the mid-1990s. For example, Kim (1998) and Kim and Koh (2004) compared the level of news coverage by gender. Analyses of gender bias in media text and picture images of women's sports include Koh and Kim (2004) Lee and Kim (1996), Nam (2004) and Nam and Kim (2003). Many of these analyses focused on international tournaments, such as the summer Olympics. Few studies involve longitudinal research that includes an Olympic period and a non-Olympic period. However, according to these studies, news coverage of women's sports by daily newspapers in Korea has steadily increased, yet remains male-oriented.

Kim and Koh (2004) compared the number of pictures of men and women athletes in Korean daily newspapers from 1948, when the Korean government was established, to 2003. They found that there were fewer pictures of women's sports than of men's sports in all periods, but the gap between the two narrowed over time. There were almost no pictures of women's sports until the 1950s. However, the number of pictures increased to 10.13 per cent (pictures of men's sports accounted for 61.29 per cent) in the 1960s and to 22.90 per cent (pictures of men's sports accounted for 68.49 per cent) in the 2000s. According to Koh (2008), articles and pictures depicting women's sports during the 2004 Athens Olympics accounted for 15.6 per cent and 25.3 per cent, respectively. Nam (2004), in a study conducted during the 2003 Daegu Summer Universiade, showed that five major Korean dailies allocated 36.5 per cent to 41.7 per cent of Universiade-related photo space to women's sports while men's sports and mixed-gender photos took 42 per cent to 57.3 per cent and 3.4 per cent to 18 per cent of the space, respectively. Meanwhile, another South Korean study conducted during one year of a non-mega event period (Cho and Cho, 1998) showed that two major Korean dailies which were included in Nam's (2004) study posted only 19.9 per cent and 20.1 per cent of women's sport photos while men's sport photos were 80.1 per cent and 79.9 per cent of total photo numbers.

In a recent study Koh (2008) found that the sports receiving the most media attention were soccer (24 photographs, 32 articles) followed by archery (23 images, 32 articles) and judo (22 images, 28 articles). Marathon (19), table tennis and track and field (18), artistic gymnastics (15), swimming (12) and badminton, shooting, weightlifting and taekwondo (10 each) were also strongly represented. During the 2004 Athens Olympics, Korea won a total of 30 medals, including nine gold medals. Female athletes brought home a total of 12 medals, including three gold, five silver and four bronze. A considerable number of news articles and pictures of the Olympics focused on sports where Korean athletes won medals. Track and field, swimming and gymnastics were also frequently covered by the media during the Olympics. On the other hand, Lee and Kim (1996), Koh and Kim (2004), Nam (2004) and Nam and Kim (2003) revealed how the South Korean media reinforce gender stereotypes and further confirm gender difference in Korean society. Like many other countries in Korea there is an increase in the number of newspaper reports on women's sports during the Olympics. Kim and Koh (2004) state that the sharp, temporary rise in the level of news coverage of women's sports during major sporting events like the Olympics derives from nationalism rather than the advancement of women's sports or changes in the media's attitude. In other words, while sports reports normally focus on men's sports – especially professional men's sports – during major sports events athletes who are likely to win medals will receive coverage regardless of their gender.[1]

Method

The mass media influence how we structure the world we live in. Newspaper pictures, in particular, have a strong visual impact that can capture the readers' immediate attention (Hartley, 1992). Sports reports are commonly accompanied by many pictures and the reader learns how to understand and interpret sports as well as society as a whole according to how mass media 'shows the content'. Therefore, analysing sports media reports and pictures can be an extremely effective way of understanding the ideologies that dominate a specific society.

There are nine daily newspapers and five sporting newspapers with nationwide distribution in South Korea.[2] Of the so-called three major dailies published in South Korea (Korean Association of Newspapers, 2008), *Donga Ilbo* (*Donga Daily*) was chosen for analysis.[3] The period of analysis were the 27 days from 7 August to 8 September 2004, which started six days prior to the opening ceremony and ended seven days after the closing ceremony of the 2004 Athens Olympics, excluding Sundays, when the daily was not published.

The data were analysed thematically. The first step was data selection: 373 articles and 345 images were selected as Olympic articles and images out of 550 articles and 415 images. Then articles and images of non-human subjects, such as pictures of facilities or scenery that did not include people or an article on doping, were excluded from the analysis. A total of 291 articles and 287 images were chosen for analysis. During the second step data were coded using an MS Excel program. The data were numbered according to the order of dates and coded with title, sport, gender, nationality, article/image location (e.g. front page, sports page) and position (on the page).

The final step was data categorisation and analysis. The Excel table constructed in the second step was used to extract ideologies from the materials. A comprehensive consideration was given to the location of the articles or images, roles of captions, relationships of pictures and relevant articles, and relevance to surrounding articles or pictures. In detail, an upper or central position for pictures was considered to be of more importance. Whether the captions matched the pictures was considered carefully: was the article relevant and if so, what was its relevance to the picture. In addition, the article or picture size, location and image in comparison to surrounding articles and pictures were examined.

In order to minimise potential errors during the coding, categorisation and analysis of data, observer triangulation and peer review methods (Padgett, 2001) were used. Two research assistants participated in the entire data analysis process and the results of the study were reviewed by two researchers working in the field of sociology of sport.

It was found that the coverage of 2004 Athens Olympics by *Donga Ilbo* confirms and reinforces nationalism and sexism in Korean sports and society. In what follows I discuss nationalism and the marginalisation, trivialisation and sexualisation of female sporting bodies in detail.

Medals, tears and heroes: confirmation of nationalism and gender difference

Parallel to the previous findings (Kim and Koh, 2004) Korean athletes who won a gold or silver medal were put in the media spotlight in *Donga Ilbo* during the Olympics. The public praised them for their heroic performances after news reports detailed the competitions in which the athletes participated and their lives as athletes. The male medal winners were commonly pictured performing their sport with great force and energy. These pictures were located in key spots and were accompanied by related articles and smaller pictures of the athletes wearing a medal around their neck. In contrast, where female medal winners were pictured wearing a medal the accompanying photos and articles emphasised their emotionality: they were pictured shedding tears of joy rather than playing their sports. In other words, all Korean athletes who won a medal became subjects of major news reports regardless of their gender, but the focus of the coverage was different. The outstanding performance of male athletes during the competition and winning a medal for the nation were highlighted. In contrast, news reports of the female athletes first emphasised their achievement in winning a medal, but then focused on the athletes' emotions. One exception was a picture of the archer Park Seong-hyeon, a gold medalist, aiming at the target, which took up more than half a page. However, half of the picture was overlapped with a close-up of the athlete's face which somewhat negated the dynamic image of her performance.

As an example, I contrast four pictures of two Korean athletes, who won a silver and a gold medal respectively. The first picture was included in an article dated 23 August which took up more than a half a page in the sports section. This picture had no separate title, just a caption which read: 'Jang Mi-ran, who won the silver medal during the women's 75 kg plus weightlifting, looks disappointed as she waves her hand'. This picture was placed next to another picture of her rejoicing as she anticipated a gold after successfully lifting 172.5 kg in her third attempt in the clean and jerk. In contrast, the full-page article titled 'Winning the gold with octopus-like defensive skills' on the athlete Jeong Ji-hyeon, who won the gold in the 60 kg Greco-Roman wrestling, had a big, dynamic picture of him performing, headed by the caption: 'I continued the flow of gold medals'. The picture was surrounded by relevant articles. In the centre of the second half of the article was a small picture of Jeong biting his gold medal.

Reports that depicted women and men competing in the same sports (e.g. taekwondo) were characterised as displaying similar tendencies. The pictures of the taekwondo women's gold medalists Jang Ji-won and men's gold medalist Moon Dae-sung circling the competition venue holding the Korean national flag after winning appeared in the upper section of a page of *Donga Ilbo* (28 August and 30 August, respectively). The titles of the related articles read: 'Jang Ji-won gives "a golden kick" taekwondo' and 'Moon Dae-sung wins the medal with a knock out'. Both pictures, however, were titled 'Pride of the nation of origin', confirming the strong nationalistic characteristic for reporting mega-sport events in Korea. Although for Koreans taekwondo is a traditional martial arts rather than a modern Olympic sport, the detailed reports on the sports pages clearly demonstrated gender differences. An article about Moon Dae-sung's victory ('Taekwon V ends the match with one strong kick')[4] starts with details of how Moon won the match by knocking out his opponent, Nikolaidis of Greece, who is 8 cm taller than Moon. The article ends with a comprehensive analysis of Korea's strength in taekwondo. In addition, more than half the article, which was half a page long, was occupied by a picture of Moon delivering the kick that won him the gold.

In contrast, an article on Jang Ji-won (' "Taekwon lady" mines the vein of gold') described her as 'a tenderhearted lady' despite her strength as a taekwondo athlete. The article focused on Jang's story of winning the gold as a result of four years of strenuous effort after failing to qualify in the trials for the 2000 Sydney Olympics. In the picture that illustrated the middle of the article the athlete was shown being embraced by her coach, not performing or celebrating her win. The short article that accompanied the main article was headed: 'Finally she becomes the "Taekwon Queen" after washing away the "tears of Sydney" '. The report further emphasised Jang Ji-won's emotionality, an issue which I elaborate in the next section:

> She had to wait patiently for four years for something that happened only in ten seconds. She promised herself that she would not cry again, but she couldn't help it after achieving what she had so earnestly hoped for. She is a heroine whose left spin kick can make even a big, healthy man faint. But she is still a woman full of emotions. That's why they call her the 'Taekwon lady'.
>
> (Donga Ilbo, 28 August 2004)

The articles covering the 2004 Athens Olympics focused on the victorious Korean athletes to create a sense of nationalism. This is where sport successfully supports the celebration of the 'love of nation' (Appadurai, 2000, p. 130). However, at the same time the focus on nationalism resulted in gendered representations of sports and athletes. News reports focused on male athletes' performance during the finals, while they exposed female athletes' emotions hidden behind the image of a strong athlete. This outcome supports the results of earlier studies in which, in the case of international sports events, such as the Olympics, emphasis is placed on medal-winning athletes, who then come to symbolise the nation (e.g. Borcila, 2000; Bruce and Hallinan, 2001; Eastman and Billings, 1999; Wensing and Bruce, 2003). However, these findings echo earlier findings of the trivialisation and marginalisation of women athletes in the media which highlight the feminine and everyday activity-related aspects of sport women's lives (Creedon, 1998; Duncan, 1990; Jones, Murrell and Jackson, 1999; Kane and Greendorfer, 1994; Lumpkin and Williams, 1991). The following section looks more closely at the marginalisation and feminisation of women athletes.

Emotional women: the marginalisation and feminisation of women athletes

As discussed earlier, the news reports on the Athens Olympics emphasised 'women's tears'. Women athletes who won a medal as well as those who failed to do so were pictured shedding tears, accompanied by words of encouragement telling the athletes not to cry. For example, an article on Jang Mi-ran, a silver medalist in weightlifting, was headed 'Don't cry Mi-ran. Your silver is as beautiful as gold' (23 August 2004).

An article titled 'Don't forget your tears and don't lose hope' (16 August 2004) focused on emotional stories about athletes who were expected to win a medal, but failed to do so, with a large picture captioned: 'Your tears are beautiful because you did your best'. The article included Seo Seon-hwa, who failed to reach the finals of the women's 10 m shooting; Jo Seong-min, who failed to make it to the finals in the men's parallel bars in gymnastics; Lee Eun-hui, who lost during the second round of the women's 52 kg judo; Kim Hui-jeong, who did not make it to the final eight in the women's fencing epee; and Bang Gui-man, who failed in the first round of men's 66 kg judo. However, all of the pictures were of female athletes crying after losing.

I mentioned Moon Dae-sung, who won the gold in men's taekwondo, earlier in my chapter (30 August 2004). Below the article featuring him was a report of the women's handball team, which won a silver medal. This article ('Beautiful match, even though we lost') begins with a description of how the women handball players shed tears of disappointment after losing the game. This came before an analysis of the game during which the Korean team lost after twice going into extra time. While it might be pointed out that the silver medal is excessively under-valued compared to the gold, the difference between the two was not what was emphasised here. Instead, the focus was on the women players showing their weakness by crying after losing. An accompanying picture showed Heo Soon-yeong in tears while hugging another player, Oh Seong-ok, and was titled 'Don't cry. It's all right'. The accompanying article described the players' feelings:

> They tried to stop the tears, but just couldn't. They tried harder, but we felt worse ... Oh Seong-ok, a married player, taps the shoulders of Heo Soon-yeong, saying, 'Don't cry.' The eyes of Oh are filled with tears too.
> (*Donga Ilbo*, 30 August 2004)

As the article reveals, some of the players were married. I return to this point later in this section.

Both foreign and Korean women athletes were pictured in tears. Many foreign athletes were depicted crying in pictures without specific captions, titles or related articles. For example, the pictures of Melania Grego, a member of the Hungarian team which lost to the Italian team in the women's water polo semi-finals, the Swedish soccer players who lost to Brazil in the women's soccer semi-finals, and Paula Radcliffe, the British world record holder in the women's marathon, who abandoned the race due to heat stress, were all posted on the same sports page of *Donga Ilbo* (25 August 2004) in tears after their unsuccessful performances.

Another means of marginalisation and feminisation of women athletes is to refer frequently to their roles as mothers or wives. In this context, women athletes were often called by the Korean media 'umuni/umma' (mother), 'unni' (older sister to a woman), 'noona' (older sister to a man) or 'ajumma' (a married woman or woman old enough to get married, but which has negative connotations). For example, an article about the women's gold medal winning archery team was titled 'Unni [the older sisters] were brave' (22 August 2004), whereas an article on the men's archery team winning the gold was titled 'Men's archery team hit's the bull's eye for two consecutive matches' (23 August 2004). This demonstrated a clear gender difference when gold-winning performances were reported on the same event. Similarly, the descriptions 'Taekwon V' and 'Taekwon lady', used to describe the taekwondo gold medalists, mentioned in the previous section, can be understood in the same context. Even articles that covered both male and female athletes showed such a tendency. An article on the men's judo 60 kg athlete Choi Min-ho and the women's judo 63 kg athlete Lee Bok-hui training in Greece before the opening of the Olympics was accompanied by a picture of the athletes using the sparring technique (August 11, 2004). The title of the article was 'Take it easy, noona [older sister]'. Although the article was about male and female judo athletes in a similar weight category training together, it seemed to make fun of the strong, female judo athlete, who was effectively pushing Choi down and attacking him. Another article presented the handball player Lee Sang-eun on her return to Korea after the Athens Olympics. In a picture caption, Lee was introduced as a ' "tough heroine" who has returned to her tender character' after coming back home. Lee, who was one of the key players bringing the silver medal to Korea, is described as a good daughter at home. The article added that four members of the Korean handball team were married and two had children. The team was referred to as the 'ajumma team':

> Our national team was an ajumma team. Four of the players are married: Oh Yeong-ran (aged 33), Heo Yeong-sook (29), Im Oh-gyeong (34), and Oh Seong-ok (33). Im and Oh are even mothers. Despite this fact, they showed what they have until the very end. Where do they get their strength from?
>
> *(Donga Ilbo, 2 September 2004)*

An American athlete, Susan Williams, who won the bronze medal in the Triathlon, was introduced with a similar theme. A picture of her was titled 'Mom, you did a great job'. Triathlon is not a popular sport in Korea; nor is this athlete well known in the nation. This athlete didn't win the gold, either. A picture of her on the winner's podium, hugging her daughter, was posted to emphasise that a woman athlete is a mother before she is an athlete.

As well as this strong focus on women athletes' feminine characteristics or their roles at home, they were also described as strong and determined. In an article titled 'Second Kiss', Lee Bo-na kisses her silver medal on the winner's podium with a big smile on her face. She won the silver in the double trap shooting after winning a bronze in trap shooting. This picture was published together with an article headed 'Heart of a woman soldier fights and wins against the strong winds of the Athens'. Located in the central upper half of the sports page (19 August 2004), the article described and evaluated the competition during which Lee Bo-na gave an outstanding performance despite the strong winds. However, when the article stressed that Lee was an army sergeant, it praised her performance as a military officer, not as a woman. Because the military or military personnel can be used as a symbol for a nation and patriotism, the emphasis of her occupation contrasts with the feminisation of other women athletes.

Beauties in the sport pages: the sexualisation of female sporting bodies

The women's sports that received the most photo coverage during the Athens Olympics in *Donga Ilbo* were archery and track and field, followed by swimming and the marathon. Previous studies have noted the higher percentage of archery photos in Korean Olympic coverage due to the success of Korea's women's archery team (Koh, 2008; Kim and Koh, 2004). However, pictures that emphasised the 'sex appeal' of the female body could also be found in this Olympic coverage. The sexualisation of the female body was most evident in beach volleyball (see also Koh and Kim, 2004). Without exception, beach volleyball pictures appeared without an accompanying article; examples of captions for such pictures included: 'Let's try to look at the ball' (20 August 2004), 'Olympics is fun' (20 August 2004) and 'Too hot' (13 August 2004). The focus was on the bodies of the players, who wore revealing clothing. For example, one player was pictured putting sun cream on the other. Synchronised swimming photos also focused on the female swimmers' appearance, although their bodies were not highlighted as much as the bodies of the beach volleyball players. In fact, one caption referred to judges and spectators becoming distracted by the swimmers' beauty. It is clear that these pictures have been posted to lure the readers' attention.

It is noteworthy that these sexualised representations are all of western female athletes. Koh and Kim (2004) pointed out that unlike in the West, the sexualisation of the female body in Korean daily newspapers began only in the late 1980s, when the commercialisation of mass media increased. Furthermore, the tendency to sexualise the female athletes' bodies was limited to reports of foreign athletes. The researchers explained that the comparatively delayed sexualisation of the female sporting body in the Korean media was related to nationalism in Korean society as well as to conservatism from the Confucian tradition. With a unique history of colonisation, the Korean War and its consequent division into two countries in twentieth century, Korean sporting images have been shaped for the purpose of strengthening the nation and enhancing its reputation rather than for commercialism. Because Korean athletes are identified with the nation, their representation, unlike that of foreign female athletes, remains unsexualised. None of the news reports on the Athens Olympics depicted Korean women athletes sexually or focused on their bodies because they are the 'symbol of the nation' and at the same time 'our mothers and sisters'.

The only picture of a Korean woman wearing something revealing was of Lee Hyo-ri, a celebrity singer, cheering Korean soccer players with the Korean national flag in her hand. This picture was used twice, once in colour and once in black-and-white, during the Olympics, something that seldom occurs in daily newspapers. A clear contrast with this picture is an image of the athletes (9 August 2004), with the national flag attached to the front of their uniforms, entering the Olympic village saluting the national flag with stern faces.

There were, however, articles and revealing pictures of women athletes who were completely unrelated to the Olympics. *Donga Ilbo* devoted an entire sports page to women's sports (20 August 2004). Surprisingly, the main article with pictures at the top of the page, titled 'Sports stars take off their clothes', talked about women athletes in foreign national teams who featured in adult magazines. This article listed female sports stars who have posed for adult magazines, including Logan Tom, a member of the US women's volleyball team, whose picture, along with a picture of her colleagues, was published in *FHM*, an US adult magazine; Amy Acuff, a high jumper from the US whose picture was published in *Playboy*, another adult magazine; Svetlana Khorkina, a popular Russian gymnast, who appeared topless in a Russian *Playboy* magazine in 1997; and other female sports stars in nude or semi-nude pictures. The article declared:

> Stars are taking off their clothes because of money and to lure interest. ... Some criticise it saying, 'sports became polluted with the commercialisation of sex', but what can we do? There are still people who want to see, and people who are willing to show ...
>
> (*Donga Ilbo*, 20 August 2004)

Ironically, the main title of the page was 'Olympics and women', a seemingly factual title for an article about women's sporting achievements. There were several articles and images that provided contrasting representations of gender. Under the aforementioned article located on the central upper half and taking up a third of the page, the biggest picture showed a beach volleyball player. Her name was not mentioned but her buttocks drew the readers' attention. In contrast, on both sides of the picture of the beach volleyball player there were three reports that talked about women making rapid progress in sports and breaking the glass ceiling in the Olympics. An article headed 'Women are inferior? Don't be biased' introduced seven sports women who changed the history of Olympics, including Nadia Comaneci, who became the first gymnast in Olympic history to receive a perfect score of 10 during the 1976 Montreal Olympics and who scored seven perfect 10s during the Olympics; Florence Griffith Joyner, who reduced the gap between women's sprint record with that of men's to 1 second; and Hassiba Boulmerka from Algeria who contributed to the improvement of the rights of Islamic women by becoming a double gold medalist during the 1992 Barcelona Olympics. An article titled 'Strong winds by women' introduced

Korean women athletes who won a total of 19 gold medals in the Olympics after the first one in 1984. An article titled 'There is nothing off-limits to women' talked about the fact that women's participation was not permitted when the modern Olympics were created, but nevertheless has steadily grown. The article added that 44 per cent of the athletes participating in the Athens Olympics were women and that women took part in all sports, excluding boxing. These three articles effectively describe the achievements made by women in the Olympics. However, the page as a whole marginalised and trivialised women's sports by placing those articles around 'soft-porn' pictures from adult magazines and the highly sexualised picture of a beach volleyball player.

Conclusion

The significant features of Korean daily newspapers' reports on sportswomen at the 2004 Athens Olympics can be summarised as the confirmation of nationalism, marginalisation of women athletes, emphasis on femininity and sexualisation of female sporting bodies. Unlike many Western studies, nationalism appeared to be the defining ideology – stronger than sexism – and constructed the media representation of women athletes. Korean sportswomen, especially during international sport events, are regarded as the symbols of the nation and are often used as a means to reinforce nationalism. As Korean sport and society become more globalised and new generation have began to represent the popular voice in sport, attitudes towards women athletes have also changed. However, although change has brought about some new trends in sport reporting since 1980s, athletes continue to be identified with the nation, particularly during the Olympic Games.

Women athletes were, however, frequently trivialised and marginalised through an emphasis on femininity or the domestic roles of the athletes. For example, women athletes' tears were often used to show their feminine side but, at the same time, to trivialise their performance. Detailed descriptions of the athletes as mothers, sisters or daughters functioned as a mean to marginalise them. Both Korean and foreign women athletes were trivialised and marginalised while their male counterparts were depicted as strong sportsmen. This tendency was evident even in the coverage of sports, where both Korean men and women won gold medals. Although women gold medalists received plenty of coverage, their femininity was emphasised by a sentimental writing style and pictures showing them in tears. On the other hand, remarkable performances in so-called female-appropriate sports such as rhythmic gymnastics and synchronised swimming, frequently those by foreign sport women, were covered by pictures – without a related article – to show the feminine beauty in sport.

The sexualisation of female sporting bodies has widely been criticised by the Western feminist sport media research but reflected the nationality of the athletes. That is, only foreign athletes appeared in the sexualised images. The only Korean woman, a pop star in a stadium seat at a soccer match, shown wearing a revealing costume, was not an athlete. It was clear that Korean athletes and teams, proudly sporting the national flag on their uniforms, are often regarded as the symbols of the nation regardless of gender. On the other hand, there were pictures that focused on specific body parts or the figure-hugging uniforms of Western women athletes. An additional review of other Korean daily newspapers' articles during the Athens Olympics was conducted to examine further the different portrayals of Korean and foreign women athletes. The results confirmed that all the other daily newspapers (although there were differences in the numbers) exclusively presented the sex appeal of the foreign athletes. While one can conclude that Korean media sexually discriminate against the foreign athletes, it must be noted that Korean media companies – presumably like many companies in other countries – acquire their picture coverage from the databases of famous foreign media companies or image distributors. These media companies can obtain pictures from major events at less cost than dispatching reporters to the Olympics or famous overseas tournaments. In Korea, AFP, GettyImages and Actionimages are the major distributors. Actionimages, which is a subsidiary of Reuters, provides pictures mostly of English soccer. Pictures of the Olympics are mainly provided by AFP and GettyImages. AFP and GettyImages contract photographers from across the globe, build databases and sell the pictures around the world. In the case of Korea, all contracts related to the sales of these images from AFP and Gettyimages have to go through Multibits, an image importer operating since 2006. To select pictures, media companies access the database and perform a search using a keyword or picture content. During the Athens Olympics, Korean media companies dispatched journalists to the venues but couldn't acquire all the pictures that they needed and obtained further coverage from the image databases. The main purpose of the Olympics-related pictures provided by foreign media was to 'grab the attention of the readers' such as the salacious images of foreign female athletes in the *Donga Ilbo*. These pictures reflect the sexually discriminatory perspectives of both the foreign journalists who took the pictures and the Korean media company that selected the pictures.

Korean daily newspapers showed diverse and somewhat contradictory attitudes which reflected the strong nationalism in Korean sport, but also the gendered gaze of both the media companies and the readers. As Wensing and Bruce (2003) contend, a focus on nationalism can change the conventional media coverage of women athletes. At the same time, commercial sensationalism of the media favoured pictures that sexualised the female sporting bodies. We should also note that women are still portrayed as 'others', regardless of the celebration of women athletes of national heroes or commodities to sell sport.

Acknowledgements

Quotation marks used in the articles and captions of illustrations are the exact forms published in *Donga Ilbo*.

The author would like to thank Hanbeom Kim and Yoonso Choi for their efforts in classifying, coding and reviewing data and two anonymous reviewers for their comments.

Notes

1. South Korean research on other sports media issues (see Koh, 2008) include: newspaper sport coverage trends during the twentieth century (Ha and Yang, 1991; June 1989), journalism in sport media (Choi and Chung, 1998; Kwon and Won, 1998; Song, 1998), ideologies and values delivered in Korean TV sport coverage texts (Kim, 1994, Lee, 2003; Yoon, H-J, 1998; Yoon, T-J, 1998), the portrayal of sporting heroes and celebrities (Kim and Kwon, 2005; Yoon and Lee, 2005), the influence of sports media consumption on sporting event attendance (Seo, 2000) and how gender bias in the sports media influences high school students' perceptions (Kim and Lee, 2006).
2. Daily newspapers include *Donga Ilbo*, *Chosun Ilbo*, *Choong Ang Ilbo*, *The Hankyoreh*, *Kyunghyang Shinmun*, *Kookmin Ilbo*, *Segye Ilbo* and *Maeil Economy*. Sports newspapers are *Sport Chosun*, *Sport Seoul*, *Daily Sport*, *Sport Donga* and *Sport Kahn*. Newspapers with on-line publication only are excluded.
3. These are *Donga Ilbo*, *Chosun Ilbo* and *Choong Ang Ilbo*.
4. Taekwon V is the title of a famous Korean animation and the name of the robot in it.

References

Appadurai, A. (2000). The grounds of nation-state: Identity, violence and territory. In K. Goldmann, U. Hannerz and C. Westin (eds.), *Nationalism and Internationalism in the post-Cold War Era* (pp. 129–42). London: Routledge.

Borcila, A. (2000). Nationalizing the Olympics around and away from 'vulnerable' bodies of women. *Journal of Sport & Social Issues*, 24(2), 118–47.

Bruce, T. and Hallinan, C. (2001). Cathy Freeman and the quest for Australian identity. In D. L. Andrews and S. J. Jackson (eds.), *Sport Stars: The Cultural Politics of Sporting Celebrity* (pp. 257–70). New York: Routledge.

Cho, S-S. and Cho, K-M. (1998). The marketing strategies for the photographic coverage of athletes by gender. *Korean Journal of Sport Management*, 3(2), 229–47.

Choi, B-H. and Chung, C-S. (2003). TV sport journalism deployment with the change in Korean broadcasting environment. *Korean Journal of Physical Education*, 42(6), 129–40.

Creedon, J. P. (1998). Women, sport, and media institutions: Issues in sports journalism and marketing. In L. A. Wenner (ed.), *MediaSport* (pp. 88–99). London: Routledge.

Duncan, M. C. (1990). Sports photograph and sexual difference: Image of women and men in the 1984 and 1988 Olympic Games. *Sociology of Sport Journal*, **7**, 22–43.

Eastman, S. T. and Billings, A. C. (1999). Gender parity in the Olympics: Hyping women athletes, favoring men athletes. *Journal of Sport & Social Issues*, 23(2), 140–70.

Ha, N-G. and J. A. Mangan (2003). Ideology, politics, power: Korean sport transformation 1945–92. In J. A. Mangan and Fan Hong (eds.), *Sport in Asian Society: Past and Present* (pp. 213–42). London: Frank Cass.

Hartley, J. (1992). Publicity. In J. Hartley (ed.), *The Politics of Pictures: The Creation of the Public in the Age of Popular Media* (pp. 1–11). London: Routledge.

Jones, J., Murrell, A. J. and Jackson, J. (1999). Pretty versus powerful in the sports pages: Print media coverage of U.S. women's Olympic gold medal winning team. *Journal of Sport & Social Issues*, 23(2), 183–92.

Jun, S-D. (1989). The trend of sport coverage in Korean newspaper since the liberation of Korea. Unpublished MA thesis, Seoul National University, Seoul, Korea.

Kane, M. J. and Greendorfer, S. (1994). The media's role in accommodating and resisting stereotyped images of women in sport. In J. P. Creedon (ed.), *Women, Media and Sport: Challenging Gender Values* (pp. 28–44). Thousand Oaks, CA: Sage.

Kim, B-C. and Kwon, S-Y. (2005). Gender and media sport: A content analysis of media portrayal of Se Ri Pak. *Korean Physical Education Association for Girls and Women*, 19(1), 89–101.

Kim, H-J. and Koh, E. (2004). Photographic coverage of women's sport in a daily newspaper: *Donga Ilbo*, from 1948 to 2003. *Korean Journal of Physical Education*, 43(4), 101–14.

Kim, Y-J. (1994). Influences of mass media on values in sports. *Korean Journal of Physical Education*, 33(2), 2156–69.

Kim, Y-R. (1998). A study on the media coverage of male and female athletes and audience's satisfaction. *Korean Journal of Physical Education*, 37(3), 64–78.

Koh, E. (2003). Chains, challenges and changes: The making of women's football in Korea. *Soccer & Society*, 4 (2–3), 67–79.

Koh, E. (in press). Media portrayal of Olympic athletes: Korean printed media during the 2004 Athens Olympics. In T. Bruce, J. Hovden and P. Markula (eds.), *Sportswomen at the Olympics: A Global Comparison of Newspaper Coverage.* Rotterdam: Sense Publishers.

Koh, E. and Kim, H-J. (2004). Gender and nationalism in sport pages: Photographic coverage of women's sport in a Korean daily newspaper. *Korean Journal of Sport Science,* 15(4), 172–83.

Korea Sports Council (1990). *70 years of Korea Sports Council.* Seoul: Korea Sports Council.

Kwon, W-D. and Won, Y-S. (1998). Sport journalism and culture on Korean newspaper: From 1920 to 1992. *Korean Journal of Sociology of Sport,* 10, 31–44.

Lee, J-O. and Kim, S-G. (1996). Gender discourses in mediasport. *Journal of Korean Physical Education Association for Girls and Women,* 10(1), 123–34.

Lee, K-W. (2003). Ideological practices of media sport texts. *Korean Journal of Sociology of Sport,* 16(1), 171–88.

Lumpkin, A. and Williams, L. D. (1991). An analysis of *Sport Illustrated* feature articles, 1954–1987. *Sociology of Sport Journal,* 8, 16–32.

McCombs, M. (1994). New influence on our pictures of the world. In J. Bryant and D. Zillmann (eds.), *Media Effects: Advances in Theory and Research* (pp. 1–17). Hillsdale, NJ: Lawrence Erlbaum Associates.

Na, Y-I. (2001). Development of sport in modern Korea. *Proceedings of 2001 International Conference on Sport Management and Sport History: Humanities and Social Science of Sport in 21st Century* (p. 1089). Taiwan, July, 13–14.

Nam, S. (2004). Content and meaning analysis of female athletes' photographs on sports section in daily newspaper. *Korean Journal of Physical Education,* 43(4), 101–14.

Nam, S., and Kim, J. (2003). Analysis of photographic image of female athletes in daily newspapers. *Korean Journal of Sociology of Sport,* 16(2), 456–77.

Padgett, D. K. (1998). *Qualitative Methods in Social Work Research: Challenges and rewards.* London: Sage.

Seo, H-J. (2000). The influence of sport media on professional sport event spectating. *Korean Journal of Sociology of Sport,* 13(2), 253–62.

Song, H-R. (1998). Sport journalism in Korea. *Korean Journalism Review,* 26(1), 42–52.

Vincent, J., Imwold, C., Masemann, V. and Johnson, J. T. (2002). A comparison of selected 'serious' and 'popular' British, Canadian, and United States newspaper coverage of female and male athletes competing in the Centennial Olympic Games: Did female athletes receive equitable coverage in the 'Games of the women'? *International Review for the Sociology of Sport,* 37(4), 319–35.

Wensing, E. H. and Bruce, T. (2003). Bending the rules: Media representations of gender during an international sporting event. *International Review for the Sociology of Sport,* 38(4), 387–96.

Yoon, H-J. (1998). Meaning structure of TV sport coverage. *Korean Journalism Review,* 26(1), 66–76.

Yoon, T-J. (1998). Non-professionalism and ideologies in sport coverage. *Korean Journalism Review,* 26(1), 52–60.

Yoon, Y-K. and Lee, I-H. (2005). Reporting sports heroes in Korean journalism and perception of the audience. *Journal of Communication Science,* 5(3), 373–410. http://www.gettyimageskorea.com; http://www.multibits.co.kr.

10

An Analysis of Amaya Valdemoro's Portrayal in a Spanish Newspaper during the Athens Olympics 2004

Montserrat Martin

In this chapter I focus on how Amaya Valdemoro, the captain of the Spanish basketball team, and the Spanish basketball team were represented in the Spanish newspaper *El País* during the 2004 Athens Olympic Games. The analysis of this representation is based on a poststructuralist sexual difference theory. This approach derives fundamentally from the Belgian philosopher, psychoanalyst and linguist Luce Irigaray's theory of sexual difference as the original and primary human difference. Irigaray calls for a focus on the radical difference between the two sexes, and therefore aims to build a theory based on the uniqueness and irreducibility of femininity and female ways of being. In order to make sense of Irigaray's theory, I shall use a narrative to examine the content and structure of the articles centred on Amaya Valdemoro and then discuss how Irigaray's concepts can be used to analyse the Olympic media coverage.

Narrative writing as a way of representing feminist sports research

One of the main goals of this chapter is to challenge the dualistic understanding of gender in sport through a feminist poststructuralist lens. In order to do so I shall first challenge the dichotomy between scientific, factual, 'plain' language, objective writing and literary, fiction, rhetorical and subjective writing (Richardson, 2000). Furthermore, following Denzin (1994, 1997) and Richardson (1994, 1997, 2000), who have written extensively on alternative and creative writing in qualitative research, I have chosen to represent my research as a narrative to describe, interpret and explain (Markula and Denison 2005, p. 169) Valdemoro's and the Spanish basketball team's portrayal in *El País* during the Olympic Games in Athens. I have chosen to embark on this narrative writing for the following reasons. First, poststructuralists have challenged the belief that scientific language transparently expresses experiences, reality and knowledge. During the so-called crisis of representation (Denzin, 1997) social scientists began increasingly to acknowledge that writing contributes to how experiences, reality and knowledge become to signify (Derrida, 1976; Foucault, 1979). Moreover, poststructuralist researchers are not detached from the subject they are analysing (Denzin, 1994). In this sense, I take for granted that my subjectivity is part of the research process, and I make it visible through narrative writing. Second, the researcher subject and the researched subject are neither linear; nor static, they are both partial, multiple and even contradictory in their actions and meanings (Richardson, 1994). Narrative writing allows the subjects of my research and me, as the author of the text, to fluidly interchange multiple voices at different levels of the portrayal of Valdemoro: the voice of the journalist in *El País*, the voice of the student who reads these portraits and tries to interpret them through feminist theories, the voice of the university lecturer, the voice of her friend in class and my own voice. It is only by narrative writing that all these voices can completely intertwine and allow the reader to contribute her/his own voice to the narrative.

Moreover, narrative writing provides an evocative text which captures the attention of the readers and allows them to feel part of the research by contrasting their own learning experiences with that of the subject (Richardson, 1994, 2000). Lastly, from a feminist perspective, writing needs to challenge 'the monolithic, objective, dominant male voice of traditional social sciences writing' (Denison and Markula, 2003, p. 6). Currently, several feminists in sport studies have experimented with the new insights provided by narrative writing which allows us to gain other kinds of knowledge beyond the patriarchal gender order (e.g. Bruce, 1998; Markula, 2003; Tsang, 2000). In addition, narrative writing corresponds with Irigaray's endeavour to create a new language to express women's original ways of being and existence in this world as subjects in their own right. I return to this point later in this chapter.

In-the-name-of-the-mother

The 2004 Athens Olympic Games finished three weeks ago and I am in my first class of media and sport, reading a headline of a newspaper article: *Valdemoro se da un atracón,*[1] while waiting for the lecturer to arrive. When I enrolled on this course I read in the outline that we would need to do a piece of research on media coverage of a famous sports athlete from the last Olympic Games in order to pass. I hope that Amaya Valdemoro will fulfil the criteria.

After a few minutes the lecturer enters. 'Hello everybody. My name is Susan Forcadell and we will be sharing a few sessions on media and sport. As I hope you have read in the outline we will be analysing how various Spanish athletes are represented by the media. Could each of you please write on the board the name of the athlete you are interested in.'

'Why do you want to concentrate on her?' the lecturer asks me when I write Amaya Valdemoro's (basketball, sixth place) name on the blackboard. My choice follows the names of Conchita Matínez (tennis, silver medal), María Quintanal (shooting, silver metal) and Patricia Moreno (gymnastics, bronze medal). The rest are all sportsmen: David Cal (rowing, gold and silver medal) and of course Pau Gasol (basketball, seventh). *He is currently playing in the NBA and he was one of the most covered Spanish athletes in the last Olympic Games, even though he didn't get a medal. I wonder what the criteria is for reporters to decide who and what to write about in the Olympic Games.*

'I think she is an intriguing athlete, I like her character on the court very much, she is … she … is gutsy,' I answer, not very enthusiastically, thinking that Susan will suggest I substitute another more famous and more successful Spanish athlete from the Olympic Games.

Damn! It was a real shame. They started really well, and against all expectations got through the quarter finals. Hopes for them were high. Yet it was the first time the Spanish women's basketball team had qualified for the Olympic Games – they played in Barcelona 1992 just because it was their home ground. This time it was completely different, they reached the Olympic Games on their own merit. They could make history for the Spanish Basketball Union, and women's team sports in general. Nobody had any confidence in them before the Olympic Games. The first game wasn't very good but they beat the Czech Republic, they were warming up. Amaya wasn't yet 100 per cent ready to start the competition. The second game was another thing. Amaya had the game of her life – she scored 22 points in the first ten minutes. What a score! They hammered China, and the audience, including me, encouraged by the media, started to believe that bringing a medal home was more than a mere likelihood. In the next match they easily beat New Zealand and they looked unstoppable. A medal was getting closer and closer.

Inevitably, the lack of height in the team began to count and they could not beat the USA, the best team with the best league in women's basketball.

Even with the significant physical discrepancy in height and speed between the Americans and the Spaniards, they played outstanding basketball. They never gave up and they made the Americans sweat for every single point they scored. Unfortunately, all Spanish hopes in this mad adrenaline rush came to an end when Spain lost by a fraction in a frantic game to Brazil (67-63). Bloody Brazilians, they were much taller than the Spaniards. Always the same! Nevertheless, Amaya played an amazing tournament. Without doubt, she gave it her all every time she was on court. It is not by chance that she has been chosen as one of the best five players in Europe. I wonder how much Susan or the rest of the class know about Valdemoro's basketball career?

'Is that all? Is that the only thing that attracts you, that she's gutsy? Most, if not all, sportswomen who participate in the Olympic Games must have some character and courage to get there, haven't they?' The lecturer looks quickly to the whole class.

'Yup ... I suppose so.' Unable to avoid blushing and looking at the blackboard I continue, 'I think she is an outstanding player.' I turn towards the class, 'Did any one know that she is the highest ever paid Spanish female basketball player? I don't understand this huge difference in coverage between Amaya Valdemoro and Pau Gasol, I guess because Valdemoro is a woman and Gasol is currently playing in the NBA.'

'I agree!' Another student intervenes. 'I read somewhere that for three years she was champion of the WNBA with the Houston Comets. A male Spanish basketball player has never achieved this feat.'

'Champion of what?' A very tall guy behind me asks scornfully.

'I can't believe it, Ivan,' Eli, the student who has just spoken, replies derogatorily, 'You don't know what the WNBA is? And you play basketball ...? The WNBA is the most important women's basketball league in the world, well at least the most professional one.'

'Yes it is!' I interject getting excited and believing that Valdemoro is worthy enough for this course. *I didn't know that Eli knew so much about women's basketball. She is a gymnast and I thought she didn't give a fig about team sports.* 'But now Amaya Valdemoro is playing in Russia with the best team in Europe.' I continue, 'She is an awesome player, she is the kind of player everyone would like to have on their team ... my dream is to be like her, she is good in every single aspect ... she is just perfect, skilful, brave, efficient, a leader, she has a very strong character ... and ... she is even pretty.' *Whoops! I suddenly felt very conscious of what I had said. They may think I am lusting after her. That wasn't my intention; I just wanted to show that outstanding players don't have to be physically unattractive. I need to control my admiration for her.* I look at Ivan and, as I expected, he's looking at me slyly while wetting his upper lip. *Yuck!*

'OK, OK.' The lecturer intervenes. 'It seems that Amaya Valdemoro has all the attributes to be a successful basketball player. It will definitely be interesting to analyse in what terms the printed press has portrayed her during the Olympic Games. As you say, she complies with all the masculine attributes to achieve the necessary success in basketball and at the same time she still looks pretty.' Then, she turns to Eli, 'Well, we have seen that Emma is really interested in how the press has treated Amaya Valdemoro. What about you Eli? Why have you chosen Patricia Moreno?'

Involuntarily, I drift off. *I know why Eli is interested in Patricia Moreno, and also Ivan in Pau Gasol, and pretty much the whole class. This is our third year together. As soon as the class finishes I need to go to the library and get all the newspapers from the period of the Olympic Games. I am going to enjoy this essay and I am going to become an expert on Amaya Valdemoro. Maybe if I know her inside out I'll become a better player and better captain for my team. This lecturer is cool. I like her.*

'All right.' The high pitch of Susan's voice brings me back to the class. 'Now that we all know the sports interests in the class and all the sports people we are going to analyse through the media, let's get started. For the next week each of you has to bring at least a couple of articles.'

'Can they be from different newspapers? What if there are lots of them?' Ivan asks arrogantly. 'I was following Pau Gasol's trajectory in Athens and I got most of the articles that focused on him I think I have around ... fifty or something like that.'

'Wow! Fifty articles on Pau Gasol in the same newspaper? I don't think any Spanish sportswomen would ever dream of getting such extensive coverage,' Eli exclaims sarcastically. 'You guys are so lucky that you have such good male sports examples in the media. Instead look at us, poor women, we hardly have any female sport models to follow, to analyse ...'

'I didn't say they were all in the same newspaper,' Ivan replies sharply. 'And if you don't have female athletes to follow you could always choose a man. For instance, Gervasi Defer got a gold medal in gymnastics.'

'Why should I have to choose a man in order to analyse a famous athlete? Everything about sport always has to have a male bias. Why is that?' Eli asks hopelessly.

'Hey, hey, you said you didn't have a model of a sportswoman to follow in the media and I'm telling you that you could choose a sportsman to analyse. Do you really think the sex of the athlete matters in order for a sports person to become famous? Why can't basketball girls mirror their game on Pau Gasol, or gymnasts on Gervasi Defer?'

For a moment silence descends on the class. I want to raise my voice and say: *No stupid, don't you see that we are completely different? I'll never be able to be a Pau Gasol, even if I could play better than him and win more games than him.* But I can't because I can't explain why mirroring my basketball to Valdemoro seems more realistic, more plausible than looking at or imitating the famous Gasol. *Is it just because she has a female body as I do?*

It looks like the lecturer doesn't know what to say when suddenly she states in a very thoughtful tone, 'This question reminds me of what Ucendo[2] claims, that women who play sport are invisible and that girls have no role models in the way boys do. Anyway, I'm glad Eli and Ivan have raised one of the most important issues in sports media: "How does the gender of the athlete affect her/his representations in the media?" As we'll see next week, gender is the first key issue through which to analyse sports media coverage.'

I breathe a sigh of relief. 'So, this Ucendo supports the idea that the gender of the athletes on whom girls or boys model themselves in order to pursue their dreams of becoming sports stars matters, does she?'

'I think so, yes. But it isn't that straightforward. Next week we will talk about all these gender-related issues. At the moment, please concentrate on finding the articles you would like to analyse.'

In less than a minute everybody has disappeared, except Eli who comes to me as soon as she has tidied her folder. 'What do you think?' she asks me.

'About what?'

'About the lecturer, about the project we need to do, about the class. Have you been in class? Or have you been spacing out, as usual?'

'I think the project is very interesting. I really want to know more about Amaya Valdemoro. And Susan seems very cool too. She is really trying hard to contain Ivan's arrogance. Don't you think?'

'Yeah. I'm glad she has realised that Ivan is kind of chauvinistic.'

'Well, I'm sure most of the guys in our class think like him. Sport is so male-oriented. For instance, look at our class: there are 70 per cent guys and 30 per cent girls. My female friends from my hometown are less interested in sport than the guys and when I go to a bar to watch an NBA basketball match the vast majority are guys. I wonder why?'

'As Susan might say,' adopting a solemn tone and trying to imitate our lecturer, Eli states: 'I don't know Emma, there isn't a straightforward answer to your question, but I suggest you go to the library and ...' She winks exaggeratedly at me, 'Bloody work ...'

We both burst out laughing.

* * *

'Good morning! Have you been working on your newspaper articles? Please sit down.' Susan raises her voice to make sure Ivan and his clique listen to her.

Giving up on any chance of silencing the class, she comes to me. 'Let's see what you have got on Amaya Valdemoro.'

'Not much from *El País*. I got two headline articles on her and then six more talking about the team and also underlying Valdemoro's performances on the court as the main star of the team. As expected much less than on Gasol,' I say while I give her a folded newspaper page with the headline: 'Amaya Valdemoro outdoes herself' and the subheading: 'Spain does superbly well the first quarter, with 22 points off the shooting guard and defeats China with authority.'

It takes Susan a couple of minutes to have a quick look at the rest of the article. 'This is very interesting. It seems the whole article is about the extraordinary sports performance of the team led by Amaya Valdemoro, isn't it? I never knew that the women's basketball team did so well in the Olympic Games.'

I nod slowly. She looks at the folded page again and continues, 'Well it looks like this article does not fully reproduce gender stereotypes in sport.'

'What gender stereotypes?' I ask curiously.

Susan returns the article to me and replies, 'Wait and see.' She leaves me to get back to her notes on her desk.

'Please, are you ready? We are going to start.' The last students enter the class and Susan closes the door and starts talking.

'In order to understand and analyse gender differences in sports media we need to review previous studies on it.' She picks up two papers from her desk and begins:

'First of all we need to bear in mind that from a feminist perspective sport has been viewed for a long time as a sexist institution, male-dominated and masculine in orientation'.[3]

Susan raises her eyes to make sure the class is paying attention, and continues.

'Many studies on sports media and gender[4] have used the concept of hegemony[5] to explain how power works through relations of gender and are reflected in sport. For these sport feminists, hegemony is grounded in the assumption that "cultural practices, including sport, are arenas in which values, meanings, and ideologies are contested."[6] This means that sport is a constantly changing process, an assumption that challenges the basics of hegemony. The hegemony approach acknowledges that hegemonic male power in sport is not coercive or violently imposed against the will of women who want to play sports. As MacNeill says "hegemonic relations are thus 'silently' maintained without coercion."[7] Consequently, power operates through more subtle forms of socialisation and ideological influence, which supports the belief that sport is "naturally" appropriate for boys and men, and also, "naturally" inappropriate for girls and women. As you might guess, not all sports are appropriate for men or inappropriate for women.'

'No, of course not. For instance in gymnastics there are disciplines, like the uneven bars, which are only for women. In this case it would be totally the opposite, wouldn't it?'
'Good point, Eli,' Susan continues the lecture.

'In order to explain why some sports activities are considered to be appropriate for women and why some others are not, it is necessary to engage with the idea that sport as part of society is organised according to "traditional" and constricted gender roles: feminine and masculine. It is argued that, from an early age, we learn feminine- and masculine-appropriate behaviours which are based on an ideology. To understand further how this dualistic gender pattern is reproduced and maintained, it is necessary to grasp the meaning of ideology.

'Ideology is a set of ideas that works to maintain the hegemonic power that dominant groups exercise in society. The interesting notion here is that subordinated groups accept their subordination as "common sense" and "natural" and as a result, there are no straightforward confrontations against this power.[8] For example, there is general acceptance that gender inequalities are "natural" consequences of sexual differences and this common sense is supported and maintained without coercion by an ideology of masculinity. Therefore, according to Theberge,[9] "the ideology of masculinity is the dominant way of seeing the world that works to keep social gender order structures in place". This ideology is rooted in the binary opposition of the two genders and the belief of hierarchical "natural" superiority of masculine characteristics above the feminine ones. Thus, there are feminine and masculine stereotypes which cannot be mixed up. For instance, the feminine includes being emotional, passive, dependent, maternal, compassionate and gentle, whereas being strong, competitive, assertive, confident and independent represents masculinity.[10] There is a parallel assumption that the display of superior masculine characteristics is linked to a male biological body that is considered naturally stronger than the female body. Therefore, the ideology of masculinity converts male dominance in sport into common sense, largely proved by biological sex differences. Consequently, one of the key tasks of most sports feminists is to unmask the social constructions derived from biological differences between men and women and show that they are ideological constructions. Therefore, sports media analysis on gender has become an important study area to understand how male dominance works and how it can be resisted.'

Susan slows her delivery for emphasis then continues:

'As a conclusion, on the one hand, sport feminists look at sport as a masculine domain that oppresses women.' Susan raises her eyes looking for complicity in the class, I nod, and she continues.

'On the other hand, sports feminists analyse women's participation in sport as a possible terrain for women's resistance and alternative practices to male hegemonic ones.'[11]

Susan stops again to make sure that we have processed all this information. Then Eli raises her hand, 'So, feminists must deal with sport as a contradictory issue? It seems that at the same time sport oppresses but helps to resist this oppression.'

'Good point, Eli. They do. One of the main premises in sport feminist research is to understand in which ways and under what circumstances, social, historical, political, economical, women resisted the gender order by participating in sport. However, very often researchers have found that at the same time as resisting gender order, some sport practices have also reproduced this gender order. And vice versa, practices which look like they collude with the established gender order in sport in some way also resist it in other ways.'

'I don't understand.' Marie Ann, a long-haired student who is wearing high heels and seated the front row intervenes. 'How can the same action be both resisting and reproducing the gender status quo? As a soccer player, I always feel that I'm resisting what people think about me because they can't understand why a woman lives and dies to play soccer, as I do.'

Susan looks thoughtfully at her, and then cautiously smiles. 'Let me explain it with an example of women's rugby coverage in the media by Wright and Clarke.[12] For these authors women's rugby challenged the gender order in sport for obvious reasons: rugby is considered a very masculine, aggressive, high-contact game. The coverage of the Games during 1996 and 1997 didn't take the women's game seriously as it described the rugby players applying make-up and dressing up after the Games,[13] as if the rugby players are trying to compensate for the extreme masculinity of the game with an extreme femininity out of it.

'As you can imagine, these kinds of comments confirm what feminist studies have claimed for long time. First, it was and still is hard for female sport to reach the media circuits. Secondly, once journalists have realised women are part of the sport phenomenon, mostly in big events, like the Olympic Games, media coverage tends to highlight the personal characteristics of female athletes, such as their attractiveness, their family and their domestic interests, and their vulnerabilities and weaknesses[14] instead of the importance of their achievements and their high levels of commitment ...'

'I agree with all this, but in gymnastics very often the media comments are about the long hours, the need to start training very young, the high levels of sacrifice and commitment to reach a final in the Olympic Games of female gymnasts,' Eli interrupts.

'Yeah, of course, we all know this, but it might be because gymnastics is seen as a very feminine sport, not like soccer or rugby,' Marie Ann replies. 'Keep going Susan,' Marie Ann encourages her as she gets back to her notes.

'You are all right. For instance, Jones et al.[15] argue that the women's sports that tend to get more words and minutes in the media are those emphasising grace, balance and aesthetics, attributes consistent with traditional gender ideology and images of femininity. In contrast, the most popular men's sports emphasise height, physical strength, speed and the use of physical force and intimidation to dominate opponents, all qualities consistent with traditional images of masculinity. As a consequence, sports media studies of gender have found that there are important differences between coverage of male and female sports and subtly these differences contribute to confirm the belief that sport is more appropriate for men than for women, and more importantly that there are some sports that are unnatural for women to play.'

Susan picks her papers up again. 'Let's relate all we have been talking about to media studies.

'For instance, if one picks up the sports section of any newspaper it is quite shocking to witness how men's sport dominates the coverage and how little, if anything, is reported about women's sport. There is plenty of evidence that women's sports have far less presence in the media.[16] This confirms what we were talking about last week – without much effort we can follow Pau Gasol's trajectory in the NBA because we have access to lots of information. In contrast, if we want to follow Amaya Valdemoro's performances in Russia we'd really need to make an effort to find the information in specialist magazines or on the Internet. This is considered the first subtle discrimination: most women's sports achievements and participation in international contests are invisible to the public because the media don't take the trouble to cover them regularly.

'Feminists assert that this lack of regular women's sport media coverage is not innocent and it tells us that women's sport is less important and is subtly convincing us that it is not for women to play sport seriously. Likewise, in qualitative terms there are also huge differences between female and male exposure. For instance, sportswomen tend to be depicted wearing light or "sexy" clothes, or in poses that emphasise their sexiness. Furthermore, in sports that are not considered appropriate for women their achievements tend to be trivialised by the focus on their feminine domestic roles as wives, mothers, girlfriends, and very often they talk about the relationship with their coaches ... Other times journalists write about how some female players look masculine – very loosely, they imply they are lesbians, and depict their actions in sport as unnatural as possible ...'

'I don't want to finish the class without telling you that there is a very interesting study[17] being carried out by researchers from the University of Liverpool and Liverpool John Moores University on the representation of female athletes in Athens 2004 in two Spanish newspapers, which you know very well, one sport newspaper, *El Marca*, and one broadsheet, *El País*. I'm sure you will look at some of the articles they are currently analysing. Fortunately, they have just presented the first results at an international conference, last week.

While they confirm pretty much all the issues we have been revising, they have also identified asymmetrical gender markings. This means that the surname is used to address men, but the first name is used more with women. What is this telling us?'

'Bastards! Another subtle discrimination' a by now deflated Ann Marie exclaims.

Susan pretends she hasn't heard the last word. 'Why discrimination? Is it not better to be called by your first name?'

'In this case, no, because it shows that women become more familiar to the readers. This can easily mean that what women do in the Olympic Games is less important than what men do.' Ann Marie murmurs another insult under her breath. 'Tell us more results.'

'Well, another one is about the need that women have to gender mark their sporting events.'

'What does that mean?' Eli asks.

'If you look at the football premiership you will hardly ever read "male football". Now tell me if you remember reading news about female sport and not having the female stated explicitly?'

'Bastards. Another subtle discrimination,' a by now deflated Ann Marie exclaims.

'Ann Marie if you want the researchers' emails, I can provide you with them, just come to see me in a tutorial.'

Quickly, Susan checks the time. 'Oh well, I think I've been talking too much. Now it's your turn. As part of this course you'll be looking at gender differences in media coverage. For this I need you to find a partner who is analysing the opposite sex but a similar sport. For instance, it would be great if Emma and Ivan could work together and at the end of the semester present to the class the main differences they have found between the Valdemoro and Gasol coverage in the printed media. Any questions?'

Before leaving the class I approach Susan's desk and while she is putting her folder in her bag I say, 'I don't mind working with Ivan for the final comparison.'

'Oh good, I'm glad,' she smiles.

'But, you know, I think I now understand what you meant by reproducing gender stereotypes early on.'

Susan seems busy organising her things and doesn't pay attention to me. I keep talking while I take the article out of my folder, 'I don't think this article does, though. Actually it says that because the Spanish players are so short in height they need to balance it through creativity and intelligence in their outside game. That's where Amaya's shots are crucial.' I start getting excited and begin talking faster.

Surprisingly Susan replies, 'That's right.' She hangs her bag on her shoulder while she takes the article from my hand. 'Furthermore, there is nothing about the personal lives of the players outside of the basketball court. I mean, it looks like the reporters don't feel the need to emphasise the basketball players' roles as girlfriends, wives or even mothers. However, let me see it again. I have noticed that in the introduction Amaya's feat is compared to Pau Gasol. This is also one way to trivialise women's sport, showing that women's sport, in one way or another, always has to be compared to men's sport. Has Gasol ever been compared to Valdemoro?'

Changing the topic, suddenly Susan asks me, 'You are a basketball player, aren't you? I heard you are a semi-professional player.'

Feeling my face going red I answer, 'Well, I play in the premiership and I was selected a few times to play in the Spanish team when I was a junior. I haven't played with Amaya Valdemoro yet, but I hope that one day I will!'

'Very good! Look, why don't you have a look at the Jones et al. article I mentioned earlier?[18] In this article the authors have classified basketball as a male-appropriate sport. They state that in this kind of sport, sports media frequently uses male-to-female comparisons. I think the comparison of Valdemoro to Gasol will fit in this category. They also state that women's male-appropriate sports coverage has less to do with sport or the players' performance than in more female-appropriate sports. Is this happening in the case of Amaya Valdemoro? From what you have told me it looks like it doesn't ...' She takes another quick look at the article.

My expression is enough for Susan to understand that I'm not interested in this kind of stuff.

'OK, I can imagine that to you basketball is not masculine at all. But why don't you go to the library to read the paper and start analysing the articles you have? And then we'll see what you understand from them and go from there.'

She is obviously in a rush, but before she leaves the class I tell her, 'Yeah, but there is this other article on Amaya Valdemoro that has really attracted my attention. I don't think it classifies her as being either feminine or masculine...' My voice rises as I realise that I'm talking to myself, the class is completely empty. I pack my bag and leave the room.

On my way to the library I read the bottom article heading: 'In the Name of the Mother' and subheading: 'Amaya displays her mother's

maiden name Madariaga on her T-shirt, to pay homage to her mother.'
I keep reading:

> Amaya Valdemoro was neither happy nor sad yesterday. She scored
> 22 points in 10 minutes against China. She scored 30 overall at the
> end, one of her best performances in her basketball career. One could
> say she had reason to be celebrating. However, she was sad. She didn't
> outwardly express it but someone was missing in her life. She missed
> her mother to whom she gave an emotional homage. Nine years after
> her death Amaya displays her mother's maiden name Madariaga on
> her T-shirt. This gesture confirms the sensibility of this woman who
> on the court transforms and becomes hard like a rock. These are two
> of her big qualities, heart and strength. With them and her unques-
> tionable talent she has set a gold standard in Spanish basketball.
> In Houston her name is written in golden letters amongst the cham-
> pions of the WNBA, the best female league in the world.

*Hmm! Does this depiction of Amaya Valdemoro's homage to her mother fit
into the feminine stereotype? Well, I guess it does if one considers that being
sensitive on the basketball court means being vulnerable and I'm sure this is
the last thing that a professional basketball player wants to show: dependence, subservience to her mother. However, the reporter frames it in a way
that it doesn't look like Valdemoro is the kind of woman who needs her
mother next to her to be successful. When she was 21 she left Spain for the
States and she played there for three years, without her mother. She has
become without doubt the best player in the Spanish team, again without her
mother. For me this homage sounds more like a very creative initiative:
acknowledging the importance of her mother in her basketball career without
undermining her situation or without feeling it is a moral duty.*

*Funny though! This reminds me of my relationship with my mother and basket-
ball. While my father was working long hours, and my sisters never played sport,
my mother was the one who took the trouble to find a basketball team for me.
I was ten and she called the Basketball Union for me to find the nearest teams to
home. Since then basketball has become my whole life. Is it thanks to my mother
that basketball is my life? Is this what Amaya Valdemoro feels about her mother
and she needs to publicly acknowledge it? How odd! It never occurred to me.
I guess because I have the image of the father taking the son to the football match.*

*I imagine Amaya's display of her mother's maiden name was a public recog-
nition that doesn't conform to the male gender order in basketball but shows
resistance to it. It doesn't mean that Amaya is not going to wear her father's
name or she is going to relinquish it from now on. The article also says that*

she has a very close relationship with her father. It clearly means she has decided to show respect and give visibility to her mother's influence in her basketball. But why? What does she intend by this? Furthermore, the Union had to know in advance because they had to print the T-shirts before the Olympic Games. What did she tell the old boys who run the Union? Fascinating!

Every time I find out more about this woman I like her more and more. She's got it all. Is she really like this or is the media constructing this ideal Amaya Valdemoro on and off the court? However, I shouldn't speak too soon because maybe, after all, the feminine stereotype is also reproduced in Amaya Valdemoro's coverage as Susan said this morning.

I continue reading the same article:

'It was an incredible experience, but when I was there I missed jabugo ham too much,' says Amaya when she is asked about her time in the States. Lover of food, there is nothing that could make her happier than a good plate of lentils, even though she doesn't get her hands dirty in the kitchen. 'I do what I can' she says. More than cooking Valdemoro likes reading. She likes good movies and she reveals she is quite eclectic regarding her music taste. Valdemoro recognises herself as a woman 'with lots of manias'. She doesn't want to elaborate on that, but she says she is 'an impatient and stubborn person, I'd say they are my major defects.'

So, the article reports personal information about Amaya Valdemoro which is not relevant to her sports performance. In this way it does follow the feminine stereotype. However, the information in itself doesn't follow such a stereotype. She doesn't like cooking, she likes reading. Is the reporter's intention to show an intellectual Amaya Valdemoro? Being a female professional athlete doesn't mean being stupid. Why is showing the personal life of athletes classified as derogatory in the sport world? Why don't we know if Gasol likes cooking? More than 'Pretty versus Powerful' it should be 'Powerful, Intelligent and Pretty'. I need to talk to Susan about it.

'Hey.'

Suddenly a hand touches my shoulder from behind 'Ahhhhh!!!' My body unconsciously trembles, 'Oh, it's you!' I say, disappointed.

'Shhhhh!' a student at the next table tells me off.

'Who else were you waiting for?' Eli asks, as shocked as me. 'Amaya Valdemoro?'

'Tee, hee, very funny!' I reply in rather a sarcastic tone. 'No one. I was just concentrating on reading Amaya Valdemoro's articles.'

'And? What have you found out? Is she still the woman of your dreams?'

'Shut up!' I move my hand down. 'This analysis is serious, nothing to do about liking or not liking her. I'm researching!'

'Yeah, and now you're going to tell me that it's by chance that you have chosen her?'

'No, of course it's not by chance, are you stupid? I have an interest in knowing more about her, you know basketball is my life and making the Spanish team my goal for this season. Of course I admire her, but it doesn't mean that my research is going to be biased because of that.' I answer getting upset. 'What are you trying to say?'

'Of course not, Emma,' Eli utters in an ambiguous tone. 'But you can't deny that you already have a pre-notion, a pre-knowledge of Amaya Valdemoro, a feeling for her, and I guess in your case it is stronger than my feeling for Patricia Moreno. So, you can't be neutral about the new stuff you are reading about her. You just need to acknowledge that all this is going to affect your thoughts and as a result your conclusions in this "research" essay.' I look at her with disdain. I hate it when someone gestures quotation marks with their fingers.

'Maybe, but apart from my personal reasons, I love basketball and she is what I want to become. I don't need to follow Pau Gasol anymore because Amaya Valdemoro is strong enough.' I start talking in an over-confident tone, 'I have found that the overall depiction of Amaya Valdemoro doesn't follow the whole male/female binary concept of gender. In most of the cases she is portrayed as masculine and feminine at the same time or, I would say, as neither one nor the other. I don't think her actions can be easily classified into one or the other gender category. I really think this gender dualism constrains the richness of an extraordinary female player like Amaya Valdemoro. It cannot be so simple: male on the court, female off of it.'

'So ...?'

'So what?' I ask impatiently.

Eli looks at the shelves in front of us. 'You might need another feminist theory that gives you other concepts and elements to analyse the extraordinary case of Amaya Valdemoro, as you said, beyond female/male stereotypes in sport,' she says in a melodramatic tone.

'Do you think I'm resisting classifying her because I'm infatuated with her?'

'Nah, I think you are looking for something that is not in Amaya's coverage.'

'What do you mean?' I ask completely lost.

'Nothing ...' she says looking away from me. 'You should keep looking for it, I'm sure there must be other gender media sport studies that suit your experiences and thoughts on Amaya Valdemoro. Why don't you ask Susan? I know she did her PhD on women's sport. I'm sure she knows more about feminist theories and gender stereotypes in sport.'

'Did she? I didn't know that.'

'Why do you think she is making us work on the gender issue?'

'Well, I thought it was the key issue. After all, we are all either women or men. Aren't we?'

Suddenly, Eli looks at her watch. 'I think she's still in her tutorial.'

Looking at my watch I say in a hurry, 'Yeah! I think she is.' I manage to tidy up my things in less than a minute and I whisper, 'I'll see you later.'

'Bye!' Eli shouts as I'm running.

'Shhhhh' The same student tells Eli off this time.

* * *

'Come in.'

'Oh hi, are you busy?'

'No, no, I'm just trying to finish a paper on qualitative analysis of sport media. Are you OK?'

'Yeah, yeah I just ran here because I thought I was late for the tutorial.' I say panting and I sit at her desk.

'Oh, no. I still have one more hour of tutorial.'

'Cool!'

'What is it?'

'I've been reading and thinking about Amaya Valdemoro and I have found this article.' I give her the folded article.

'In-the-Name-of-the-Mother,' she reads.

Without giving her time to catch her breath I quickly say, 'I don't think I can classify Amaya Valdemoro and her homage to her mother in either feminine or masculine terms. I think there is something else. I need other concepts that can help me to understand and to celebrate her creativity, sensitivity and extraordinary basketball talent. A theory that doesn't classify actions only as masculine or feminine. The article says that Valdemoro is sensitive and at the same time she is hard like a rock when she plays on court. I mean a theory that can help me to explain how women can have all these attributes and show that it does not mean that when women play inappropriate sports they are not women. A theory that doesn't take for granted that the universal model of sport is only male-oriented. I'm fed up of having to think about/like Pau Gasol if I want to become a basketball star. A theory that recognises women's sports activities in and out of the sport as intertwined and impossible to isolate because being a woman is that, you know ... A theory ...'

'OK, OK. I get it. Calm down, otherwise what you'll need is not a theory, but an ambulance!' For a second the sound of the printer is all that can be heard in the room.

I sit back in the chair and I feel dizzy. I don't say a word. One thousand and one thoughts are coursing through my mind. I can't talk anymore. I feel I'm going to collapse.

She gets up very slowly and while she picks the papers up off the printer and gives them to me she says to me as she looks out of her window, 'Look Emma why don't you go under that tree? It's autumn and the leaves are becoming brown. It is beautiful, isn't it? I love autumn. Don't you? As I said, why don't you go under that tree and read a part of this draft that I think will interest you? I have a feeling it can help you to analyse the Amaya Valdemoro coverage in all its complexity.' She hands me two pages. 'And ... why don't we talk more calmly about it tomorrow at 1:30?'

'OK,' I reply. I was rather taken aback. I thought we would discuss my concerns, but instead I am being hurried out of the office. *How odd ...*

Leaving the building I am intrigued by the papers I am holding in my hand and can't wait to begin reading. However, I decide I'll be more comfortable at the coffee shop than outside. Approaching the place I see that my favourite table by the window is free. I don't hesitate. I go in at once, buy some Early Grey tea, put in the right amount of milk and start reading slowly.

A Poststructuralist Feminist Approach to Analysing Gender in Sport Media Texts

Poststructuralist theory proposes a closer analysis of language use in media texts, because from this perspective, language is not only assumed as a tool to reflect unambiguous and linear reality. Language, in the form of competitive discourses, creates different versions of reality. Poststructuralist theorists strongly believe that it is through language that individual experience and the common sense about appropriate gender behaviours – gendered subjectivity – becomes fixed, natural, real, and therefore, true. Consequently, it is also through a detailed analysis of language and the belief that language constructs reality that it is possible to contest and change fixed and universal ideas on gender. A poststructuralist approach focuses on how language gender categories or concepts shape or mediate our perceptions of media texts. Moreover, it also acknowledges the influence that the text might have on a reader's identity and understanding of the world.

One of the starting points of poststructuralist analysis of the media is to demonstrate how feminine and masculine categories that are constructed as opposites, might be redefined because they actually overlap. For instance, by examining the underlying distinctions between feminine and masculine representations in sports media one may note that 'being feminine' isn't necessarily always the negative or the opposite of 'being masculine'. One important concern of poststructuralist feminism is to inquire into new linguistic forms of representing the feminine that escape the constricted limits of gender dualism. Particularly, some French feminists have worked intensely on new possibilities to create and develop women's language as a way to resist male definitions, and therefore as a way to overcome male oppression and discrimination.

What is sexual difference?

According to a poststructuralist perspective, sexual difference is not the one that culture has constructed from 'biology' and imposed as gender. Instead it is a difference that goes beyond mere physicality, 'a difference of symbolization, a different production of reference and meaning' (de Lauretis, 1994, p. 2). Furthermore, Braidotti (2003) asserts that sexual difference is to be understood as neither a biological nor sociological category, but rather as a point of overlap between the physical, the symbolic and the material social conditions. As such in sexual difference theory, difference 'is conceived in positive terms, rather than in terms of opposition' (Weedon, 1997, p. 123). One of the key feminists, who has developed sexual difference theory from a poststructuralist notion of language and gendered subjectivity, is Luce Irigaray.

Luce Irigaray is a philosopher, linguist and psychoanalyst. She was also an active member of l'Ecole Freudienne de Paris during the 1970s, a psychoanalytic school directed by Lacan. Since the 1980s, Irigaray has conducted research on the difference between the everyday language of women and men. As a result she found out that men encourage their relationship with the self, whereas women use language to make connection and relationships (Ives, 1996). Her work exposes the masculine ideology underlying language and gestures towards a 'new' feminine language that would allow women to express themselves if it could be spoken. Her work is deeply influenced by Jacques Lacan's ideas to understand the importance of language as the primary and elementary structure of the unconscious and the acquisition of gendered subjectivity. For Lacan, language assumes an important role in shaping unconscious meanings and desires (Lechte, 1994). Therefore, gendered subjectivity is a construction and it is through language that gendered subjectivity differences acquire meaning for the individual. Drawing from psychoanalytic theory Irigaray's working premise is that 'femininity as it currently exists is male-defined' (Weedon 1997, p. 60). In order to resist this definition we need to challenge the language that legitimises this definition as the holder of truth.

The assumption that guides Irigaray's theoretical position is that men and women constitute two separate and independent entities. Sexual difference in Irigaray's work does not refer to a bipolar understanding of gender (male/female) although much of Western thought is engrained in such a logic of binaries. On the contrary, the originality of Irigaray's sexual difference theory is based on her emphasis on the need to radicalise the duality of gender instead of blurring the two poles of the binary. Eventually one sex is irreducible to the other. This means that female beings and femininity cannot be compared or measured against males and masculinity because they work in completely separated and unrelated settings, scales and rhythms. While this might appear like a self-evident assumption, it sets Irigaray profoundly apart from many other feminist perspectives.

The key concept in this definition is *irreducibility*, which means that one sex – the female sex – cannot be reduced to a variation or be defined according to the characteristics of the other sex, the male sex. In the words of Irigaray, 'I shall never take the place of a man; never will a man take mine. Whatever identifications are possible, one will never exactly fill the place of the other – the one is irreducible to the other' (1987, p. 124). According to Irigaray, therefore, sexual difference is *the originary-primary* human difference, which we need to respect and work through in all our attempts to analyse and interpret reality.

Irigaray's central thesis derives from her psychoanalytic critique of Jacques Lacan's conception of woman. For Irigaray, Lacan's definition of woman and her sexuality responds more to the interpretation of what a woman is for a man than what or who she is for herself. In Lacanian thought the feminine only makes sense by being the negative, the complement or in some cases the imitation of the masculine. As a consequence, the dependence of the feminine on the masculine is total, which for Irigaray means the total neglect of women's representation in a symbolic sphere, a sphere that transcends materiality and it is represented by language. Furthermore, within psychoanalysis, women are always defined negatively because female sexuality is related to male sexuality in terms of deficiency, atrophy or lack. Irigaray's (1985a, b) main focus in her earlier works was to prove that women need to create new spaces, new definitions where representing their sexuality positively might become the starting point the thought that women are irreducible to men. This would allow women to create new definitions of femininity that are able to escape the male-phallocentric.

Consequently, one of the most controversial aspects of Irigaray's work in American and English feminism has been her constant references to the female body, and her research on the uniqueness of female sexuality. Therefore, Irigaray has been able to confirm the existence of a female libido and female sexual economy, which does not need the phallus to pursue its desire (Ives, 1996, p. 60). For this reason, Irigaray was expelled from the École Freudienne after her first controversial publication: *The Speculum of the Other Women* ([1975], 1985a), in which Irigaray showed the limits of Lacan's mirror stage that explained little girls' introduction in the language and cultural world. Irigaray uses the metaphor of speculum, the medical curved mirror used for inspecting the vagina, to show the specificities of female sexual organs which cannot be explained or defined through phallocentric tools. In this sense, Irigaray, from her analysis of women's multiple sexuality and pleasures, coined the concept of 'two lips in continuous contact' meaning 'both at once' (Fuss, 1992, p. 97). As Irigaray asserts, 'when one starts from "the two lips" of the female sex, the dominant discourse finds itself baffled: there can no longer be a unity in the subject'. She continues, 'they [two lips] are always at least two, and ... one can never determine of these two, which is one, which is the other: they are continually interchanging' (1985b, p. 83). In other words, women are at the same time singular and doubled, two lips that are continually in touch and cannot be isolated, she is 'already two – but not divisible into one(s)' or 'neither one nor two' (Irigaray, 1985b, p. 24). While the meanings of the two lips displace male sexuality as the only reference able to produce language, subjectivity and truth based on concepts like production, property, order, form, unity, visibility and erection (Irigaray, 1985b, p. 77), female sexuality is associated with continuous, compressible, dilatable, viscous, conductible and difussable (Irigaray, 1985b, p. 111). These terms become a starting point to produce woman's language and new subjectivities without male interferences.

Lastly, Irigaray points out another original female source to produce women's language and subjectivity, the figure of the mother in our lives and the great impact that she has in our existence. She emphasises the need to retrieve the primary relationship between two women and explore the meanings of the relationship between mother and daughter. This relationship is an elemental structure which does not have a presence in patriarchy, and even further, the lack of acknowledgement of this elemental relationship between two women contributes to the perpetuation of the belief that phallocentrism is the only possible existential order. This lack of representation between mother and daughter is due to what Irigaray calls matricide: 'Patriarchy is founded on the murder of the mother, which was committed to safeguard the power of the father and the husband' (cited by Muraro, 1994, p. 327). Due to matricide the father becomes the only recognised author of life. Accordingly, Irigaray (1993) asserts that 'Lacan relegates the maternal woman's body to the "real" of biological reproduction that lies outside of culture or the symbolic' (p. 58). Thus the mother originates biological life, but it is only the father who can provide access to the symbolic order – the order in which, through language, the child becomes a social human being. Irigaray recognises the figure of the mother as the cornerstone in transcending the meanings, the significance, that women's *personal* relationships have for women's politics. I believe that one of the tasks we face as feminists is to discover this symbolic bond and to develop it in our own terms in order to create an alternative to a symbolic order founded only on male subjectivity. It is, then, to acknowledge the symbolic effect of the mother on each of us that could make a substantial contribution to the resistance of male gender order.

What a coincidence! This is exactly what Amaya did. Did she read this Irigaray thing before the Olympic Games? Unconsciously I smile. *Her case could be interpreted as the vital impact of her mother in her development as a professional basketball player. Somewhere else I've read that her mother regarded Amaya's participation in the Olympics as the highest achievement for a sportswoman. I guess she had already passed away when Amaya got the contract with the Houston Comets. My mother has never showed such high expectations for my basketball career. The first time I played for Spain, when I was in the junior team, I remember she was happy and she never denied the importance of it, but she didn't get very excited about it. Mothers and sport, what a complex and fascinating issue to study!*

The Production of Language, Subjectivity and Truth

Irigaray's sexual difference ascribes the poststructuralist premise that language does not merely reflect reality but rather constructs and limits its possible meanings. As such, language creates reality and therefore, language is a powerful expression of the structure of subjectivity and social organisation (Weedon, 1997). Whether reality can exist beyond language is a philosophical matter that exceeds the aim of this paper. However, from a poststructuralist and psychoanalytic standpoint language significantly intervenes in the construction and shaping of our unconsciousness and reality. Women are only able to think of themselves as subjects through a language that has already defined their existence in male terms.

In this light, Irigaray insists on the need to create a new language, a language in which not only men are the subjects, for women to overcome male oppression and discrimination in everyday life. Moreover, she asserts that this language has to ignore male preconstruction, male subjectivity, rationality and linearity in order to create a space for women to invent and reinvent themselves and their realities, along with their experiences and their feelings. In Irigarayan vocabulary a language, which instead of legitimising the unspeakable female difference, is able to articulate women's pleasures and desires. The idea of making the female body speak and not only to speak *about* the body has led Irigaray to experiment with language in a very creative manner with the content as much as with the syntax. In this sense, Irigaray's praxis is positive because, instead of merely critiquing the lack of feminine language and thinking that women will never reach the same subjective status as men, she is constantly and intensely working on possible *original female sources* that can produce discourse and therefore, create realities in which women are full subjects.

One of the main pursuits of Irigaray in linguistic research is to gather enough data to prove that the continual denial of gendered discourses is in men's interest: 'Men and women produce different utterings and thereby reveal and produce elements of sexual difference' (Hass, 2000, p. 70). This confirms what we have seen above: sexual difference is not biological or social, it is produced and given existence through language and the symbolic order in which language originates. As a consequence, language is among the key sites to identify sexual difference.

Unconsciously I checked the name of the reporter: Noelia Román. 'She's a woman!' I exclaim. *Maybe this explains why Valdemoro is portrayed through adjectives that are not stuck in gender dualisms which are purely male or female, dualisms which do not accept both concepts at the same time. What was that sentence I just read in Susan's paper ... the concept of 'two lips in continuous contact' meaning 'both at once'.*

Nervously I look for the sentences I underlined in the article: 'This gesture confirms the sensibility of this woman who on the court transforms and becomes hard like a rock. These are two of her big qualities, heart and strength.' That's it! *Taking on board Irigaray's concept of two lips will help me understand the reason behind Valdemoro being portrayed in both male and female stereotypes ... they are no longer contradictory terms but merely interchangeable, interconnected.* Wahoo! I can't avoid smiling. *Where do I start? Do I need to write poetry to achieve and express my female subjectivity? I can't write my essay on Amaya Valdemoro in the traditional style. That will be unconsciously male-oriented.* Feeling more nervous, I get up from the table. *I need to talk to Susan soon. Maybe I need to take a creative writing course, in which new language can be invented as this Luce Irigaray suggests.*

'Aha! Here you are! I've been looking for you for ages. So ...? How did the tutorial go?' Eli asks excitedly.

'I don't know. She gave me this paper on poststructuralism and a feminist called Irigaray which I've just read.' I show her the pages. 'You were right. There are other theories and concepts to understand gender differences in the media but it's not at all easy to grasp their meaning.'

'Why?'

'Oh well,' I take my time and I sit down again. 'They focus on production of language as production of reality, apparently language shapes our reality instead of reflecting it. So, we are at the service of language instead of language being a tool that we use to explain our experiences. Weird, isn't it?'

Eli doesn't say a word. She looks, thinking about what I've just said.

'So in my case it is not Patricia Moreno who performs gymnastics, gymnastics is performing her?'

'Well, now think about it in writing.'

'What do you mean?'

'For instance, if you write about Moreno in your analysis you could think that the media are merely describing her in the Olympic Games and you are describing her from the media, all very straightforward, isn't it?' I slow my pace, 'then you would take for granted the media's interpretation of Moreno as true and objective if you believe that language is just a tool to reflect reality, meanings or experiences. Now look at it from a poststructuralist perspective.' I can't avoid getting worried when I realise how intensely Eli is listening to me. 'The media, with its use of language, are creating, producing a Patricia Moreno, aren't they?' I raise my voice and open my mouth ...

'Why?'

I stop in order to compose myself. I'm not very sure how to frame it. Eli is nodding very slowly. 'Because portraits of Patricia Moreno like Amaya

Valdemoro in the media can only be partial, local and situational,[19] and therefore, it can have multiple meanings and very often contradictory meanings.' Eli really looks lost in space whereas I feel more and more confident.

'For instance, if I interpret Valdemoro's display of her mother's family name in the Olympic Games from Irigaray's perspective, it means that she is recognising the important role that her mother played in Valdemoro becoming a professional and an Olympic-level basketball player. She is not only recognising her biological mother and being thankful because she gave her physical existence. Don't you see it? She's giving her mother more than that; her mother is right at the centre of Valdemoro's most important achievement in her life. This has more symbolic meaning than merely being a daughter. Most importantly, she can escape the male definitions of her as a player, because she has found a way to make her mother present in the symbolic sphere of her sport, something that only men, as Irigaray says, could previously do through male language.' Eli looks at me as if I have lost the plot.

'Don't look at me like that,' I interject. 'This means that Valdemoro is creating a new female language by including her mother in her game and this can only be done symbolically.' I smile. 'Imagine the chaos that would ensue if her mother was really playing with her on the court.'

Eli smiles at me uneasily. 'I don't know if you are right, but it sounds very innovative I would never think about it in these terms. How do you know you're right?'

'That's the interesting part of poststructuralism. I don't know if it's right and probably for some sports feminists it's not. However, it's another interpretation that will help me to expand my thinking and analysis of sportswomen's representation in the media. And – who knows? – maybe in the future other professional players will do the same as Valdemoro and more symbolically, mothers will have a presence in our sports. And – who knows? – maybe this is a way to gradually redress the imbalance. Don't you think?'

'Let's have a beer. I can't think any longer, can you? My head is going to explode,' I assert, not very convinced that Eli or I can consistently think in such terms.

'Aren't you training later?' Eli asks, surprised

'Yes, but today the coach is going to scream and tell us off because we lost on Saturday. I didn't play very well. He just doesn't get it. We are different from guys, and sometimes he needs to listen more to our needs and worries than his own problems. Treat us as full thinking subjects not only as his players. Oh well, let's enjoy ourselves before the storm. The first one is on me.' I wink at her as I stand up and pick up my bag.

Epilogue

Through this narrative which is based on the learning process of an undergraduate student, Emma, in a sport media class, I hope to engage with the experiences of other students who might have undergone a similar experience of a need to challenge established theories in order to understand the cultural context and their own experiences in sport. The story I have told about Emma, her learning of feminist theories through sport media analysis, aims to contribute to current discussions of gender (in sport) as a dualistic concept. My narrative of Valdemoro's media portrayal aims to show the inadequacy of defining women's sport through gender dichotomy. To illustrate my point, I structured the narrative in three main parts.

First, although Emma is unfamiliar with feminist theory, she plays semi-professional basketball and is aware that she has limited opportunities compared to men who play basketball in Spain. I created Ivan, Emma's classmate, who plays basketball and admires Pau Gasol (the even more successful Spanish basketball player) to show how men's and women's basketball coverage is extremely unequal in Spanish sport media, but also demonstrates the common understandings of the necessary differences between men's and women's sport.

Secondly, the lecture setting and the dialogue between lecturer and students was designed to show Emma's introduction to feminist theory through the concept of hegemony through which she could start analysing the gender inequalities in the sports media. She clearly agreed with some aspects of this theory, but her own experiences in playing basketball and her budding analysis of Valdemoro's media coverage cannot be explained fully in the light of this theory. On the contrary, my narrative gradually brings out the contradictions and the limitations of classifying women's sport as feminine or masculine. One way I illustrate these limitations is through a new character, Marie Ann, who with her feminine looks and her passion for football embodies many contradictions in women's sports.

Lastly, I introduce the scholarly work of Irigaray in the narrative through Emma's search for solutions for contradictions and limitations of hegemony theory. Susan, Emma's lecturer, introduces Emma to poststructuralism and, more specifically, to sexual difference theory, through tutorials and informal conversations in class. In addition, it is necessary to recognise the importance of Eli, Emma's best friend in class, in the narrative. Eli always encourages Emma to go further in her inquiry and also listens to Emma's doubts during the process of discovery. In addition, Eli tries to understand all the new knowledge Emma is acquiring. In some ways, Eli represents the reader who is reading about the new concepts by Irigaray pondering how they can be applied to analyses of gender in the sport media.

My chapter has focused on the analysis of one female athlete, Amaya Valdemoro, in the Spanish media, but I believe that I was able to introduce the meaning of poststructuralist feminist critique more effectively through a narrative. In addition, a narrative can bring abstract theoretical concepts closer to the lived experiences of students, athletes and researchers alike. By representing my research in this way I hope to demonstrate further the fluidity of gender and the multiplicity of voices that speak about it in a variety of cultural contexts.

Notes

1. Valdemoro outdoes herself. *El País*, 17 August 2004. Bernstein (2002, p. 415).
2. Bernstein (2002); Eastman and Billings (1999); Wensing and Bruce (2003); Higgs et al. (2003).
3. Alina Bernstain (2002, p. 415).
4. Alina Bernstain (2002); Eastman and Billings (1999); Wensing and Bruce (2003); Higgs et al. (2003).
5. 'Leadership or dominance, especially by one state or social group over others'. *Concise Oxford Dictionary*, 10th edition (1999).
6. Birrell and Theberge (1994, p. 326).
7. 1994, p. 274.
8. Hargreaves, 1994; MacNeill, 1994.
9. 2000, p. 64.
10. Krane, 2001, p. 117.
11. Birrell, 2000; Hall, 1996; Theberge and Birrell, 1994; Hargreaves, 1994.
12. 1999.
13. 1999, p. 235.
14. Eastman and Billings, 1999.
15. 1999.
16. Hargreaves, 1994.
17. Crolley and Teso (2007).
18. Jones, Murrell and Jackson (1999).
19. Richardson, 1994, p. 520.

212 *Montserrat Martin*

References

Bernstein, A. (2002). Is it time for a victory lap? *International Review for the Sociology of Sport*, 37(3), 415–28.

Birrell, S. (2000). Feminist theories for sport. In J. Coakley and E. Dunning (eds.), *Handbook of Sport Studies* (pp. 61–76). London: Sage.

Birrell, S. and Theberge, N. (1994). Ideological control of women in sport. In D. M. Costa and S. R. Guthrie (eds.), *Women and Sport* (pp. 341–59). Champaign, IL: Human Kinetics.

Braidotti, R. (2003). Becoming woman: Or sexual difference revisited. *Theory, Culture and Society*, 20(3), 43–64.

Bruce, T. (1998). Postmodernism and the possibilities for writing 'vital' sport texts. In Rail, G. (ed.), *Sport and Postmodern times* (pp. 3–19). Albany, NY: SUNY Press.

Crolley, L. and Teso, E. (2007). Gendered narratives in Spain: The representation of female athletes in *Marca* and *El País*. *International Review for the Sociology of Sport*, 42(2), 149–166.

De Lauretis, T. (1994). The essence of the triangle or, taking the risk of essentialism seriously: Feminist theory in Italy, the U.S., and Britain. In N. Schor and E. Weed (eds.), *The Essential Difference* (pp. 1–39). Bloomington, IN: Indiana University Press.

Denison, J. and Markula, P. (2003). Introduction: Moving writing. In J. Denison and P. Markula (eds.), *Moving Writing* (pp. 1–24). New York: Peter Lang.

Denzin, N. K. (1994). The art and politics of interpretation. In N. K. Denzin and Y. S. Lincoln (eds.), *The Handbook of Qualitative Research* (pp. 500–15). Thousand Oaks, CA: Sage.

Denzin, N. (1997). *Interpretive Ethnography: Ethnographic Practices for the 21st Century*. Thousand Oaks, CA: Sage.

Derrida, J. (1976). *Of Grammatology*. Baltimore, MD: Johns Hopkins University Press.

Eastman, S. and Billings, A. C. (1999). Gender parity in the Olympics. *Journal of Sport & Social Issues*, 23(2), 140–70.

Foucault, M. (1979). What is an author? In J. V. Harari (ed.), *Textual Strategies* (pp. 113–38). Ithaca, NY: Cornell University Press.

Fuss, D. J. (1992). 'Essentially speaking': Luce Irigaray's language of essence. In N. Frasser and S. Bartky (eds.), *Revaluing French Feminism* (pp. 94–112). Indianapolis, IN: Indiana University Press.

Hall, A. (1996). *Feminism and Sporting Bodies*. Champaign, IL: Human Kinetics.

Hargreaves, J. (1994). *Sporting Females*. London: Routledge.

Hass, M. (2000). The style of the speaking subject: Irigaray's empirical studies of language production. *Hypatia*, 15(1), 64–89.

Irigaray, L. (1985a). *Speculum of the Other Woman*. Ithaca, NY: Cornell University Press.

Irigaray, L. (1985b), *This Sex Which Is Not One*. Ithaca, NY: Cornell University Press.

Irigaray, L. (1993). *Sexes and Genealogies*. New York: Columbia University Press.

Irigaray, L. (2004). Beyond all judgment you are. In L. Irigaray (ed.), *Key Writings* (pp. 66–76). London: Continuum.

Higgs, C. T., Weiller, K. H. and Martin, S. B. (2003). Gender bias in the 1996 Olympic Games. *Journal of Sport & Social Issues*, 27(1), 52–64.

Jones, R., Murrell, A. and Jackson, J. (1999). Pretty versus powerful in the sport pages. *Journal of Sport & Social Issues*, 23(2), 183–92.

Ives, K. (1996). *Cixous, Irigaray, Kristeva: The Jouissance of French Feminism*. Kidderminster: Crescent Moon Publishing.

Krane, V. (2001). We can be athletic and feminine, but do we want to? Challenging hegemonic femininity in women's sport. *Quest*, 53(1), 115–33.

Lechte, J. (1994). *Fifty Key Contemporary Thinkers: From Structuralism to Postmodernity* (pp. 66–70). London: Routledge.

MacNeill, M. (1994). Active women, media representations and ideology. In S. Birrell and C. L. Cole (eds.), *Women, Sport and Culture* (pp. 273–87). Champaign, IL: Human Kinetics.

Markula, P. (2003). Bodily dialogues: Writing the self. In J. Denison and P. Markula (eds.), *Moving Writing* (pp. 27–50). New York: Peter Lang.

Markula, P. and Denison, J. (2005). Sport and the personal narrative. In D. L. Andrews, D. S. Mason and M. L. Silk (eds.), *Qualitative Methods in Sport Studies* (pp. 165–84). Oxford: Berg.

Muraro, L. (1994). Female genealogies. In C. Burke, N. Schor and M. Whitford (eds.), *Engaging with Irigaray*. New York: Columbia University Press.

Richardson, L. (1994). Writing: A method of inquiry. In N. K. Denzin and Y. S. Lincoln (eds.), *The Handbook of Qualitative Research* (pp. 516–29). Thousand Oaks, CA: Sage.

Richardson, L. (1997). *Field of Play, Constructing an Academic Life*. New Brunswick, NJ: Rutgers University Press.

Richardson, L. (2000). New writing practices in qualitative research. *Sociology of Sport Journal*, 17(1), 5–20.

Theberge, N. (2000). Gender and sport. In J. Coakley and E. Dunning (eds.), *Handbook of Sport Studies* (pp. 322–33). London: Sage

Tsang, T. (2000). Let me tell you a story. *Sociology of Sport Journal*, 17(1), 44–59.

Ucendo, N. (2003) 'La mujer deportista en los medios', *Comisión Mujer y Deporte*. http://www.mujerydeporte.com/analisis/igualdad/LaMujerDeportistaenlosMedios.pdf. Accessed 6 September 2006.

Weedon, C. (1997). *Feminist Practice and Poststructuralist Theory*, 2nd edition. London: Blackwell.

Wensing, E. H. and Bruce, T. (2003). Bending the rules. *International Review for the Sociology of Sport*, 38(4), 387–96.

11
The Media as an Authorising Practice of Femininity: Swiss Newspaper Coverage of Karin Thürig's Bronze Medal Performance in Road Cycling

Natalie Barker-Ruchti

Karin Thürig from Switzerland won the bronze medal in the 24 km road cycling event at the 2004 Olympic Games. She was the only Swiss female athlete to win a place in Athens. Despite female cycling being a relatively unknown and unpopular sport for women in Switzerland, her success received considerable media coverage. This chapter analyses Swiss newspaper articles printed the day after Thürig's medal-winning performance. I use Michel Foucault's concepts of biopower and normalisation to examine how the Swiss sports media constructed this athlete. I begin by providing an overview of Foucault's theoretical understanding of how modern forms of power affect the construction of human identity and life experiences. Second, I use this Foucauldian framework to examine how the newspaper articles represented and produced Thürig according to dominant feminine norms, as well as how the athlete herself, in her interviews, appeared to support the same ideals.

Foucauldian analysis and women's sport

Foucault did not study women, nor did he include sport as a social practice in his many academic explorations. Links to both these fields are possible and useful, however, mainly as he examined how humans develop their identities, respectively how individuals' selves are shaped by their social surroundings. Foucault himself described his scholarly endeavours with providing 'a history of the different modes by which, in our culture, human beings are made subjects' (Foucault, 1994, p. 208). In these analyses, Foucault refers to identities as 'subjectivities', which represent individual selves as products of discursive, ideological and institutional practices (McLaren, 2002). The body, in particular its inside, or its soul as Foucault writes, is central in being marked. Through this formed inside, the outside takes shape accordingly and hence determines a person's self and conduct. There is no true self, Foucault argues; rather, our identities and the way we lead our lives are shaped by our social surroundings.[1]

Foucault's main argument is that identity formation is connected to and embedded within a network of power relations. In his genealogical analyses, he links knowledge and social practices with modern forms of power (Foucault and Rabinow, 1984). This form of power emerged with modernity and involves 'a new mechanism ... possessed of highly specific procedural techniques, completely novel instruments, quite different apparatuses' (Foucault, 1980, p. 104). A bureaucratic *life-administering* force, by way of addition and augmentation, individual disciplinary techniques and tactics of *normalisation*, administer, manage and optimise the population. Foucault calls this development the 'beginning of an era of "bio-power"' (Foucault and Rabinow, 1984, p. 262).[2] Bio-power occurs on two levels: the micro-level, which disciplines the body; and the macro-level, which regulates the population. The former objectifies the body as an individual machine, disciplining and optimising it to increase its usefulness, docility and integration into political economic controls. Schools, hospitals, prisons and factories, but also sporting institutions, are examples of social institutions that organise, appraise and hierarchise bodies and minds in order to manipulate, teach and make them productive. The latter, the macro-level, target the body as a species. That is, authorities evaluate and control the population's biological processes such as birth, mortality, levels of health and life expectancy.

Foucault's acceptance that 'strategies, relations and practices of power in which knowledges are embedded and connected' explains how certain information and discursive practices develop, whereas others are ignored and made to disappear (Carabine, 2001, p. 276). Knowledge is thus not neutral, but is transformed into 'realities' or 'truths', respectively 'lies', which, through its discursive practices, are being transmitted to and inscribed on humans.

I have chosen women's artistic gymnastics as an example to illustrate how its participants are shaped, and disciplined, by this sport.

Gymnastics, like other sports, has historically been formed by gender norms and, more recently, by political, economic and media developments (Barker-Ruchti, 2007). This has resulted in a contemporary dominant gymnastics trend consisting of certain feminine aesthetics and difficult and risky aerial gymnastics sequences. Other forms of gymnastics are seen as undesirable or *passé*, as this is the case with the graceful and elegant style popular in the 1950s and 1960s (Barker-Ruchti, 2009). On an institutional level, the present requirements are manifested in the sport's rulebook, the Code of Points. Existing artistic and acrobatic gymnastics elements and their precise technical executions, athlete attire and behaviour, judging conduct, as well as coach behaviour during competitions are noted in this document. These prescribed expectations, or boundaries, generate discursive practices, of which a culture of selection at a young age and repetition of gymnastics elements and routines are two examples. With regard to the former, gymnasts' flexibility and muscular power are identified early on, which excludes the possibility that athletes might develop these qualities at an older age. With regard to the latter, the current training culture sees endless and long-term repetition as the only option for victory. A gymnastics routine must be practised until the athlete can perform it flawlessly; injuries, rehabilitation or training recovery recommendations are ignored. Gymnasts, coaches and parents *must* adhere to these requirements and regulations to operate successfully within its parameters, which means that they normalise their beings accordingly.

The subtle effects of bio-power, through institutional, social and internalised disciplinary techniques, examine, hierarchise and normalise in order to achieve and maintain political aims such as social order, class and gender structures and economic productivity, or in the case of gymnastics, a particular gymnastics hierarchy and culture. It affects the body by way of homogenisation, rather than through direct actions. This normalisation process is successful as it inscribes its norms within the individuals and offers rewards, respectively, induces punishment. Through this process, the body is:

> directly involved in a political field: power relations have an immediate hold upon it; they invest it, mark it, train it, torture it, force it to carry out tasks, to perform ceremonies, to emit signs.
>
> (Foucault, 1978, p. 25)

It successfully trains and manipulates the body so that it obeys and becomes useful economically. The body as a site of political struggle is key in this process (McLaren, 2002). Power's grip works *through* the human body, primarily by influencing people's bodies and minds to the extent that they adopt these standards. The internalisation of normalising techniques results in surveillance and self-regulation, which require 'minimum expenditure for the maximum return, [producing] subjected and practised bodies, "docile" bodies' (Foucault, 1978, p. 138). That is, without physical constraints or corporal control, but through invisible disciplinary normalisation techniques and tactics, individuals control, discipline, manipulate and improve their bodies and minds to achieve a given dominant standard. For example, gymnasts believe they adhere to the rules and expectations because of intrinsic motivation to succeed in their sport. They diligently adopt the sports' regulations by ignoring tiredness and injuries, limiting their diet and following the coach's instructions (Barker-Ruchti, 2008). Ultimately, they become efficient by eliminating distractions and ignoring difficulties. The gymnasts begin to regulate themselves.[3]

Foucault sees these normalising consequences in a productive light, but also warns of possible dangers (Foucault, 1978). The specific positioning of individuals, for instance, may have reductive and discriminating consequences. In the case of artistic gymnastics, a gymnast who does not desire to strive for perfectionism struggles with the demands of precision and the endless repetitive training requirements. Similarly, a gymnast who lacks flexibility or dislikes performing expressive dance series in front of spectators will be considered unsuitable for this sport. These disadvantages or bias may lead athletes to experience disappointments, which may lower their self-worth or lead them to retire (Barker-Ruchti, 2009).

Media coverage as authorising practice

Bio-power is validated through *authoritative channels* and reflected and produced in the language of *authorising practices* (Ramazanoglu and Holland, 2006). Authoritative channels include scientific fields such as education, psychiatry and medicine, of which sport science is a product. These fields are saturated by and influence the construction of gender knowledge, discourses and practices within. In a Foucauldian framework, media reporting can be regarded an authorising practice. By speaking to the general audience in the language of authorising channels, contemporary multi-media outlets are particularly influential in transmitting and supporting dominant images and representations of sport. The media language and images are, therefore, embedded in and saturated by social context. Sport news coverage is not a neutral medium of representation, but must be understood as a reflection of existing dominant social understandings. Through Foucault's concepts of bio-power and its normalising effects, my analysis of Karin Thürig illustrates how particular discourses, positions and practices of femininity and masculinity in sport are created and transmitted through media coverage. In addition, I examine how these discourses are inscribed on athletes, who, through their subjectivities, reinforce the validity and power of the dominant (masculine) idea of sport.

My analysis aims to combine feminist and Foucauldian thinking. This is not unproblematic. In fact, several feminists criticise and even reject Foucault's constructivist theorising (for useful examples, see Fraser, 1989; Hartsock, 1990). These scholars accuse Foucault's works of lacking a normative framework, being gender-blind and androcentric, and undermining feminist emancipatory politics. Both Foucault and feminists, however, are committed to anti-domination and freedom. While Foucault does this through critiquing phenomena such as the prison and sexuality, and the disciplinary discourses these create, several feminists have used his frameworks to analyse specific disciplinary practices of femininity within sport (Barker-Ruchti, 2007, 2009; Bridel and Rail, 2007; Chapman, 1997; Chase, 2006; Dworkin and Wachs, 1998; Markula, 2003, 2004). Studies on how female athletes are represented in the media are also popular.[4] Specific Foucauldian discourse analyses on print media articles are, however, rare, with only few exceptions (Eskes, Carlisle, Duncan and Miller, 1998; Jette, 2006; Markula, 2001). Using fitness magazines, these scholars have explored how the print media acts as a disciplinary practice of femininity. This chapter adds to the limited amount of studies that have combined feminist and Foucauldian ideas to examine women's sport media coverage. Further, by offering a discourse analysis of newspaper articles, this study extends previous media analysis to newspaper coverage and explores the normalisation of a female athlete through its particular representations.

Methodology

Foucault studied various (historical) texts to examine identity and experiences. The language these texts used, however, was never his only source for analysis. Rather, he was concerned with *discourses*. A discourse, for Foucault, uses language as a means by which discursive practices are transmitted. In his earlier works on the archaeology of knowledge,

Foucault engaged in identifying 'the objects, enunciations, concepts and theories that inform a particular discursive practice' (Markula and Pringle, 2006, p. 52). Coherences of such discursive practices form discursive spheres, which in turn reflect authoritative channels (scientific fields) and a dominant *episteme*. An episteme refers to a common ground through which existing knowledge about a certain topic, and during a particular historical moment, is described and represented (Hall, 2001). Gender relations are embedded in power, and maleness and masculinity are valued over femaleness and femininity (Bordo, 1993; Craig, 1992; Hargreaves, 1994). While interested in discourses, Foucault examined these on three distinct levels:

> Sometimes ... the general domain of all statements, sometimes as an individualizable group of statements, and sometimes as a regulated practice that accounts for a number of statements.
>
> (Foucault, 1972, p. 8)

This chapter analyses the newspaper coverage of Karin Thürig's Olympic success on three levels: 1) the articles' individual statements; 2) various concepts these statements form and refer to, and their possible meanings; and 3) the discourses these clustered concepts draw on and reinforce. I begin by showing how the individual statements and pictures construct this cyclist's athletic performance. I then illustrate how Thürig herself, by referring to her interview comments, has become inscribed with this secondary position.

Data collection

The collected newspaper articles were published on 19 August 2004, the day after Thürig's cycling success and featured in a variety of Swiss newspapers from the German-speaking region: Daily newspapers: *Tages Anzeiger* (two articles − 1 + 2), *Neue Zürcher Zeitung* (3), *Basler Zeitung* (4), *Aargauer Zeitung* (5), *St. Galler Tagblatt* (6), *Neue Luzerner Zeitung* (7) and *Zeitung im Espace* (three joint newspapers in Berne, one article each – 8); tabloid press: *SportBlick* (9); and a free newspaper: *20Minuten* (10). All articles cover at least three-quarters of a page, each includes one or more coloured photographs and were written by male journalists.

The articles were read and coded inductively.[5] The broad themes were split into the following categories: emotions showed, external help received, race plans made, athlete exceptionality and domestic roles. In addition, I analysed Thürig's interview comments. These themes are presented below as major enunciations: focus on talent and career development, focus on race tactics and external assistance, focus on emotions, focus on her life as a normal woman and her own press commentary. Throughout these descriptions, I quote the newspaper articles and Thürig's interview statements, which have all been translated from German into English by myself. After that, I draw out two concepts related to these particular representations – the combination of natural ability, age, training and planning leading to successful competitive performance for women; and emotions and everyday life roles creating a feminine athlete. I then draw on a feminist framework to offer explanations for their meaning. Lastly, in 'discursive coherence', I discuss relevant scientific discourses that support the positioning of Thürig.

Major enunciations

Individual statements are the first level in a Foucauldian analysis of discourses. They focus on what is being said, or left out, and how it is formulated. The following descriptions highlight how Thürig's personality and success were constructed in the newspaper articles and how her interview statements reflect dominant discourses of femininity.

Focus on Thürig's talent and career development

Thürig's talent was portrayed as the key factor in providing her with the 'tool' to compete at the elite cycling level and winning an Olympic medal. The adjectives 'multi-talented' (1, 2, 3, 4, 6, 8, 9, 10) and 'polysportive' (5, 6, 7) were used to describe Thürig, as well as being used in some of the headings (4, 6, 8, 10). One article even described Thürig as 'the woman for everything' (3). Thürig's achievement were thus titled as 'the craziest Swiss success' (2), hyped as 'a story that is almost unbelievable' (4), an 'adventure on the track' (8) and 'a fast track career that is outstanding and unbelievable' (9). Her natural ability is portrayed as something she was given genetically, which also explains her success. The articles further contrast her athletic exceptionality to her age – 'and then, Karin Thürig, meanwhile aged 32, fulfilled a dream at her first Olympic Games participation' (5). In so doing, the reports suggest that an Olympic success at the age of 32 is out of the ordinary.

The descriptors used for Thürig's exceptional talent were supported with detailed explanations of how this athlete, after already having been a Swiss national league B volleyball player, a world champion duathlete and a successful triathlete and ironman participant, moved into cycling as a 'traverse beginner' (title in 8).

Duathlon is not Olympic, in triathlon she could not be successful because of swimming. So, she tries it in cycling. One year later, she dares a first attempt, a year later she wins the bronze medal at the World Championships in Zolder – in the third time trial race of her career.

(2)

Her career path is further described as spontaneous, coincidental and 'impulsive', which is depicted to have begun while watching the 2000 Olympic television coverage (2). 'I want to be part of this [event]', she is quoted as saying (5, similar in 2, 4, 9). In this instance, Thürig is described as having asked herself 'in which disciplines she could find opportunities [to participate at the Olympics]?' (4, similar in 2, 9). Several of the articles also write that the 24 km race was only Thürig's tenth, 'or maybe rather her eighth', road race (1, similar in 5, 7, 10). Thürig is quoted to have said that '[the Olympic competition] is not the best moment to count [how many events I participated in previously]' (1, similar in 7). In fact, although her successes in volleyball, duathlon and triathlon are briefly mentioned, the long-term and time-consuming training these involved is left out. Two articles state jokingly that Thürig might enter the next Olympic Games in another discipline 'See you in Beijing. The question is only: Cycling or horse riding? Or why not hammer throwing?' (2, similar 5, 7).

Focus on race tactics and external assistance

The race plans Thürig used in the road event took further importance in the newspaper exposures. The articles describe how she had broken the racecourse into twelve stages, for each of which she had particular goals. The breaking up of the racecourse, however, is credited to a sport psychologist: 'it was not my idea, I have it from my sport psychologist' (1, similar in 3, 7, 9). Similar to this race plan helping her performance, other external factors are described to have assisted her success. The racecourse, which was seen to be perfectly suited to her abilities, especially her strong physical build and size, served as one such aspect (1, 4, 5). The black-and-white one-piece lycra skinsuit Thürig wore, which appears in the newspapers' photos (all articles except 2 and 6), is another such assistance. The outfit was depicted as the latest technology, whose producers did not have enough time to colour it in the red and white Swiss national flag colours.

In addition, the editorials focused on the emotions Thürig exhibited in Athens.

Focus on emotions

The newspaper coverage highlighted Thürig's emotional state before, during and after the cycling race. Before the race, Thürig is quoted to have experienced the Olympic experience 'with astonished eyes' (8) and as 'overwhelming' (1), 'great' (3) and a 'nice feeling' (5). In fact, one article credits those emotional experiences for having taken away Thürig's nervousness for the race (9). During the race, the cyclist is described to have been able to succumb to her emotions. The passages depict how she was so focused on sticking to the race plans that she did not hear her interval times (5, 7). The cyclist is also quoted to have miscalculated the final stage – 'I expected another incline, and suddenly, I found myself already on the finishing line' (1, similar in 7, 9). The emotions Thürig encountered after the race are particularly key in the descriptions. Her tears during the medal ceremony serve as important signs (2 and 9 with photo, 3, 6, 10), but also her joy and euphoric reactions are mentioned (4, 7). Her comment that winning the bronze medal 'is one of the most beautiful moments of her life' is illustrative (5). 'I cannot think yet', Thürig said, and instead is portrayed to let her heart speak. In contrast, the reporting left out that Thürig won her bronze medal fairly and deservedly. Only one article printed her satisfaction with winning a medal: 'But at the moment I am just happy. This medal is like a dessert, which I am allowed to enjoy after much hard work' (7). Further to her emotional reactions, Thürig's private life was covered in detail.

Focus on personal life aspects

One of Thürig's private aspects the coverage focuses on is her heterosexuality through her liaison with a male veterinary surgeon (5, 9). Moreover, her typical life role is ensured by the articles mentioning her professional career and part-time employment. 'She allows herself to be trained as an aerobic, fitness and spinning instructor, then she completes a diploma in marketing and management at a business school' (2) and 'by the way, works in a 50 per cent position as an operating manager' (5, similar in 4, 6, 8). Lastly, her love for horses and horse riding is mentioned: 'her preferred hobby is horse riding. Each spare minute belongs to horses' (2, similar in 5, 6, 9, 10). Thürig is thus described as a woman with normal interests outside of sport (2, 5, 6, 9, 10). The newspaper articles also include various interview statements from Thürig.

Athlete's comments

Thürig's honesty and modesty in particular can be drawn from her interview statements. She comments, for instance, that while she had given everything in the race, 'silver or gold [would not have been] possible' (5, similar 7, 9) and admits that the sport psychological help she had received in developing the race plans were key for her success. When asked about her next competition, she further admits that it will be difficult for her to win a medal in the 3000 metre indoor pursuit race (1, 5).

Also, as we have seen, Thürig does not inhibit her emotions, but gives her feelings voice by marvelling about the Olympic experience, the ambience in the athlete village and the team spirit of the Swiss team – 'the entire life in the Olympic village is impressive. I met athletes that I only know from television. I was able to have a long conversation with Roger Federer, for instance, and other athletes that I only knew from television' (4, similar in 1). Her impressions of the Games are so intense that she thanks 'Greece for these great games' at the press conference after the race (8). She also speaks of the medal ceremony in a way that suggests overwhelming feelings: 'I can't think yet' she is quoted, and 'everything went so fast, I was racing for half an hour, and now I am sitting here with a medal around my neck' (1, 4). Further, when asked about the amount of road cycling races she had completed, she was unsure whether she had participated in eight or ten. Lastly, she reasons her choice of road cycling in order to be able to participate in the Olympic Games with her inability to swim well enough for the Olympic triathlon distance (this is despite top ten placings in the 2002 and 2003 ironman events in Hawaii). She does not see her cycling ability and conditioning as the basis for this choice. Rather, as the articles' references to her talent do, Thürig explains her swimming results by a physical shortcoming.

Groups of statements or major concepts

The second level of Foucault's discourse analytic process focuses on concepts that individual statements refer to and explores possible meanings. The above enunciations portray Thürig in two ways: as a female elite cyclist and as a 'normal' woman. As a cyclist, Thürig's successful *performance* was seen as possible through a combination of natural ability and talent, race planning and tactics, and external performance assistance, all in spite of her advanced age. Her achievement in Athens is built around those factors, and not, in contrast, on necessary long-term training efforts in cycling and other sports, and her mental toughness and drive during the Olympic race. Thürig's *self*, on the other hand, is constructed using dominant attributes of femininity: her emotional reactions, coupled with her everyday life roles outside of sport. In so doing, Thürig is portrayed as a typical woman, who has, despite her 'abnormally' advanced age and unusual sporting career, managed to reach the level of elite cycling. Her 'normalcy' was constructed through the appeal of technological implements and scientific aids that allowed her to achieve Olympic success at her age. Her abnormality as a successful cyclist is further countered by concentrating on her emotional reactions in Athens and her interests and commitments outside of sport. When Thürig's success was explained through various factors that made it 'normal' and meaningful in the context of the Olympic sports, her achievements could be lifted at the centre of Swiss Olympic media coverage.

The ten newspaper articles covering Thürig's success in Athens did this by 'naturalising', psychologising and spectacularising her performance, as well as by focusing on her life roles and interests outside of sport.[6] The commentaries' foci on Thürig's biology, rapid career development and outside assistance draw on her dependence on outside help. Thürig did rely, therefore, on external factors. In the above representations, Thürig's exceptional and unusual talent, specific fortunate constellations (her rapid career path, the race track suited to her abilities) and particular external assistance (sport psychologist, race attire) are used to illustrate her dependence. Her long-term hard work in training, and her determination and focus with regard to her sporting career, are, on the other hand, ignored in the coverage. Moreover, the emphasis on her impulsive choice of competing in road cycling and becoming an Olympian, as well as her quick career development, further suggest that female road cycling is a minimally competitive sport, where Thürig was able to come in at an advanced age and win a medal after only three years of competitive experience. This rationale further normalises, or makes possible, her career move to cycling with little race experience at the elite level, but undervalues her previous long-term cycling conditioning.

Thürig was further constructed as a normal woman athlete by focusing on emotional reactions. This is done as emotional reactions and irrationality are considered as due to women's 'feminine emotional instability' and perceived typical female qualities (Bordo, 1993; Hartmann-Tews and Rulofs, 2003). Thürig's euphoric feelings for the Games, her need for sport psychological assistance, as well as her tears during the medal ceremony and the thank you gestures at the subsequent press conference, are illustrative examples. Additionally, the newspaper articles' reference to Thürig's male partner, her profession and part-time position, and her love for horses ensure that Thürig is seen as a normal, yet very fit, woman, despite her exceptional achievements in elite sport. Thürig's personal comments suggest modesty, honesty and emotionality. She plays down her swimming ability, for example, despite excellent ironman triathlon achievements, and is unsure how many road cycling competitions she has participated in. Further, her interview comments in Athens are emotionally reactive. Drawing from Foucault's ideas of normalisation and how subjectivity is inscribed into an athlete's body, I argue that Thürig's mediated femininity reflects the feminine qualities culturally defined as 'normal'.

Foucault's third level of discursive analysis refers to how clustered concepts draw on and reinforce certain discourses. The above-identified foci of the newspaper articles include talent and career development, race tactics, emotional reactions and personal life aspects that normalised Thürig into a certain type of femininity. They draw on particular discourses with certain coherences. I identify (historical) medical sciences and sport sciences as some of such discourses that construct elite female athlete's identity.

Discursive coherence

Nineteenth-century medical science problematised, and subsequently investigated, female biology (Hargreaves, 1994). Their research persuaded 'numbers of influential social theorists, politicians, medical practitioners and educationalists [to use] scientific arguments to depict women as passive victims of their biology' (p. 44). This nature was believed to be governed by a fixed amount of energy for all physical, mental and social actions. If this was exhausted, pathological conditions would be the consequence. Physical activities were thus restricted or discouraged. It is this connection between too much or too vigorous exercise and negative health outcomes that still influences beliefs about what women can or should do in sport. If women challenge these boundaries, as Thürig did, they are not only perceived as abnormal, but as threatening the status quo. Further, nineteenth-century medical science assumed that the biology was responsible for female emotional instability and various nervous and hysterical illnesses. Today, women are still seen to react emotionally rather than objectively or rationally. The medical sciences and medicalisation of the female body thus used biological sex differences to define and maintain ideological concepts of femininity.

Several concepts in the articles draw on discourses of sport science. Natural ability, race plans, psychological techniques and clothing are all sport-scientific facets. The reports' attention to these aspects was taken to defy Thürig's abnormal status as a woman in elite sport and her abnormally fast rise up the ranks of women's elite cycling. This, however, could not be achieved without carefully planned sport science assistance and technological innovation. While this does not belittle her performance *per se*, it does indicate that Thürig's 'natural' talent could only be harnessed through scientific intervention, which then acts as a technology of dominance over the athlete's body. While similar normalisation might be evident in men's sport, women's sport representation includes additional elements that make women athletes not only normal athletes, but normal women.

The media representations of women in sport ensure that athletes are feminised. The conceptual representations cohere, for example, to indicate that women athletes are, despite their exceptional achievements, normal women: they display emotions and conduct their lives outside of sport as non-sporting females would. Thürig is not, however, explicitly compared to a male cyclist or the characteristics these athletes are perceived to have. Although male sport is not mentioned explicitly, a male standard, is hidden behind the explicitly feminine media representation.

Secondly, this differentiation of women and men athletes through discourses of femininity and masculinity has naturalising effects. That is, Thürig's emotional outburst and her dependence on external help, for instance, are portrayed as a natural female reaction, rather than being one that has social origins and one that was specifically selected and exaggerated by the newspaper coverage. The naturalisation of gender differences also feeds into other discourses, of which heterosexuality and homosexuality are two examples. By naturalising the differences between men and women, heterosexuality is confirmed, while gay and lesbian people are left un-naturalised and stigmatised.

The meanings of the discursive sphere influence the athletes. Foucault's theory of normalisation, through a process of inscription and embodiment, helps explain how particular positions – in this case gender roles – are adopted and performed. For example, Thürig's interview comments illustrated how she had adopted the 'normal' feminine athletic identity. My analysis thus demonstrates how the process of subjectification (normalisation), through various *gendered* social influences, operates and has real-life effects.

Conclusions

This chapter has used a feminist Foucauldian framework to examine sport newspaper coverage from the 2004 Athens Olympic Games. In particular, it has investigated how Karin Thürig's success was represented in the Swiss newspaper media. Foucault's three-level discourse analytics served as a tool to study the representations, while common feminist themes and reasons for media representations of female athletes served as thematic explanations. The analysis of the first level, the individual statements, highlights how newspaper statements produced Thürig as a cyclist, Olympic medal winner and female elite athlete. As a cyclist, she was portrayed as a newcomer, lacking experience, but who was able to use her exceptional talent for cycling successfully. Her achievement was described as possible thanks to external factors such as her cycling suit, the racetrack and sport psychological counselling she received. Her hard work and determination was overlooked. As a medallist, her emotions before, during and after the competition were in the foreground. Lastly, as an elite athlete, her self and achievements were emphasised as they were compared to her age and non-sport roles as a part-time worker and hobby horse-rider.

Individuals are, as Foucault suggests, inscribed by discursive practices. The inscription, or positioning, of female athletes means that women themselves adopt and identify with its discourses. The analysis of Thürig's interview statements illustrate how this athlete, due to her honesty, modesty and emotionality, embodies the traditional version of femininity. Hence, while the newspaper coverage constructs Thürig in a particular way, she reinforces the same subjectification in her interviews. Thürig's inscription and embodiment also illustrate how power, through its various authoritative channels, in this case particularly the media, shapes individuals. While this moulding may not be solely negative, it may also have positive productive consequences, the analyses demonstrate how subjects and subjectivities are socially constructed.

Thürig's identity was constructed within dependence, emotional instability, inadequacy and normal womanhood, or, as Foucault calls them, coherences that constitute femininity. This sphere constructs Thürig as an elite athlete, but also ensures that she is portrayed as womanly and, in this sense, *normal*.

The identity construction of a female elite athlete is made possible by and is a part of what Foucault labelled a field of scientificity – in this case medical and sport sciences – that enables certain knowledge to be separated out as the 'true' and 'valid' understanding of female elite athleticism. There are other possible versions of the female elite athlete, but the newspaper comments normalise and reduce individual differences into one version of the female elite athlete. This singular and currently dominant version reflects modern epistemological assumptions. With regard to sport, this modern episteme creates sporting discourses that devalue female athletes' selves and performances.

The discursive explorations in this chapter highlight how knowledge, power and discourse must be seen in conjunction with and in relation to each other. The media and its journalists, the newspaper articles and its contents, Both Thürig and the readers are involved in the reflexive triad of power, knowledge and discourses. Therefore, all factors and participants are entrenched within, affected by and ultimately maintain the framework of modern power.

Notes

1. In his later work on sexuality, Foucault recognised that individuals are able to constitute their selves.
2. Foucault moved away from the term 'bio-power' in 1978, employing *governmentality* instead. The concept governmentality includes the institutional, procedural, analytical, calculative and tactical techniques characteristic of bio-power, but extends them to the 'process by which this type of power has become pre-eminent in Western societies, leading to the formation of a whole series of governmental ' "apparatuses" ... and "knowledges"' (O'Leary, 2002, p. 29). Lois McNay (1992) writes that governmentality extends sovereignty and bio-power with the *efficient* management of the population. The juridical system is one such way to efficiently control the population.
3. Foucault uses Jeremy Bentham's concept of the panopticon to illustrate how self-regulation can operate in a prison. His prison design consisted of an observatory tower in the middle, with the prisoners' cells built around it. Each cell is placed in such a way that the prison guard can observe the prisoners, but the inmates cannot see the supervisor or the other prisoners. Because they can be observed at any time, the prisoners conform to prison regulations. They have internalised the rules.
4. For useful examples see Alexander, 1994a, 1994b; Blinde, Greendorfer and Shanker, 1991; Crossman, Hyslop and Guthrie, 1994; Daddario, 1994; Duncan, 1990; Duncan and Hasbrook, 1988; Hargreaves, 1994; Hartmann-Tews and Rulofs, 2003; Kane and Parks, 1992; Lee, 1992; Lumpkin and Williams, 1991; Messner, Duncan and Jensen, 1993).
5. I realise that 'induction' *per se* is an illusive concept. Ideas or themes cannot be drawn from a text objectively; such a process is always affected by social factors, primarily by the researcher's own subjectivity.

6. Daddario and Wigley (1998; 2007), Hartmann-Tews and Bettina Rulofs (2003) and Riitta Pirinen (1997) in particular have previously worked with these or similar themes. These authors used other themes, including sexualisation, naturalisation, nationalism and racial stereotyping. These were, however, not found to be relevant in this study's selected newspaper articles.

References

Alexander, S. (1994a). Gender bias in British television coverage of major athletic championships. *Women's Studies International Forum*, 17, 647–54.

Alexander, S. (1994b). Newspaper coverage of athletics as a function of gender. *Women's Studies International Forum*, 17, 655–62.

Barker-Ruchti, N. (2007). *Women's Artistic Gymnastics: An (Auto-)Ethnographic Journey*. St Lucia: University of Queensland.

Barker-Ruchti, N. (2009). Ballerinas and pixies: A genealogy of the changing female gymnastics body. *International Journal of the History of Sport*, 26(1), 43–61.

Barker-Ruchti, N. (2009). 'They *must* be working hard': An (Auto-)Ethnographic account of women's artistic gymnastics. *Cultural Studies – Critical Methodologies*, 8(3), 372–80.

Blinde, E., Greendorfer, S. and Shanker, R. (1991). Differential media coverage of men's and women's intercollegiate basketball: Reflection of gender ideology. *Journal of Sport & Social Issues*, 15, 98–114.

Bordo, S. (1993). *Unbearable Weight: Feminism, Western Culture and the Body*. Berkeley, CA: University of California Press.

Bridel, W. and Rail, G. (2007). Sport, sexuality, and the production of (resistant) bodies: De/re-construction of the meanings of gay male marathon corporeality. *Sociology of Sport Journal*, 24(2), 127–44.

Carabine, J. (2001). Unmarried motherhood 1830–1990: A genealogical analysis. In M. Wetherall, S. Taylor and S. J. Yates (eds.), *Discourse as Data: A Guide for Analysis* (pp. 267–307). London: Sage.

Chapman, G. E. (1997). Making weight: Lightweight rowing, technologies of power, and technologies of the self. *Sociology of Sport Journal*, 14, 205–23.

Chase, L. F. (2006). (Un)disciplined bodies: A Foucauldian analysis of women's rugby. *Sociology of Sport Journal*, 22(3), 229–47.

Craig, S. (1992). *Men, Masculinity and the Media*. London: Sage.

Crossman, J., Hyslop, P. and Guthrie, B. (1994). A content analysis of the sports section of Canada's national newspaper with respect to gender and professional/amateur status. *International Review for the Sociology of Sport*, 29, 275–88.

Daddario, G. (1994). Chilly scences of the 1992 winter games: The mass media and the marginalisation of female athletes. *Sociology of Sport Journal*, 11, 275–88.

Daddario, G. (1998). *Women's Sport and Spectacle: Gendered Television Coverage and the Olympic Games*. Westport, CT: Praeger.

Daddario, G. and Wigley, B. J. (2007). Gender marking and racial stereotypig at the 2004 Athens Games. *Journal of Sports Media*, 2(1), 29–51.

Duncan, M. C. (1990). Sports photographs and sexual difference: Images of women and men in the 1984 and 1988 Olympic Games. *Sociology of Sport Journal*, 7(7), 22–43.

Duncan, M. C. and Hasbrook, C. (1988). Denial of power in televised women's sports. *Sociology of Sport Journal,* 5, 1–21.

Dworkin, S. L., & Wachs, F. L. (1998). 'Disciplining the body': HIV-positive male athletes, media surveillance, and the policing of sexuality. *Sociology of Sport Journal,* 15, 1–20.

Eskes, T. B., Duncan, M. C. and Miller, E. M. (1998). The discourse of empowerment: Foucault, Marcuse, and women's fitness texts, *Journal of Sport & Social Issues,* 22, 317–44.

Foucault, M. (1972). *The Archaeology of Knowledge,* trans. A. M. Sheridan Smith (April). London: Travistock.

Foucault, M. (1978). *Discipline and Punish: The Birth of the Prison.* New York: Random House.

Foucault, M. (1980). *Power/Knowledge: Selected Interviews and Other Writings, 1972–1977.* Brighton: Harvester Press.

Foucault, M. (1994). The subject and power. In J. D. Faubion (ed.), *Power: Essential Works of Foucault 1954–1984,* Vol. 3, (pp. 326-348). London: Penguin.

Foucault, M. and Rabinow, P. (1984). *The Foucault Reader.* London: Penguin.

Fraser, N. (1989). *Unruly Practices: Power, Discourse, and Gender in Contemporary Social Theory.* Oxford: Polity.

Hall, S. (2001). Foucault: Power, knowledge and discourse. In S. Taylor, M. Wetherell and S. J. Yates (eds.), *Discourse Theory and Practice: A Reader* (pp. 72–81). London: Sage.

Hargreaves, J. (1994). *Sporting Females: Critical Issues in the History and Sociology of Women's Sports.* London: Routledge.

Hartmann-Tews, I. and Rulofs, B. (2003). Sport in den Medien - ein Feld semiotischer Markierung von Geschlecht? In I. Hartmann-Tews, P. Giess-Stüber, M.-L. Klein, C. Kleindienst-Cachay and K. Petry (eds.), *Soziale Konstruktion von Geschlecht im Sport* (pp. 29–68). Opladen: Leske & Budrich.

Hartsock, N. (1990). Foucault on power: A theory for women? In L. J. Nicholson (ed.), *Feminism/Postmodernism.* New York: Routledge.

Jette, S. (2006). Fit for two? A critical discourse analysis of *Oxygen* fitness magazine. *Sociology of Sport Journal,* 23, 331–51.

Kane, M. J. and Parks, J. (1992). The social construction of gender difference and hierarchy in sport journalism – few new twists on very old themes. *Women in Sport & Physical Activity Journal,* 1, 49–83.

Lee, J. (1992). Media portrayals of male and female Olympic athletes: Analyses of newspaper accounts of the 1984 and the 1988 Summer Games. *International Review for the Sociology of Sport,* 27, 197–219.

Lumpkin, A., & Williams, L. (1991). An analysis of *Sports Illustrated* feature articles, 1954–1987. *Sociology of Sport Journal,* 8, 16–32.

Markula, P. (2001). Beyond the perfect body: Women's body image distortion in fitness magazine discourse. *Journal of Sport & Social Issues,* 25(2), 158–79.

Markula, P. (2003). The technologies of the self: Sport, feminism, and Foucault. *Sociology of Sport Journal,* 20, 87–107.

Markula, P. (2004). 'Tuning into one's self': Foucault's technologies of the self and mindful fitness. *Sociology of Sport Journal,* 21, 302–21.

Markula, P. and Pringle, R. (2006). *Foucault, Sport and Exercise: Power, Knowledge and Transforming The Self.* London: Routledge.

McLaren, M. A. (2002). *Feminism, Foucault, and Embodied Subjectivity.* Albany, NY: SUNY Press.

McNay, L. (1992). *Foucault and Feminism: Power, Gender and the Self.* Cambridge: Polity.

Messner, M. A., Duncan, M. C. and Jensen, K. (1993). Separating the men from the girls: The gendered language of televised sports. *Gender & Society,* 7, 121–37.

O'Leary, T. (2002). *Foucault: The Art of Ethics.* London: Continuum.

Pirinen, R. (1997). Catching up with men? Finnish newspaper coverage of women's entry into traditionally male sports. *International Review for the Sociology of Sport,* 32(3), 239–49.

Ramazanoglu, C. and Holland, J. (2006). *Feminist Methodology: Challenges and Choices.* London: Sage.

12
Reproducing Olympic Authenticity: Representations of 2004 'Olympic Portraits of US Athletes To Watch'

Nancy Spencer

On Monday, 2 August 2004, a photograph of the swimmer Natalie Coughlin appeared above the fold on the front page of *USA Today* Sports. The first in a series of Olympic portraits was shot by the *USA Today* photographer Robert Hanashiro and included stories about 'U.S. athletes to watch' in the future Athens Olympics (p. 1C). In addition to Coughlin, the series featured six male athletes and seven female athletes wearing 'handmade costumes styled from classical Greek sculpture' ('Olympic portraits', 2004, p. 2A). Among the signifiers used to conjure up images of the ancient Olympic Games were: wreaths of vegetation (used to honour winners in antiquity); flowing robes worn by the athletes; and photographs cast in sepia hues with ragged borders, in an apparent attempt to evoke authenticity and nostalgia.

In this chapter, I draw on the concepts of 'critical' or 'reflective nostalgia' (Boym, 2001; McDermott, 2002, 2004) and 'reading sport critically' (McDonald and Birrell, 1999) to explore the portraits of US female athletes that appeared in *USA Today*. These specific photographs provide a means to 'read sport critically' (McDonald and Birrell, 1999), as they 'offer unique points of access to the constitutive meanings and power relations of the larger worlds we inhabit' (p. 283). While these larger worlds include twenty-first- century global culture, I also wish to explore two other historical moments evoked by these photographs – the contexts in which the ancient Olympics began in 776 BC and the late nineteenth century when the modern Olympics were restored. Of greatest interest to me 'is the movement of narratives beyond their apparent time and place of origin – expanding, converting, multiplying, and contradicting as they encounter and are taken up by new audiences/subjects who are characterized by different cultural locations' (McDonald and Birrell, 1999, p. 293). Before exploring specific narratives related to each female athlete, I shall explain the theoretical meanings of nostalgia that I use to read the multiple and contradictory encounters elicited by these photographs.

Using 'critical nostalgia' as a tool to 'read sport critically'

The notion of 'critical' (or 'reflective') nostalgia has been forwarded by several scholars (Boym, 2001; McDermott, 2002, 2004), who distinguish it from a more conservative type known as 'restorative nostalgia'. The term nostalgia itself comes from *nostos*, meaning to return home, and *algia*, or longing; thus nostalgia is 'a longing for a home that no longer exists or has never existed' (Boym, 2001, p. xiii). This notion of returning home is especially relevant for analysing the 2004 Athens Olympics since the Olympics were returning 'home' to the site of the ancient and modern Olympic Games (Apostolopoulou and Papadimitriou, 2004).

Not only can nostalgia be linked to a different place, but it may also refer to 'a yearning for a different time – the time of our childhood, the slower rhythms of our dreams. In a broader sense, nostalgia is rebellion against the modern idea of time, the time of history and progress' (Boym, p. xiv). While the object of nostalgia may be elusive, Boym (2001) suggests that 'the ambivalent sentiment permeates twentieth-century popular culture, where technological advances and special effects are frequently used to re-create visions of the past, from the sinking *Titanic* to dying gladiators and extinct dinosaurs' (p. xiv). Technological effects played a key role in producing the sense of nostalgia evoked by these portraits of male and female Olympic athletes.

The two distinct types of nostalgia that I have identified are not meant to be 'absolute types, but rather tendencies, ways of giving shape and meaning to longing' (Boym, 2001, p. 41). The first is 'restorative nostalgia', which emphasises *nostos* 'and proposes to rebuild the lost home and patch up the memory gaps' (p. 41). Boym considers restorative nostalgia to operate as a 'kind of history-making employed by nations in order to provide a coherent narrative and to lay claim to ownership of the past. Because it seeks to recover the past, it glosses over contradictions and discrepancies, and elides other histories' (McDermott, 2004, p. 262). It is more likely that restorative nostalgia operates through the Olympic portraits in this special series, as readers are asked to overlook historical discrepancies. Most notably, these photographs of female athletes wearing the garb of ancient Greek goddesses invite readers to overlook the reality that women were not included in competitions of the ancient or early modern Games; in fact, they were not even permitted to attend the ancient Games, at the risk of death (Metheny, 1965).

'Reflective nostalgia' (Boym, 2001), also known as 'critical nostalgia' (McDermott, 2004), 'is less interested in providing a linear, progressive narrative of history than in exploring detours, noticing the gaps and discrepancies between past and present' (p. 262). In this chapter, I am especially intrigued by how these historical gaps have been elided to create the appearance of a linear progression from mythical athletes of ancient Greece to athletes of the early modern Games, as well as the US Olympic athletes of the twenty-first century. Therefore, I wonder how we might tell different stories about the links between these imagined athletes of ancient Greece and contemporary (female) athletes. Thus, I ponder how 'critical nostalgia' can be employed to tell different stories. First, I would like to discuss the possibilities of using critical nostalgia as a tool specifically for feminist research of sport media.

Using 'critical nostalgia' in feminist sport media research

Many feminist scholars have taken up debates regarding feminist uses of nostalgia. From one perspective, women are often interpreted as engaging in restorative nostalgia, having been 'deprived of outlets in the present, they live more in the past' (Greene, 1991, p. 295). As a result, Greene suggests that women are more likely to be 'keepers of diaries, journals, family records, and photograph albums' (1991, pp. 295–6). In this regard, it is no wonder that some feminists regard nostalgia as a taboo emotion that is conservative or regressive. As McDermott (2002) explains, nostalgia 'is often seen as a conservative and regressive impulse, a form of escapism in which the past is idealized in contrast to an unsatisfactory present' (p. 390). From this perspective, women may have little to be nostalgic about since the good old days were not necessarily good after all (Greene, 1991). Women who employ restorative nostalgia by dwelling on imagery of Greek goddesses might conclude, erroneously, that women have participated in sport since antiquity; they might also assume that the images of Greek goddesses provide evidence of a time when women were able to resolve the predicament of being athletic while also performing traditional femininity. In both cases, women would be dwelling on an idealised past that is likely to have never existed.

While this first type of nostalgia ('restorative') can be perceived as problematic for women, McDermott (2002) suggests that 'reflective' nostalgia can be recuperative if it provides 'a politically valid strategy' for reflection rather than simple escapism (p. 389). Thus, instead of dwelling on a past that was oppressive, women may envisage a future with opportunities that were not available to them in the past. In that sense, the Olympic project may be perceived as a way for girls and women to visualise the gains by which they have become active participants in a tradition from which they were once excluded. This is where 'reflective' or 'critical' nostalgia may be especially useful, since it 'treats the past differently: rather than viewing it simply as the forerunner to the present, or as a place of stasis, the past is seen as a source of unrealized possibilities' (McDermott, 2004, p. 265). As McDermott (2004) explains: 'In Boym's (2001) reading, the past becomes a medium for seeing otherwise: critiquing the status quo by creating other narratives of how things might have turned out, and perhaps might yet be. In this way, rather than functioning as a conservative harking back to 'the ancient regime or fallen empire', nostalgia becomes a revolutionary reminder of 'the unrealized dreams of the past and visions of the future that became obsolete (Boym, 2001, p. xvi)' (p. 265). Thus, 'critical nostalgia' can serve as a feminist tool to detect multiple meanings. As a result, I shall attempt to read the series of photographs through the lens of critical nostalgia. In addition, I shall reflect upon these twenty-first-century photos as they are juxtaposed against two other moments – the Ancient Olympics and the late nineteenth-century United States when the modern Olympics began – using Olympic history as a detour to understand the current representation of women athletes in the United States. My focus will be specifically on the centrality of 'the statue' in the history of women's physically active bodies. I begin with women athletes in the Ancient Olympics.

'The magnificent statue of Athena': the ancient Olympic portrayal of women athletes

Contemporary notions of ideal athletic bodies derive from ancient Greek mythology and sculptures that reflect 'the concept of the athlete as a godlike being' (Metheny, 1965, p. 42). The archetype that transferred from the ancient to modern Olympic Games symbolised 'man's conception of himself as a consequential force within the grand design of the universe' (p. 42). And yet, when the ancient Games began in 776 BC women were excluded from 'the sacred precincts of Olympia' (Metheny, 1965, p. 43). Nonetheless, the prototypes of masculinity and femininity that inform our contemporary ideas about gender identities stem from ancient Greece. In particular, the term *masculine* was embodied in Heracles, 'the legendary hero of pre-Homeric Greece', a great man of strength who was 'sometimes credited with founding the earliest form of the Olympic Games' (Metheny, 1965, p. 46). The term *feminine* was linked to the ancient image of Pandora, the legendary first woman, who was 'lovely to behold', yet showed little interest 'in overcoming the inertia of mass' (Metheny, 1965, p. 47). Based on Pandora's image, it is not surprising that the early Greeks 'could not reconcile feminine desirability with athletic prowess' (Metheny, 1965, p. 46).

There were other Greek goddesses who portrayed notions of femininity that *did* reconcile with athletic activity. Artifacts such as statues and vases from ancient Greece suggest that Artemis, Aphrodite, Atalanta and Athena were admired for their physical prowess and were depicted in active poses as swimmers and runners (Spears, 1978). However, these images did not appear to correspond to the lived realities of most Athenian women in ancient Greece. Many authorities believe that in contrast to their immortal counterparts, 'Athenian women were confined to special quarters where they supervised the house, the slaves, the education of the young children, and spent long hours making themselves attractive. Such a life did not include sport' (Spears, 1978, pp. 4–5). It seems curious that these remnants of mythological women were so different from their mortal counterparts. Even more intriguing is how these mythological images have survived the centuries to contribute to the construction of femininity in contemporary portraits of US women athletes in the 2004 Olympics.

The story of Athena seems particularly relevant to understanding how Greek mythology may have inspired meanings embedded in the Olympic portrait project. Athena, who was 'born from the head of Zeus', was the patron goddess of Athens (Woodford, 2003, p. 240). Known as the 'warrior goddess', Athena was recognised for wearing a woman's long skirt, while being 'armed, carrying a spear and shield, and wearing a helmet' (Woodford, 2003, p. 29). This description appears to be congruent with certain photographs in the 'Olympic portrait project', especially that of the fencer Sada Jacobson. Despite being the warrior goddess, Athena was referred to as 'a helpful deity' who often provided support (Woodford, 2003); she was also regarded as the 'goddess of wisdom' (Murphy and Merrill, 2004, p. 16C). A festival honouring Athena, the 'Great Panathenaia', was held every four years and featured 'athletic contests and sacrifices and concluded with a procession culminating in the presentation of a new, elaborately woven robe (a peplos) to an old, highly venerated statue of the goddess' (Woodford, 2003, p. 226). According to the Greek art hstorian Amalia Amvradivou, the garment worn by female athletes in the Olympic portrait project resembled the peplos (personal communication, 15 August 2007). Meanwhile, the Panathenaia may have been a precursor to the modern Olympic Games.

Athena's importance to the Greeks is evidenced by the 'magnificent statue' that was sculpted by Phidias in the decade following 447 BC; the statue 'was placed in the Parthenon, the largest temple in Athens dedicated to the city's patron goddess' (Woodford, 2003, p. 123). At the time of the 2004 Olympics, the Greeks were in the process of refurbishing the Parthenon, hoping to complete its restoration by 2006. During the Athens Olympics, *USA Today* devoted an entire page to the restoration project, which had begun in 1975.[1] The restoration of the Parthenon signifies the Greeks' history-making claim to ownership based on restorative nostalgia (Boym, 2001). However, in this chapter, I am more interested in using critical nostalgia to explore the movement of narratives about the statue of a goddess (Athena) in order to consider how these narratives have been taken up by new audiences in different cultural locations (McDonald and Birrell, 1999). While the statue of a goddess (Athena) might be central to narratives about the restoration of the Parthenon, critical nostalgia enables us to see that Athena does not embody a monolithic representation of Greek understandings of femininity. Furthermore, we can see that the portraits of US 'Athletes to Watch' do not appear to be faithful replicas of the Greek ideal of womanhood, even if they seem to have some connections with the way Athena was pictured in the statues representing her. Nevertheless, the Greek ideals have been employed variously to represent femininity at several historical junctures in US history. I next discuss the influence of Greece to 'living statues' which were fashionable among middle-class women at the turn of the twentieth century in the United States.

'Living statues': expressing cultural legitimacy in the United States

Towards the end of the nineteenth century, many middle- and upper-class American women began to practise 'artistic statue posing'. The impulse for this popular practice was the 'renewal of the Olympic Games in 1896', as it 'sparked interest in the Greek ideal of the body' (Daly, 1995, p. 103). This ideal had become especially important to Americans, who perceived the association with Greece as providing 'cultural legitimacy' (Daly, 1995, p. 103). The notion of cultural legitimacy mattered to Americans who aspired to world class status, yet lacked 'a pedigreed past equal to that of the great European states' (Daly, p. 103). Regardless, like Britain, France and Germany, the United States 'envisioned itself as the true heir of the great Greek civilization, in all its political, economic, and artistic glory' (Daly, 1995, p. 103).

In the midst of this era of modernity, Americans experienced uneasiness about the swift economic growth following the Civil War and had begun to feel anxiety over 'the effete, overwrought, and nervous condition of their age' (Daly, 1995, p. 120). Within this cultural climate, many Americans feared losing a sense of self in the increased material comforts and spiritual blandness. 'Expression' was considered as one way to give substance to the self: through bodily expression, the authentic 'American self' could be located – 'a pioneer style self, independent and individual, unencumbered by external pressure but capable of outward projection' (Daly, 1995, p. 120). The body was perceived as the medium for expression with several forms of bodily exercises, or physical culture, developed to foster expressiveness in individuals. The physical culture movement also extended to women, who became enamoured with enacting 'living statues' – a practice informed by the work of François Delsartes, a French actor and singer.

The popularity of 'artistic statue posing' which captivated American middle- and upper-class women took its cue from 'the Delsartean fad', which gained momentum in the 1880s and up to the outbreak of the First World War (Daly, 1995). For American women, the ideal of the expressive body was an apt response to the strictures of nineteenth-century Victorianism. In contrast to the constraints that had previously been imposed on them, Delsartes conceived of the expressive body as depth, believing that,

> the force of its depths streamed outward, unconstrained. It subverted the dividing line between the inner and the outer, between the private and the public, and in obliterating those boundaries, it held the promise of personal, political, and religious liberation.
>
> (Daly, 1995, p. 120)

The living statues were 'moving statues' modelled after images of classical Greek sculptures in books and manuals. Daly describes the actual practices of living statues: 'Women with cornstarch-powdered hair, wearing gauzy Greek gowns and cheesecloth underskirts, melted seamlessly from one statue pose to the next' (Daly, 1995, p. 125). The gestures and postures were carefully designed to express the harmony of the body and mind. To obtain an expressiveness of physical, mental and spiritual states, an individual woman had to practise moving fluidly, in a wavelike sequence, dynamically moving the body parts in opposite directions. The physical culturists did not promote physicality or sport *per se*, but bodily activity rooted in the mind and emotions to cultivate 'self-improvement'. Such bodily expression also became an important marker of beauty and social grace for American women. At the same time, with the physical culture of bodily expression, the development of photography enabled the representation of the expressive feminine self.[2]

Just as models of classical Greek sculpture motivated the enactment of 'living statues' popularised by Delsartes, it appears that the photographs in Hanashiro's Olympic portrait project are inspired by ancient Greek statues. One could also argue that to a certain extent these contemporary photographs resemble the turn-of-the-century photographs of serious women posing in modified Greek apparel. And yet, at the dawn of the twenty-first century, the postmodern contexts of US/global cultures differ dramatically from turn of twentieth-century US (modern) culture, and the (pre-modern) society of ancient Greece. Thus, as I attempt to read meanings of these images of 2004 female Olympians whose portraits appeared in this series of 'Athletes to Watch', it is important to consider the postmodern context in which they have been produced. In particular, I reflect on the kind of 'feminine self' these photographs convey. Using critical nostalgia, I interrogate how these images operate within the contemporary postmodern contexts of gender, nation and consumer capitalism.

'Athletes to watch': the Olympic portrait project

In the days leading up to the 2004 Athens Olympics, 13 portraits of US 'Athletes to Watch' appeared in *USA Today*. Among the Olympians included in these portraits were 'high-profile athletes like gymnasts Carly Patterson and Paul Hamm as well as wrestler Rulon Gardner': in addition, there were 'several athletes who prepared and competed out of the limelight', such as the water polo player Tony Azevedo, triathlete Barb Lindquist and boxer Andre Ward (Hanashiro, 2004, para. 51). Of the 13 portraits, there were six male Olympians[3] and seven females. For the purpose of this chapter, I focus primarily on the seven portraits of eight US female athletes (with the dates of their appearances in parentheses), namely: the swimmer Natalie Coughlin (2 August 2004); the fencer Sada Jacobson (4 August 2004); the triathlete Barb Lindquist

(5 August 2004); the freestyle wrestler Patricia Miranda (9 August 2004); the softball pitcher Jennie Finch (10 August 2004); and the gymnast Carly Patterson and beach volleyball players, Kerri Walsh and Misty May (13–15 August 2004). In addition to describing these portraits, I highlight salient sections of the narratives that accompanied each of the athletes.

Natalie Coughlin

The first photograph in the 'Portraits of Athletes to Watch' featured Natalie Coughlin, who appeared on the front page of *USA Today* on Monday, 2 August 2004. In the accompanying article, Coughlin was described as having an 'all-American smile and engaging personality', and she was anticipated to become one of America's new sweethearts by the end of the Olympics (Dodd, 2004, p. 1C). Yet, the portrait in *USA Today* featured a grim-looking Coughlin standing on a pedestal in the pose of a Greek statue. More specifically, Coughlin stood with arms at her side and fingers clasped, wearing a long flowing robe gathered by two rope belts, and a wreath on her head. The Greek art historian Amalia Amvradivou explained that the 'dress she [was] wearing recalls the ancient Greek *peplos,* a heavy woollen garment worn over a much thinner *chiton.* The stripes indicate some activity and are usually found on charioteers or hunters' (personal communication, 15 August 2007). Her garment was comparable to 'a formal, matronly dress befitting older women – married, that is – and goddesses such as Hera, or Athena'. Her stance [was] in accord with statuary types and representations of static figures on reliefs and vases of the fifth century BC and later. Amvradivou emphasised that these images have nothing to do with ancient athletics, but instead 'come from a mythological or religious context' (personal communication, 15 August 2007).

Entering the 2004 Olympics, Coughlin was described as the 'most versatile U.S. female swimmer' (Dodd, 2004, p. 1C), holding five world records and 18 national records, and having 'broken American records 35 times' (p. 1C). Given her past success, Coughlin was projected to win as many as five Olympic gold medals, which would make her the first US woman to win that number (competing in the 100 metres backstroke, 100 metres freestyle and three relay races) (Dodd, 2004, p. 1C).[4] In retrospect, the coverage of Michael Phelps' Olympic achievements completely overshadowed the accomplishments of the US swimmers Natalie Coughlin, who 'quietly won five Olympic medals', and Jenny Thompson, who 'won her 11th Olympic medal to equal the career total of Spitz' (Shevin, 2004, pp. 5–6). Perhaps not surprisingly, neither Coughlin nor Thompson ranked in the top ten most covered US athletes.

In her photograph, Coughlin portrays a woman who seems poised and confident, while the retro look suggests that this was how women athletes might have been depicted in ancient Greece. If we were to compare Coughlin's photo to the artistic statue posing of American women at the turn of the twentieth century, her pose seems to convey a much more sombre tone. She appears to express her determination to compete successfully for medals instead of expressing an inner calm through her body. Thus, the portrait may represent the dichotomy that many US female athletes now face: having made significant strides in sport, by winning greater participation opportunities, they have become part of the harsh competitive climate of international sport. Thus, rather than expressing the harmony of body and mind, the American feminine self is now incorporated into the realm of 'brute' physicality, in sharp contrast to the physical culture movement of early twentieth-century America.

Sada Jacobson

The Olympic portrait of the fencer Sada Jacobson appeared above the fold on the front page of the regular Sports section on 4 August 2004. Below the photo, a large bold caption read: 'Wielding a powerful, swift sword' (2004), and beneath that a smaller caption also in bold, indicated that she was 'pointed to Athens' (p. 1C). Following the caption, it was noted that 'Sada Jacobson comes from a fencing family. Her father represented the USA in 1974, and her sister, Emily, was to be a competitor in Athens'. Sada, 'pushed into fencing by accident', was ranked No. 1 in the world in saber (p. 1C). Like the photo of Natalie Coughlin, Jacobson stood at attention with her eyes focused directly ahead and a determined look on her face. She held her helmet in the crook of her right elbow while her left hand was inserted into the hollow of her sabre which she held upright and diagonally across her right shoulder. Jacobson wore a loosely pleated gown gathered just above the waist where it was held by four rope belts. The lighting in the photo casts shadows against the rough-edged sepia-hued finish. Notably, Jacobson was the only athlete to resist the idea of wearing traditional Greek garb for her photo, until her mother observed that she looked like a Greek goddess; with that observation, Jacobson's misgivings were apparently assuaged (Hanashiro, 2004).

At 21, Jacobson was ranked No. 1 in the world in women's sabre – a distinction that made her 'the first U.S. fencer in history, male or female, to hold the world's top spot for an entire year' (Lieber, 2004, p. 6C).

Athens was slated to be the first Olympics to feature sabre for women and Jacobson was the favourite to win gold based on her world ranking. Leiber (2004) reported that in order to win gold, Sada might have to beat her sister, Emily, who was also one of 13 members of the US Olympic fencing team, which was anticipated to be among the world's strongest. Yet despite the strength of the team, the US had not won 'an individual medal since 1984' when Peter Westbrook won bronze, nor had they won a team medal since 1948[5] (Lieber, 2004, p. 6C).

There is an interesting connection between women's fencing and the physical culture movement I discussed earlier. Namely, women's participation in fencing began in the late 1800s when American 'society women' and actresses were introduced to the pastime as part of the physical culture movement ('The foil', 1893). In a *New York Times* article, enthusiasts promoted the efficacies of fencing, including 'increased strength of limb, suppleness, quicker movements, a more erect bearing, a loss of unnecessary weight ... the sum of which means greatly increased grace' ('The foil', 1893, np). However, none of these elements was emphasised in narratives about Sada Jacobson. Instead, like many of the other narratives, Jacobson's story highlighted her potential to win gold medals. More recently, some journalists have criticised the United States' over-emphasis on winning medals (Brennan, 2004). Ironically, for women, the Olympics provide arguably the only international platform where winning a medal has the same value whether it is won by a male or a female.

Barb Lindquist

The triathlete Barb Lindquist, aged 35, was the third female to appear in *USA Today* and the fifth in the series of 'U.S. Athletes to Watch'. The front-page photo of Lindquist was shot from slightly above, creating the impression that she was smaller than previously featured athletes.[6] In the photo, Lindquist stands with her arms bent at the elbows, hands on hips, wearing a flowing gown with fabric gathered to reveal her strong slender arms. Her garment is gathered at the waist, and held in place by a thick rope belt. Lindquist appears to be wearing a small necklace in the shape of a cross. The foliage on her head blends with her short hair to give the impression of a feathered look. Although shadows obscure the left side of her face, it appears that her lips are pursed and she has a determined expression on her face. In her Olympic portrait, the short garment worn by Lindquist might be similar to the *chiton* worn by females in the foot races honouring Hera.

The brief history of the triathlon competition began in 1974 with the first swim–bike–run competition, staged in San Diego, CA (Wallechinsky, 2004). The triathlon was first introduced as an Olympic event for both men and women at the 2000 Sydney Games. The Olympic event features 'a 1500-metre open water swim' followed by a 40-kilometre cycling leg, and ending with a 10,000 metre run (Wallechinsky, 2004, p. 1021). Given its recent introduction to the Olympics, there is really no comparable event held in the ancient Games, although events for both men and women featured running as well as swimming competitions. Lindquist's participation in the triathlon at the age of 35 speaks well for her fitness as well as her persistence. Yet, her age and marital status do not reflect legendary practices of women who typically participated in foot races[7] as virgins in ancient Greece (Scanlon, 1988).

Patricia Miranda

The 'Olympic portrait' of the American woman wrestler Patricia Miranda appeared the front page of *USA Today's* Sports on 9 August 2004. In her cover photograph, Miranda is featured in bare-feet and seated with her legs bent and arms clasped around her knees. The photo is shot from slightly above and to her right.[8] Miranda wears a two-piece garment that exposes her arms and most of her right leg. While her limbs do not reveal muscular definition, her arms and legs appear to be thick and strong. The bottom portion of her garment is a flowing skirt with a pattern on the hemline reminiscent of decorative ancient Greek vases trimmed with mini-labyrinths.[9] Miranda's short curly hair reaches just below her ears and, like other athletes in the Olympic project, she wears a laurel wreath.

Beneath the cover photo of Miranda, the headline reads in large bold letters: 'Making the grade as a wrestler' (2004, p. 1C). The explanation of the caption reveals that Miranda's father 'was not keen on her joining the wrestling team in the eighth grade. But he said if she earned all A's, she could do as she wished with her spare time' (p. 1C). Not only did she fulfil her father's expectations, but she also proceeded to 'become a Phi Beta Kappa graduate at Stanford', (p. 1C) where she practised with the men's wrestling team (Mihoces, 2004). In Athens, Patricia Miranda was among the favourites to compete in the 105$\frac{1}{2}$lb weight class for the US. To win the gold, she would have to beat her nemesis, Irini Merleni of the Ukraine, the three-time world champion, who had beaten her 5-4 'in the 2003 world finals' (Mihoces, 2004, p. 3C). After competing in women's free-style wrestling at Athens, the 25-year-old planned to attend Yale Law School (Mihoces, 2004).

In the ancient Games (pre-modernity), wrestling was one of three com-
bative sports staged, the other two being boxing and *pancration*, a brutal
combination of boxing and wrestling (Young, 2004). The 2004 Athens
Olympics marked the first time that women would compete in freestyle
wrestling (Mihoces, 2004). Despite being slated to become an Olympic
sport for women, narratives reported that the US offered few opportunities for girls and women to pursue their dreams of wrestling competitively
at high school or collegiate levels.[10] In the debut of women's free-style
wrestling, Miranda hoped to become the first American woman to win a
gold medal.

In her portrait of an athlete to watch, Miranda hardly looks like an
intimidating athlete who is about to compete in a once brutal sport. In
fact, both the photo and the narrative about her seem to undermine her
participation in a physical contact sport. Perhaps the strategy of posing
her as small and non-threatening is more palatable to US consumers
who 'still see women's wrestling as taboo', according to the USA
wrestling's national women's coach, Terry Steiner (Thomas, 2008, p. 24).
Yet, what are we to make of the emphasis on her academic achievements? There are several ways that these narratives may have operated
to produce our understandings of Miranda. One possible explanation is
that by highlighting her academic proficiency coupled with her physical
prowess, the Greek ideal of mind and body is evoked. This strategy may
also link to Delsartes's encouragement of women's development of
mental as well as physical acuity. Finally, it may be that such narratives
work to offset the plethora of stories about (mostly male) collegiate
athletes who fail to attain high academic standards. Whatever the strategy, narratives about Miranda do not work to produce her marketability
as is the case with other female Olympians.

Jennie Finch

The softball pitcher Jennie Finch appeared on the full front page of the
newspaper on Tuesday, 10 August. The 'Olympic Portrait' of the stat-
uesque Finch features her smiling, with long shoulder-length blonde
hair apparently ruffled by a slight breeze. Although known primarily for
her pitching, Finch stands curiously with a bat resting on her right
shoulder, a view that provides a glimpse of the engagement ring on her
left hand.[11] Beneath the photo is a caption in bold that poses the question, 'Goddess of marketing?' The phrase that follows the bold heading
informs readers that 'Jennie Finch's 71-mph softball pitch could lead to
Olympic and marketing gold' ('Goddess of marketing', 2004, p. 1A). So
potent was Finch's appeal that Horovitz (2004) predicted she 'could

give some of the Greek goddesses a run for their money' (p. 2A). From the outset, it is clear that the construction of Finch is meant to evoke her commodity appeal to consumers.

While the photo visibly establishes Finch's heterosexual appeal, the cover story that continues on the next page reveals how her off-the-field marketing stature is linked to her pitching performances on the field. A smaller photo features Finch looking in a mirror as she appears to apply make-up. The reflection from the mirror discloses that she is actually applying eye black, despite wearing a dark evening dress and having her hair pulled tight. Beneath the inside photo is an ad for Mizuno (sports equipment) that reads 'Your passion is our obsession'; next to the Mizuno logo is a small bat. A box below the second photo of Finch is a list of all the companies 'Betting on Finch' (headed by Mizuno) that have signed up for endorsements totaling $400,000 entering the Athens Olympics (Horovitz, 2004).[12]

In the article that accompanies the two photos of Finch, three aspects of her appeal are highlighted in bold: her golden arm, her golden face and her golden marketing future (Horovitz, 2004). The performance statistics provided to reinforce that she has a golden arm mention her being named NCAA 'college player of the year' while pitching for the University of Arizona in 2002 (Horovitz, 2004, p. 2A).[13] Describing her golden face, Horovitz (2004) notes that 'at 6-foot-1, she has hazel eyes, blond hair and a smile that make her look more like a runway model than a runaway Olympic gold candidate' (p. 2A). Based on her good looks, Finch was named in *People Magazine's* list of the '50-most-beautiful people'. According to the *People* representative Cynthia Wang, 'Jenny is a bombshell' (Horovitz, 2004, p. 2A). Her good looks prompted the former US Olympic swimmer Summer Sanders to conclude that Finch was 'teaching young boys and girls to look at women athletes as sexy' (Horovitz, 2004, p. 2A). Despite the appeal of her beauty, Finch had turned down lucrative offers to be photographed for magazines like *Playboy* and *Maxim* (Horovitz, 2004). While she may not have capitalised as fully as she might have, her decision to forgo the potential earnings from such sources meant that Finch probably enjoyed greater appeal with some because of her 'family values'.

Finch's marketability was further underscored by sports marketers' likening her to 'perky gymnast Mary Lou Retton' who 'enchanted a nation two decades ago' (Horovitz, 2004, p. 1A). The only other US Olympic athlete expected to outstrip Finch in terms of marketability was the swimmer Michael Phelps, who hoped to exceed Mark Spitz's record of seven gold medals at the 1972 Olympics. As it turned out, Finch garnered more photographic coverage (4286.86 cm^2) than any other American female athlete and was second only to the gymnast Carly Patterson in terms of article space (7213.65 cm^2) (Spencer, in press). According to Paul Swangard, a sports marketing professor at the University of Oregon, Finch faced one of the few downsides to her marketing appeal because she played a sport that is not traditionally considered appropriate for females (Horovitz, 2004). While she participated in a sport that received very little media coverage, the fact that the Olympics are staged every four years potentially registered as a negative for her marketability as well.

In arguably the most provocative statement referring to Finch, Horovitz suggested that her sex appeal could provide 'the simplest diversion of all' for 'an Olympics so beset by terrorism fears that the athletes have been issued gas masks' (p. 1A). In the aftermath of 9/11, concerns over threats of terrorism at the 2004 Olympics were frequently voiced (Toohey and Taylor, 2008). According to Toohey and Taylor (2008), 'the intensity of media and governmental moral panics and event organizers' responses to terrorism since 9/11 … brought the issue to the attention of the world in a manner similar to the aftermath of the 1972 Munich Olympic attack' (p. 451). As a result of security concerns, Athens spent more than any other modern Olympics to ensure the safety of the Games (Toohey and Taylor, 2008).

While it is beyond the scope of this chapter to probe in depth the relationship between commodities and global capitalism, it is important to point out that this connection plays a key role in understanding how these Olympic portraits of 'Athletes to Watch' have been used to produce ideas about American women athletes. In particular, these portraits communicate certain versions of femininities that reflect the conjuncture between nation and gender. Perhaps Finch, more than any other US female athlete in the 2004 Olympics, represents the 'preferred' or 'emphasised' image of femininity (Connell, 1987; Hargreaves, 1994) that is disbursed through Hanashiro's project.

Carly Patterson

The Olympic hopeful 16-year-old gymnast Carly Patterson appeared on the front page of *USA Today* on Friday, 13 August 2004. The caption in bold below Patterson's photo proclaims that she is the 'Golden favorite' who 'could become the darling of the Games if she rises to the occasion' (p. 1A). In the photograph, a smiling Patterson strikes a pose that could be used for a senior picture, with her arms bent, elbows on knees, and her face resting against the palm of her right hand. Her head is tilted slightly to her left with her hair pulled back, and the vestiges of a laurel wreath on her head. Her bare arms appear to be strong, albeit not muscularly defined, and her pose gives the impression that she is small, as we have come to expect, especially of female gymnasts.[14]

Descriptors of Patterson confirmed that she was expected to be the star of the US women's gymnastics team, with references to her as the 'pony-tailed princess of the team' (Boeck, 2004b, p. 6D) and the 'jewel of the U.S. women's gymnastics program' (Boeck, 2004c, p. 6D). She was the only American gymnast expected 'to compete in all four individual events – vault, uneven bars, balance beam and floor exercise – and the all around' (Boeck, 2004a, p. 2A). As the 'two-time American Cup champion (2003, '04)' ('Six vying', 2004, p. 2A), she was perhaps the most motivated of all the American competitors since she had a score to settle with her nemesis, Svetlana Khorkina (Boeck, 2004a). In fact, their return match promised to be 'a central storyline in the 2004 rendition of the Games' most captivating show' (Boeck, 2004a, p. 1A).

Gymnastics, perhaps more than any other sport for girls and women, held the promise of instant stardom for those who won gold. According to Boeck (2004a), gymnastics was 'the magical arena where instant fame awaits the medalist, likely still in her teens, who stirs hearts and somersaults in to stardom' (p. 1A). One has only to recall names such as Nadia Comaneci, Mary Lou Retton and Kerri Strug to evoke reminders of gold medal performances that became part of the historical landscape of gymnastics lore. Retton herself predicted that Patterson could become 'our next queen of gymnastics' (Boeck, 2004a, p. 2A). That kind of success could land her on the box of the breakfast cereal 'Wheaties' and among the most marketable of Olympians following the Games.[15] Interestingly, in these multiple texts and narratives about Patterson, her youth is celebrated through her 'cuteness'.

Misty May/Kerri Walsh

The final portrait of 'U.S. Athletes to Watch' featured the beach volleyball players Kerri Walsh and Misty May whose photo appeared on the eve of opening ceremonies (Friday, 13 August 2004). In their portrait, the duo stands on the beach wearing two-piece garments that bare their midriffs, yet are not nearly as revealing as the skimpy bikinis worn during play. Each also wears a skirt extending below the knees and trimmed with a pattern of mini-labyrinths. Walsh stands on the left, the taller of the two at 6'3" and holds a volleyball against her hip, cupped in her right hand, with her left arm bent and her left hand on her waist. Despite being described as the more emotional of the two, Walsh glares intently at the camera, striking an authoritative pose.

Standing next to her, Misty May is slightly shorter at 5'10" but also looks determined and serious as she clasps a volleyball against her stomach with both hands.

Prior to the 2004 Athens Games, Walsh and May had become 'more visible than the rest of the women athletes who compete in skimpy bikinis' (Moore, 2004, p. 1C). They had garnered endorsements including a Visa commercial that aired during the 2004 Super Bowl as well as McDonald's ads displaying their likenesses (Moore, 2004). Walsh and May had not won gold before entering the 2004 Athens Olympics, but had dominated the 'AVP tour and internationals FIVB tour', winning '13 of the 16 tournaments they entered' (Moore, 2004, p. 2C). Their dominance is clearly prefigured by the photograph on the front page of *USA Today's* Sports, beneath which the title in bold announces their 'Net supremacy at the beach' (p. 1C).

The most notable difference between men's and women's beach volleyball[16] is that women wear significantly less clothing (i.e. bikinis), which may account for the overwhelming popularity of the women's game. The appeal of the modern game of beach volleyball clearly relies on the sex appeal of the women's game. The portrayal here, while not overtly sexualised, revealed the players' bare midriffs, but also depicted both women as determined and serious. As with previous portraits of female athletes, the main themes that are conveyed by the portrait and accompanying narrative include an emphasis on dominance, the potential to medal and the emphasis on sex appeal of the competitors.

Using 'critical nostalgia' to tell different stories

In this chapter, I have explored seven portraits of US female 'Athletes to Watch' that appeared in *USA Today* in the days leading up to the 2004 Olympics. By reading sport critically, I have endeavoured to follow the movement of narratives surrounding three distinct moments of Olympic history constituted by pre-modernity (776 BC), modernity (1896) and post-modernity (2004). When the ancient Olympics began in 776 BC, ideals of womanhood were personified by mythological Greek goddesses. These exemplars would later provide the basis for 'artistic statue posing' by middle- and upper-class American women at the turn of the twentieth century; they also appear to have informed the portraits of US 'Athletes to Watch' in the 2004 Olympics. Yet, despite the persistent influence of mythological Greek goddesses over time, these images were not congruent with the reality of most Greek women during pre-modernity, much less with American women during eras of modernity and postmodernity.

Restorative nostalgia suggests that there is a direct link between the imagery of ancient Greek goddesses and the production of the American feminine, athletic self during modern and/or postmodern times. By contrast, reflective or critical nostalgia encourages us to observe the gaps and discontinuities that make it possible for us to see that these images hark back to a time that never existed, and yet have been used to build new images appropriated for the needs of each era. Therefore, while Hanashiro employed numerous signifiers to evoke nostalgia – e.g. loosely flowing robes, laurel wreathes and retro look – the photographs tell us more about the contemporary postmodern moment in which we live than they reveal about ancient Greece. To analyse how these contemporary images of women athletes draw from previous Olympic moments, yet have been reconstructed to serve the present time, I shall briefly examine several themes conveyed through these portraits.

Two dominant themes produced by the Olympic portraits and their accompanying narratives emphasise the importance of winning medals and the potential marketability of US female athletes. In written narratives about each of the female Olympians, references were made to their being expected to vie for gold: Coughlin (Dodd, 2004); Finch (Horovitz, 2004); Jacobson (Lieber, 2004); Lindquist (Michaelis, 2004); May and Walsh (Moore, 2004); Miranda (Mihoces, 2004); and Patterson (Boeck, 2004a; 'Six vying', 2004). In retrospect, Hanashiro (2004) referred to this project as his 'own personal Summer Olympic Games' (para. 58). Moreover, he included his final medal count, indicating that four women won gold medals (Patterson, Coughlin, Finch, and May and Walsh); one won silver (Patterson); and three won bronze (Coughlin; Jacobson; and Miranda) (Hanashiro, 2004). Only the triathlete Barb Lindquist failed to win a medal.

Marketability was the other dominant theme conveyed through narratives about many of the US female athletes. Prior to the 2004 Olympics, sports marketers, sponsorship consultants and members of the sports media selected the five athletes with the greatest commercial appeal (Horrow and Ward, 2004). Not surprisingly, the swimmer Michael Phelps was overwhelmingly expected to be the most marketable (by 82 per cent). Finch, who was anticipated to be the 'goddess of marketing' (Horovitz, 2004), was chosen by 76.2 per cent of voters. Coughlin (39.7 per cent), Carly Patterson and Rulon Gardner rounded out the top five, with Patterson and Gardner tied at 34.9 per cent (Horrow and Ward, 2004).

Contributing to the marketability of female Olympians, the association with sex appeal was most obviously applied to Finch and May and Walsh. This strategy has been used in the past to convey heterosexual appeal – especially using images of the tennis players Anna Kournikova and Maria Sharapova, golfer Natalie Gulbis and race car driver Danica Patrick. While such images clearly follow the adage that 'sex sells', they raise the question of whether it is good 'business' or 'sexism' to employ such images on behalf of women's sport (Levin, 1992). Not only do such images operate in support of heterosexism, but they also serve to promote nationalism.

Marketability also featured through narratives about Patterson and Coughlin, both of whom were projected to become 'American sweethearts' as a result of their Olympic performances. The ages of Patterson and Coughlin enter into their categorisation as such, with an emphasis on likeability and cuteness, rather than sexual attractiveness. Many young female tennis players have been promoted as having such qualities when they entered the limelight as teenagers (e.g. Chris Evert, Tracy Austin and Jennifer Capriati). While narratives about Jacobson, Lindquist and Miranda do not really emphasise their potential marketability, each is lauded for having strong family ties, persistence and, in the case of Miranda, an enviable academic record.

How then can we understand the work that is done by these portraits of US female athletes photographed by Robert Hanashiro? In a provocative article about celebrity feminism, Cole and Hribar (1995) suggested that Nike participated in creating certain 'identities' and 'desires' that appear to be similar to the photographs in this series. In order to comprehend how these identities were created, it is important to comprehend the economic and political conditions of early twenty-first-century American and global culture. In this postmodern moment, advertising is 'central to the governing logic of consumption' (p. 355). In this case, images of female athletes 'solicit the hard body, the deep self, and free will (which arouse the desire to work on the body and consume commodities in order to maintain the body and stabilize identity)' (p. 355). In this sense, the search for the American 'deep self' appears to continue, although it takes a different feminine 'physicality': free-willed individuality is now expressed through determined competition, sex appeal and marketability instead of expressing the harmony of body and mind through controlled statue posing of the physical culture movement. The feminine identity is now stabilised, as the Nike advertisements demonstrate, through the freedom to consume commodities. While we are reminded of how athletes resemble the ancient Greek goddesses (and can perform miracles), the accompanying text tends to construct them as successful athletes and marketable commodities sold through the traditional means of good looks.

Cole and Hribar (1995) suggest that an erasure of the blatant links to commodification (achieved in this series of photos through the Greek imagery) tends to impede political action because these images work as a distraction, even going so far as to suggest that sex appeal and/or consumption can serve as an antidote to terrorism. Making such links obscures the real political conditions within US and global culture that have produced anxieties about terrorism. Furthermore, by valorising these images of US Olympians, Americans are encouraged to persist in thinking that terrorist concerns can only be perceived through the lens of events surrounding 9/11 – events that seemingly targeted primarily the United States.

While contemporary narratives about physically active female bodies (and femininity) differ from modern narratives about femininity, could these narratives produced in modernity be considered counter-narratives? Women's achievements in sport are now openly celebrated unlike they were at the turn of the twentieth century in America. This certainly marks great achievements in terms of women's access to sport. However, it appears that both of these narratives of femininity (in modernity as well as in postmodernity) sustain the dominant cultural narrative of the individualism prominent in the American national narrative. Both suggest a continued search for the same 'true', stable, American feminine self instead of encouraging critical questioning of the meaning or adoption of such a self.

Thus, we need to imagine how we might write counter-narratives, so that we create images and narratives that do not impede political action. To that end, critical nostalgia should enable us to see how more politically viable strategies can be applied to tell different stories. This aim is consistent with McDonald and Birrell's (1999) advocacy of reading sport critically with the potential to 'enact social change' by offering counter-narratives (p. 295). While it is difficult to envisage how we might provide counter-narratives that help us to see how women might be offered alternatives to the current construction of femininity, this chapter has sensitised us to be able to read the motives of employing imagery of 'Greek goddesses' differently. Furthermore, it illustrates how similar imagery can be used at different times to create different meanings. On the other hand, critical nostalgia has enabled a reading that goes beyond the surface differences to allow a critical reading that provides possibilities for political action.

Notes

1. This restoration project – like the 2004 Athens Olympics – was undoubtedly important to Greece because of the potential tourist income that might follow. Indeed, the Olympics have long served to advertise a city and/or nation in anticipation of future tourist investments. Given all that was expended in preparations, some felt that Greece stood to lose 'billions in future tourism' if they failed to pull off a successful Olympics (O' Connor, 2004, p. 3C).
2. Thanks to Pirkko Markula for pointing out the relevance of 'artistic statue posing' to this project.
3. One male athlete who was scheduled to be photographed failed to appear – the track star Maurice Greene.
4. Despite the great expectations for Coughlin entering the 2004 Olympics, she and all US swimmers basically took a back seat to the athlete receiving the most pre-Olympic hype, the swimmer Michael Phelps, who was anticipated to break Mark Spitz's record of seven gold medals set in the 1972 Olympics. Although Phelps failed to match the record (winning six gold and two bronze medals), he received more print coverage than any other US Olympian, male or female. Phelps dominated, with the most articles (28) and space (16908.31 cm2; 6.2 per cent of all Olympics coverage and 15.4 per cent of all male Olympic coverage) (Spencer, in press).
5. In ancient Greece, fencing was not initially contested in the Olympics, although it was similar to other sports in which men participated as 'a preparation for warfare or a reflection of the martial spirit' (Scanlon, 1988, p. 185). Nonetheless, men's fencing was not introduced in the modern Olympics until 1900 in Paris, where the French team dominated, winning five of seven titles contested (*Chronicle of the Olympics*, 1996). Not until the 1924 Olympics, again held in Paris, were women's events included and Denmark's 33-year-old Ellen Osilier became 'the first female Olympic fencing champion', by winning all 16 bouts in the Individual Foil (Wallechinsky, 2004, p. 600).

    Despite the traditional separation between men and women competitors, fencing encountered a brief period of controversy in 1938 when Germany's Helene Mayer 'unexpectedly defeated the men's champion' to claim the US national fencing title (Cahn, 1994, p. 210). Mayer's capture of the title presented a clear threat to the traditional supremacy of male competitors and challenged the binary distinction that created separate categories of competition as discussed by Kane (1995). Thus, the 'U.S. fencing organization hurriedly imposed a ban on competition between men and women' explaining their action as an attempt to preserve 'chivalry' (Cahn, 1994, p. 210). The rationale for separating competition between the sexes was that females needed to be protected from the threat of males' potential capacity to incur violence against women (Cahn, 1994). In defence of their actions, officials argued that 'men could not fight full force against women because fencing involved physical contact' (Cahn, 1994, p. 210). This explanation implied that the only way a woman could have beaten a man was by the man 'holding back' his use of physical force. While it was couched in the guise of preserving chivalry, perhaps the real fear was the challenge to manhood that might result from a man being beaten by a woman. However, by defining fencing as a sport that involved physical contact, it was understood as a sport that was less appropriate for women (according to Metheny's criteria), especially if it involved competition between males and females.

6. White and Gillett (1994) indicate that such a photo conveys that the reader is superior to the person in the picture. By contrast, the portrait of the boxer Andre Ward is shot from straight on and shows the boxer with a serious, almost mean look on his face. His glare makes him look intimidating, thus making the reader feel inferior, by contrast to the photo of Lindquist.

7. The foot race was one of three legs of the triathlon, the other two being swimming and bicycling. The feel-good story of the former Stanford swimmer revealed that she had qualified for the Olympics at her third attempt, after failing to make the team as a swimmer (in 1988) as well as in the inaugural triathlon held in 2000 in Sydney (Michaelis, 2004, p. 7C). In 1993, Lindquist began to compete in triathlons and quickly became one of the elite US women competitors. By 1998, she had been named the USOC's 'triathlete of the year', and a year later she was ranked No. 5 in the world, which was higher than any other American (Michaelis, 2004, p. 7C). By 2000, as 'the USA's top prospect', Lindquist failed to qualify for Sydney after crashing twice on the bicycle course and finishing twelfth. Since the triathlon held in 2000 at Sydney was the inaugural event for both men and women (Wallechinsky, 2004), Lindquist was undoubtedly devastated to miss qualifying for the 2000 US team. However, as she continued to compile impressive rankings leading up to the 2004 Olympics, she eventually qualified for Athens after winning a race in Honolulu. Entering the 2004 Olympics, Lindquist was considered 'a favorite for the gold medal' (Michaelis, 2004, p. 1C).

8. In being shot from above, Miranda's photo made her look much smaller than the photo of the wrestler Rulon Gardner, which revealed his expansive size. Of course, the distinction in weight classes (Gardner was a heavyweight; Miranda competed in the 105 wt. class) made an obvious difference. However, the angle from which each photo was shot accentuated the differences, just as White and Gillett (1994) spoke of in reading the muscular body. Ironically, as one graduate student pointed out, Gardner's expansive girth hardly made him look much like what we might imagine as a 'Greek god'.

9. The garment worn by Steven Lopez, Taekwondo athlete, also featured this pattern.

10. After joining the boys' wrestling team in junior high, Miranda competed in high school, where she became a team captain of the boys' team in her junior and senior years (Mihoces, 2004). Mihoces (2004) estimated that about 4,000 high school girls wrestled in 2004, which was a dramatic increase from 1990 when only about 100 girls competed. Hawaii and Texas were the only two states offering 'state-sanctioned girls competition' in 2004 (Mihoces, 2004, p. 3C). At the college level, there were 'only six college varsity women's wrestling programs in the USA' (Mihoces, 2004, p. 3C). According to former US world champion Tricia Saunders, as of 2004, the US had 'some catching up to do with the rest of the world', especially Japan (Mihoces, 2004, p. 3C).

11. In the accompanying story, Horovitz (2004) informs that Finch would marry then-Arizona Diamondbacks pitcher Casey Daigle at the Crystal Cathedral in the autumn. Horovitz (2004) asks whether this would mean 'more tall pitchers in the wings?' (p. 2A) As if in reply, Finch says that she would 'love to have four or five kids' (Horovitz, 2004, p. 2A).

12. Her marketing portfolio did not seem to have suffered as of 2004, when she had deals with (value in parentheses): Mizuno ($100,000, through 2005); Sprint ($75,000 through 2005); Bolle sunglasses ($50,000 through 2005); Bank of America ($50,000 through 2004); 24 Hour Fitness ($50,000 through 2005); Sportskool Sports video instruction ($25,000 through 2004); Ripken baseball sports camps ($25,000) and *This Week in Baseball*, which sponsored the Jennie Challenge ($25,000 through 2004). Given her potential exposure, sports marketers predicted that her endorsement earnings could triple following the 2004 Olympics (Horovitz, 2004).

13. In a pre-Olympic tour with USA Softball, Finch compiled a record of 15-0, while earning a minuscule 0.27 ERA (earned-run average). With pitches clocked as high as 71mph, Finch had even struck out several prominent Major League baseball players, including the New York Mets' Mike Piazza and Mike Cameron (Horovitz, 2004).

14. Patterson's senior photo pose strikes a sharp contrast to another small photo in the upper right-hand corner of the front page of the same paper, where she wears gymnastics garb. This photo serves as a bookend complementing a similar colour photo of the US diver Troy Dumais in the upper left corner, where he performs a back dive with arms extended in front of him at shoulder height. By contrast, Patterson's arms are pulled towards her torso, with her right arm across her abdomen, and left arm just below her breasts. Patterson's hair is pulled tightly into a ponytail. The muscularity of both athletes is especially evident in their strong legs. While Dumais wears only a skimpy bathing suit, Patterson wears a red and white three-quarter length sleeved leotard with blue trim.

15. Even before the Olympics, Patterson was anticipated to be among the top five most marketable US athletes.

16. As a team sport, volleyball was not part of the ancient Olympics and was not added until 1964 when the indoor game was first contested in Tokyo for both men and women (Wallechinsky, 2004). Beach volleyball was added for both men and women in 1996 at Atlanta. Unlike the indoor game which includes six players per side, the beach version features two players per team with no substitutions.

References

Apostolopoulou, A., and Papadimitriou, D. (2004). 'Welcome home': Motivations and objectives of the 2004 Grand National Olympic sponsors. *Sport Marketing Quarterly, 13*, 180–192.

Boeck, G. (2004a, 13–15 August). U.S. gymnasts look bound for glory. *USA Today*, pp. 1A, 2A.

Boeck, G. (2004b, 16 August). U.S. women alternately strong, shaky. *USA Today*, p. 6D.

Boeck, G. (2004c, 18 August). Early missteps cost USA the gold. *USA Today*, p. 6D.

Boym, S. (2001). *The Future of nostalgia*. New York: Basic Books.

Cahn, S. K. (1994). *Coming on Strong: Gender and Sexuality in Twentieth-century Women's Sport*. Cambridge, MA: Harvard University Press.

Chronicle of the Olympics, 1896–1996 (1996). New York: DK Publishers.

Cole, C. L. and Hribar, A. (1995). Celebrity feminism: Nike style post Fordism, transcendence, and consumer power. *Sociology of Sport Journal, 12*, 347–69.

Connell, R. W. (1987). *Gender and Power: Society, the Person and Sexual Politics*. Cambridge: Polity Press.

Daly, A. (1995). *Done into Dance: Isadora in America*. Bloomington, IN: Indiana University Press.

Dodd, M. (2004, 2 August). Poised for pedestal: Versatile Natalie Coughlin gets chance to shine brightest. *USA Today*, pp. 1C, 2C.

Goddess of marketing? (2004, 10 August). *USA Today*, p. 1A.

Golden favorite. (2004, 13–15 August). *USA Today*, p. 1A.

Greene, G. (1991). Feminist fiction and the uses of memory. *Signs: Journal of Women in Culture and Society*, 16(2), 290–321.

Hanashiro, R. (2004). Leading off: The three Ps. http://www.sportsshooter.com/news/1284. Accessed 30 June 2006.

Hargreaves, J. (1994). *Sporting Females: Critical Issues in the History and Sociology of Women's Sports*. London: Routledge.

Horovitz, B. (2004, 10 August). Softball's Jennie Finch ready to make her pitch. *USA Today*, pp. 1A, 2A.

Horrow, E. J. and Ward, S. (2004, 20 August). Olympians with commercial appeal. *USA Today*, p. 1C.

Kane, M. J. (1995). Resistance/transformation of the oppositional binary: Exposing sport as a continuum. *Journal of Sport & Social Issues, 19*, 191–218.

Levin, S. (1992, April). The spoils of victory. *Women's Sports & Fitness*, 62–9.

Lieber, J. (2004, 4 August). Jacobsons know power of sword: Family obsession leads sisters to Athens; Sada favored to win gold. *USA Today*, p. 6C.

Making the grade as a wrestler. (2004, 9 August). *USA Today*, p. 1C.

McDermott, S. (2002). Memory, nostalgia, and gender in *A Thousand Acres*. *Signs: Journal of Women in Culture & Society*, 28(1), 389–407.

McDermott, S. (2004). Future-perfect: Gender, nostalgia, and the not yet presented in Marilynne Robinson's *Housekeeping*. *Journal of Gender Studies, 13*, 259–270.

McDonald, M. G. and Birrell, S. (1999). Reading sport critically: A methodology for interrogating power. *Sociology of Sport Journal, 16*, 283–300.

Metheny, E. (1965). *Connotations of Movement in Sport and Dance*. Dubuque, IA: Wm. C. Brown.

Michaelis, V. (2004, 5 August). Lindquist personifies perseverance. Sixteen years after first try, she is finally going to Games. *USA Today*, p. 7C.

Mihoces, G. (2004, 9 August). Wrestler shows she learned her lessons well. *USA Today*, p. 3C.

Moore, D. L. (2004, 13 August). Net supremacy at the beach. *USA Today*, pp. 1C, 2C.

Murphy, J. and Merrill, D. (2004, 13 August). Restoring the temple of Athena. *USA Today*, p. 16C.

O'Connor, I. (2004, 29 August). Some won, some lost, but Greece triumphed over all. *USA Today*. http://www.usatoday.com/sports/columnist/oconnor/2004-08-30-oconnor_x.htm. Accessed 21 February 2007.

'Olympic portraits: U.S. athletes to watch' (2004, 2 August). *USA Today*, p. 2A.

Scanlon, T. F. (1988). Virgineum Gymnasium: Spartan females and early Greek athletics. In W. J. Raschke (ed.), *The archaeology of the Olympics: The Olympics and other Festivals in Antiquity* (pp. 185–216). Madison, WI: University of Wisconsin Press.

Shevin, C. (2004, 31 August). U.S. Women shine at Olympics, thanks to Title IX. National Organization for Women. http://www.now.org/issues/title_ix/083104 olympics.html. Accessed 13 October 2008.

'Six vying to be the next golden girls' (2004, 13 August). *USA Today*, p. 2A.

Spears, B. (1978). Prologue: The Myth. In C. Oglesby (ed.), *Women and Sport: From Myth to Reality* (pp. 1–15). Philadelphia: Lea & Febiger.

Spencer, N. E. (in press). Content analysis of U.S. Women in 2004 Athens Olympics in *USA Today*. In T. Bruce, J. Hovden and P. Markula (eds.). *Sportswomen at the Olympics: A Global Content Analysis of Newspaper Coverage*. Taipei, Taiwan: SENSE.

'The foil in woman's hand; fencing considerably practiced by New York women' (1893, 12 March). *New York Times* [online].

Thomas, K. (2008, 27 May). Women want to wrestle; small colleges oblige. *New York Times*, p. 1A. Lexis Nexis Research Database. Accessed 10 October 2008.

Toohey, K. and Taylor, T. (2008). Mega events, fear, and risk: Terrorism at the Olympic Games. *Journal of Sport Management, 22,* 451–69.

Wallechinsky, D. (2004). *The Complete Book of the Summer Olympics* (Athens 2004 Edition). Wilmington, DE: Sport Media Publishing.

'Wielding a powerful, swift sword' (2004, 4 August). *USA Today*, p. 1C.

Woodford, S. (2003). *Images of Myths in Classical Antiquity*. New York: Cambridge University Press.

Young, D. C. (2004). The roots of the modern Olympic Games. In L. R. Gerlach (ed.), *Winter Olympics: From Chamonix to Salt Lake City* (pp. 18–40). Salt Lake City, UT: The University of Utah Press.

Index